Law-Making in the International Civil Aviation Organization

Volume 7, Procedural Aspects of International Law Series

The Procedural Aspects of
International Law Series

Richard B. Lillich, *editor*

1. International Claims: Their Adjudication by
National Commissions

Richard B. Lillich (1962)

2. International Claims: Their Preparation
and Presentation

Richard B. Lillich and Gordon A. Christenson (1962)

3. The Role of Domestic Courts in the
International Legal Order

Richard A. Falk (1964)

4. The Use of Experts by International Tribunals

Gillian M. White (1965)

5. The Protection of Foreign Investment:
Six Procedural Studies

Richard B. Lillich (1965)

6. International Claims: Postwar British Practice

Richard B. Lillich (1967)

7. Law-Making in the International
Civil Aviation Organization

Thomas Buergenthal (1969)

Law-Making in the International Civil Aviation Organization

THOMAS BUERGENTHAL

SYRACUSE UNIVERSITY PRESS

Standard Book Number 8156–2139–6

Library of Congress Catalog Card: 72–80016

FIRST EDITION 1969

Manufactured in the United States of America

To Dotty

Editor's Foreword

This book is the seventh volume in the Procedural Aspects of International Law Series prepared under the auspices of the Procedural Aspects of International Law Institute and published by Syracuse University Press. The author, Dr. Thomas Buergenthal, Professor of International Law, State University of New York at Buffalo School of Law, already has established himself as a leading specialist in the field of human rights. With this volume, his first full-length book, he brings to bear on a specialized international organization the same thoroughness of research, depth of analysis and clarity of exposition that has characterized his previous work in the human rights area.

As Professor Buergenthal observes in his General Introduction, "we now have a veritable plethora of specialized international organizations, and as the problems that call for multinational cooperation increase, so do the international institutions that are designed to cope with them." An abundance of literature exists describing the activities of various international organizations, but meaningful generalization about the law and law-making processes of such organizations is rare, basically because the use of the comparative approach "presupposes that the one applying it have a thorough understanding of the constitutional development and the day-to-day practice of a large number of organizations." Such thorough knowledge is understandably lacking since "the practice of these organizations is voluminous and often not readily accessible."

The author, like the present writer, believes that there is a definite need for a number of case studies covering the law and practice of international organizations from a procedural perspective. "They alone," he notes, "can provide the requisite factual and legal background upon which any meaningful comparative research has to be based." As an earnest of his belief, he has spent the past three years working on this study of the law-making techniques of the International Civil Aviation Organization (ICAO), a specialized international organization with headquarters in Montreal which is responsible for the safe, orderly, and efficient development of international air transport, certainly one of the most important and rapidly expanding transnational businesses today.

Professor Buergenthal's book is not a definitive study of ICAO for, as he himself acknowledges, "it is by no means intended to provide a comprehensive analysis of the multitude of tasks that ICAO performs, nor does it seek to detail the various functions of legal interest that each ICAO organ discharges." Rather, he has analyzed the international organization's law and practice in the areas of membership, legislation, settlement of disputes, and amendatory matters, "primarily because the legal issues they raise demonstrate the dynamics of the ICAO law-making process more effectively than others that might have been selected."

By revealing for the first time the surprisingly dynamic and sophisticated character of this process, which is explored in terms of its political as well as legal ramifications, the author demonstrates the vast and as yet inadequately appreciated possibilities for international cooperation in handling modern technological problems. "The relative success of its law-making techniques," Professor Buergenthal concludes, "demonstrates that it is by no means impossible for an organization of some 116 states to make considerable progress in regulating the conduct of governments." Hopefully, his findings will encourage additional scholars to undertake similar studies of other international organizations.

In sum, the student of international organizations will find in this book many valuable insights concerning the nature of the law of such institutions and the effect it has on their decision-making processes, while the aviation law specialist and those attorneys here and abroad having to render advice on international civil aviation problems will discover that it offers a vast amount of highly relevant legal information that hitherto has not been analyzed adequately. On both counts, then, it is an important contribution to the literature on international institutions and a significant addition to this Series.

Richard B. Lillich

Newport, Rhode Island
May, 1969

Preface

This book explores the extent to which law affects the decision-making process of the International Civil Aviation Organization, what the nature of this law is, and how it is developed. The answers to these questions are sought by analyzing the manner in which ICAO has dealt with certain important problems having legal or constitutional ramifications; by inquiring what considerations, be they political, economic, technical, or legal, prompted a given decision; and by examining the legislative content of these decisions.

I started to work on this book during the academic year 1965–66, which I spent at the Harvard Law School on a Law Teacher's Fellowship. The study was completed in April, 1968, and submitted to the Harvard Law School as a S.J.D. dissertation. It has been extensively revised and somewhat enlarged in the meantime.

This book could not have been written without the enthusiastic encouragement, the many helpful suggestions, and the valuable counsel of Professor Louis B. Sohn of the Harvard Law School. His vast learning, his perceptive scholarship, his provocative approach to the law of international organizations, and his personal kindness not only contributed immeasurably to this book, but made the actual writing of it a most enjoyable and worthwhile experience. My debt to Professor Richard R. Baxter of the Harvard Law School is also particularly great, for I benefited immensely from his excellent course on International Air Law, his sound criticism, and his many valuable suggestions. Equally helpful to me was Dr. Gerald F. FitzGerald, Senior Legal Officer of the International Civil Aviation Organization, who was kind enough to read the manuscript and to share with me his vast legal knowledge and experience. My good friend, Professor Richard B. Lillich, contributed much to this book by his thorough editorial critique. In expressing my profound gratitude to Messrs. Lillich, FitzGerald, Baxter, and Sohn, I should note that I am solely responsible for all the shortcomings of this book as well as for the opinions that are advanced in it.

Many of my colleagues at the State University of New York at Buffalo School of Law have contributed to this book by giving freely of their time and advice, and by assisting with many of the problems that I encountered along the way. I should particularly like to express my appreciation to Dean W. D. Hawkland and to Professors J. D. Hyman, Adolf Homburger, Joseph Laufer, Wade J. Newhouse, Jr., and Saul Touster.

Thanks are also due to Dr. Vaclav Mostecky of the Harvard Law Library; to Mr. Christian L. Wiktor, Foreign Law Librarian of the State University of New York at Buffalo School of Law; and to the staff of the ICAO Library in Montreal. Their professional competence and personal kindness significantly lightened my task.

My secretary, Miss Barbara B. Goodwin, who worked on the innumerable drafts of this manuscript, struggling with great perseverance and good humor to decipher my ever-worsening handwriting, deserves my special thanks for her great skill and kindness. Thanks are also due to Mrs. Michael Gibson, who helped proofread the manuscript without losing her pleasant disposition, and to Susan and Janet Soderstrom, who performed various clerical chores and did so expertly.

I should also like to record my profound appreciation to the Graduate Division of the Harvard Law School for the financial aid I received during the academic year 1965–66, to the Graduate School of the State University of New York at Buffalo for assisting with the publication of this book, and to the Procedural Aspects of International Law Institute of New York City for sponsoring it.

This book is dedicated to my wife as a small token of my appreciation for her invaluable assistance. To catalog her many contributions to this book, beyond noting that she helped with the typing, proofreading, and revisions of the manuscript, would not do justice to the unbounded enthusiasm and energy, the ungrudging encouragement, and the unlimited tolerance with which she lightened my burden as author and my conscience as husband and father.

T.B.

Buffalo, New York
August, 1968

Contents

Law-Making in the
International Civil
Aviation Organization

General Introduction

The tendency of governments to establish special departments or agencies to deal with newly perceived problems of national importance has also become a phenomenon of international life in the last three decades. We now have a veritable plethora of specialized international organizations, and as the problems that call for multinational cooperation increase, so do the international institutions that are designed to cope with them.

Over the years, each of these many organizations has developed a relatively large body of law that governs the manner in which the organization transacts its business and exercises its functions. This law and the processes that create it have not as yet been explored as thoroughly as they should be.

Although specialized international organizations evince a great many structural and constitutional similarities, each of them has, since its establishment, tended to develop an institutional personality or *modus operandi* of its own. This institutional personality is the product of a variety of factors. Among these the organization's history, its functions, its membership complexion, and the political or economic power that it commands probably predominate. The organization's *modus operandi* in turn has a significant effect on the manner in which the organization resolves legal problems or articulates the rules that are applicable to them.

These considerations tend to be overlooked by many who have written on the law of international organizations. The literature consequently abounds with comparative studies analyzing and juxtaposing the provisions found in the constitutive instruments and resolutions of a host of organizations as if they were fungible commodities. These frequently dazzling exercises in statutory interpretation, supplemented by tidbits gleaned from the practice of one or the other organization, fail more often than not to take account of the institutional transformation that the constitutive instruments or

1

the organizations themselves have undergone. This in turn leads to factually untenable conclusions about the legal significance that attaches to the actions of these organizations. Studies of this type accordingly contribute little to an understanding of the law and law-making process of any international organization.

All this is not to say that comparative studies of one or more aspects of the law of international organizations are by their very nature conceptually unsound. On the contrary, valid generalization about the law and law-making processes of these organizations cannot be obtained without comparing their constitutive instruments and institutional practice. But the meaningful utilization of the comparative method in this area of the law presupposes that the one applying it have a thorough understanding of the constitutional development and the day-to-day practice of a large number of organizations. Regrettably, very few commentators have this understanding, because the practice of these organizations is voluminous and often not readily accessible.

The need for thorough and accurate studies devoted to the practice of each of these international organizations is therefore readily apparent. They alone can provide the requisite factual and legal background upon which any meaningful comparative research has to be based. Although the need for such studies is recognized, it has by no means been fully met.

One specialized international organization whose substantial law-making accomplishments have not received the attention they deserve is the International Civil Aviation Organization. The present study is accordingly designed to assess these accomplishments. It does so only in part, however, for it is by no means intended to provide a comprehensive analysis of the multitude of tasks that ICAO performs, nor does it seek to detail the various functions of legal interest that each ICAO organ discharges. Since others have dealt with these questions,[1] it seemed more useful and intellectually more challenging to limit this study to an analysis of the Organization's practice as it bears on four broad areas of legal concern. These subjects—membership, legislation, settlement of disputes,

---

[1] See, *e.g.*, Erler, RECHTSFRAGEN DER ICAO: DIE INTERNATIONALE ZIVILLUFTFAHRTORGANISATION UND IHRE MITGLIEDSTAATEN (1967); ICAO Secretariat, MEMORANDUM ON ICAO (5th ed. 1966); Cheng, THE LAW OF INTERNATIONAL AIR TRANSPORT 31–170 (1962); Schenkman, INTERNATIONAL CIVIL AVIATION ORGANIZATION (1955).

and amendments to the Chicago Convention—were singled out primarily because the legal issues they raise demonstrate the dynamics of the ICAO law-making process more effectively than others that might have been selected. A thorough analysis of the manner in which the Organization has dealt with these questions therefore bore some promise of yielding important new insights about ICAO's institutional personality and the effect it has on the resolution of legal problems.

The very limited scope of this study is by no means predicated on the assumption that the areas which are not explored are less deserving of attention. Rather, it was motivated by the consideration that an overly ambitious study entailed the risk of superficial coverage. Law, in one form or another, affects almost every aspect of the work of an international organization. Studies which attempt to capture this all-pervasive influence of legal norms on the conduct of an international organization therefore frequently sacrifice thorough analysis to the perceived need to touch upon each and every topic with which the institution deals. Such studies, as a result, often end up being descriptive monographs which, to be sure, have their own value. They are not, however, a substitute for studies that explore all possible legal ramifications of a limited number of legal problems. This is not to say that it is impossible to combine thoroughness of legal analysis with wide coverage of subject matter, but rather that this writer did not feel that he was ready to attempt it.

In exploring the four topics that make up this study, the author has been guided by the proposition that legal rules, whether they be domestic or international, do not exist in a contextual vacuum and that, as a result, one cannot understand the law without understanding the facts and institutional setting to which it applies. A great deal of background information that bears either directly or indirectly on the resolution of a given legal problem has therefore been supplied. The reader who is not acquainted with the activities of the International Civil Aviation Organization may, furthermore, wish to familiarize himself with its institutional structure and functions by consulting the short description that follows.

ICAO: Its Functions and Institutions

The International Civil Aviation Organization came into being on April 4, 1947, when the Convention on International Civil Aviation

—its constitutive instrument—entered into force.[2] The Convention emerged from the International Civil Aviation Conference which met in Chicago, Illinois, from November 1 to December 7, 1944. The Chicago Conference was attended by representatives of more than fifty states who had been invited by the U.S. Government to join with it in establishing a legal framework for the development of international civil aviation after the Second World War.[3]

In addition to being the constitution of the International Civil Aviation Organization, the Convention is a multilateral agreement that seeks to promote the orderly, safe, and efficient development of international aviation. With a view to achieving these objectives, the Convention defines the rights and obligations of the Contracting States in international civil aviation matters, and contains undertakings by them to cooperate in programs for the facilitation of international air transport and the improvement of air nagivation services and installations.[4]

Probably the most important substantive clause to be found in the Convention is Article 5. It provides that any civil aircraft which is registered in a Contracting State has the right, when it is not engaged in scheduled international air services, to fly over or to land for non-traffic purposes in the territory of any other Contracting State without prior authorization. Aircraft of scheduled international air services do not enjoy similar rights[5] because the states participating in the Chicago Conference were unable to agree upon a generally acceptable formula for the commercial exploitation of international air transport.[6] Under a compromise worked out at Chicago, provisions for the exchange of transit and commercial

[2] The Convention on International Civil Aviation [hereinafter cited as Convention], 61 Stat. 1180, T.I.A.S. No. 1591, 15 U.N.T.S. 295 (1948), was opened for signature at Chicago, Illinois, on 7 December 1944.

[3] For the *travaux préparatoires* of the Chicago Conference, see the two-volume PROCEEDINGS OF THE INTERNATIONAL CIVIL AVIATION CONFERENCE, CHICAGO, ILLINOIS, NOVEMBER 1–DECEMBER 7, 1944, which was published by the U.S. Department of State in 1948.

[4] On this subject generally, see Cheng, *op. cit. supra* note 1, at 106–70.

[5] See Convention, Art. 6.

[6] For a discussion of the proposals relating to this question that were considered by the Chicago Conference, see Jennings, *Some Aspects of the International Law of the Air*, 75 Recueil des Cours 513, 520–25 (1949); MATEESCO MATTE, TRAITÉ DE DROIT AÉRIEN-AÉRONAUTIQUE 170–75 (2d ed. 1964).

rights for scheduled international air services, while not included in the Convention, were embodied in two separate instruments—the International Air Services Transit Agreement [7] and the International Air Transport Agreement.[8]

In addition to the Convention and the Transit and Transport Agreements, the Chicago Conference also adopted an Interim Agreement on International Civil Aviation.[9] The Interim Agreement, which came into effect on June 6, 1945, established the Provisional International Civil Aviation Organization. Endowed with advisory powers only, PICAO's main functions were to plan the technical program and administrative structure for the permanent International Civil Aviation Organization in the period preceding the entry into force of the Convention.[10] The valuable preparatory work performed by PICAO during its twenty-months' existence [11] enabled ICAO to implement many of its programs as soon as it was established.[12]

The functions that the Convention assigns to the International Civil Aviation Organization [13] are set out in Article 44. It provides that "the aims and objectives of the Organization are to develop the principles and techniques of international air navigation and to foster the planning and development of international air transport" for the purpose, *inter alia*, of insuring "the safe and orderly growth of international civil aviation throughout the world"; of encouraging "the development of airways, airports, and air navigation facilities for international civil aviation"; of promoting "the development of all aspects of international civil aeronautics"; and of meeting

[7] The International Air Services Transit Agreement, 59 Stat. 1693, E.A.S. No. 487, 84 U.N.T.S. 389 (1951), entered into force on 30 January 1945.

[8] The International Air Transport Agreement, 59 Stat. 1701, E.A.S. No. 488, 171 U.N.T.S. 387 (1953), entered into force on 8 February 1945.

[9] For the text of the Interim Agreement, see International Civil Aviation Conference, FINAL ACT AND RELATED DOCUMENTS 44 (1945).

[10] Interim Agreement, Art. 1(3).

[11] On the functions that PICAO performed, see Le Goff, *L'Organisation Provisoire de Chicago sur l'Aviation Civile*, 9 Revue Générale de l'Air 600 (1946); Warner, *PICAO and the Development of Air Law*, 14 J. Air L. & Com. 1 (1946).

[12] See Jennings, *supra* note 6, at 544.

[13] On the similarities and differences between the Convention and multilateral international civil aviation agreements concluded before the Second World War, see Latchford, *Comparison of the Chicago Aviation Convention with the Paris and Habana Conventions*, 12 Dep't State Bull. 411 (1945).

"the needs of the peoples of the world for the safe, regular, efficient and economical air transport."

The Organization, which now consists of 116 states, discharges these functions through the ICAO Assembly, Council, and various subsidiary bodies.[14] All Member States of the Organization are represented in the ICAO Assembly, where each of them has one vote.[15] The Assembly meets at least once every three years.[16] Its major functions, in addition to electing the ICAO Council and approving the Organization's budget and expenditures,[17] are to review the activities of and to set general policy guidelines for the Organization. The Assembly has the power, furthermore, to "deal with any matter within the sphere of action of the Organization not specifically assigned to the Council."[18]

Most decisions of the Assembly are adopted by a majority of the votes cast after a quorum, consisting of a majority of the Contracting States, has been ascertained.[19] A different voting formula applies to three types of Assembly decisions. The adoption of a proposal to amend the Convention requires a two-thirds vote of the Assembly;[20] the admission to ICAO membership of former enemy states must be approved by a four-fifths vote of the Assembly;[21] and an Assembly decision to relocate the permanent seat of the Organization is subject to a vote of at least three-fifths of the total number of Contracting States.[22]

[14] For a discussion of the structure and functions of the various ICAO organs, see Erler, *op. cit. supra* note 1, at 16–32; Cheng, *op. cit. supra* note 1, at 42–56.

[15] Convention, Art. 48.

[16] Convention, Art. 48(a), as amended. Prior to its amendment, Article 48(a) of the Convention envisaged an annual meeting of the Assembly. The amendment instituting triennial meetings of the Assembly was adopted on 14 June 1954, and entered into force on 12 December 1956. For the text of the amendment, see Assembly Res. A8–1, ICAO Doc. 7499 (A8–P/9) (1954).

[17] Convention, Arts. 49(b), 49(e), and 49(f).

[18] Convention, Art. 49(k).

[19] Convention, Art. 48(c); ICAO Assembly, Standing Rules of Procedure, Rule 46, Doc. 7600/2 (1963).

[20] Convention, Art. 94(a); ICAO Assembly, Standing Rules of Procedure, Rule 54, Doc. 7600/2 (1963). An amendment to the Convention, after it has been adopted by the Assembly, must be ratified by at least two-thirds of the Contracting States before it enters into force.

[21] Convention, Art. 93; ICAO Assembly, Standing Rules of Procedure, Rule 54, Doc. 7600/2 (1963).

[22] Convention, Art. 45, as amended. This amendment was adopted by the ICAO Assembly on 14 June 1954, and entered into force on 12 December 1956.

In exercising its functions, the ICAO Assembly is assisted by a number of committees and commissions that are constituted while the Assembly is in session. In addition to the Credentials Committee,[23] the Assembly's Rules of Procedure provide for the establishment of an Executive Committee and an Administrative Commission.[24] The functions of the Administrative Commission are, on the whole, limited to budgetary matters. The Executive Committee is a steering committee which exercises substantial control over the agenda, organization, and conduct of business of the Assembly.[25] The establishment of other committees, such as the Technical Commission, the Legal Commission, and the Economic Commission, depends upon the nature of a particular Assembly agenda. When constituted, the Economic Commission reports on air transport matters and the Technical Commission on questions relating to air navigation. The Legal Commission advises the Assembly on agenda items relating to problems of public and private international air law. All Contracting States have the right to be represented in these commissions and committees by a member of their delegation.[26]

The ICAO Council is composed of 27 Contracting States [27] elected by the Assembly for a three-year term.[28] In selecting these Contracting States, the Assembly must make sure that the following three groups of states are adequately represented on the Council: states of chief importance in air transport; states which make the largest contribution to the provision of facilities for international civil air navigation; and states whose designation will insure that all the

---

For the text of the amendment, see Assembly Res. A8–4, ICAO Doc. 7499 (A8–P/9) (1954).

[23] See ICAO Assembly, Standing Rules of Procedure, Rule 6, Doc. 7600/2 (1963).

[24] *Id.*, Rule 14.

[25] *Id.*, Rule 15.

[26] *Id.*, Rule 21. It should be noted, however, that the Assembly's Rules of Procedure expressly provide that the Executive Committee shall consist of the President of the Assembly, the Chief Delegates of the Contracting States and the President of the Council. *Id.*, Rule 15. The President of the Assembly is elected at each session of the Assembly. *Id.*, Rule 8.

[27] By an amendment to the Convention, which entered into force on 17 July 1962, the Council was enlarged from a membership of 21 to 27 Contracting States. This amendment was adopted on 19 June 1961. See Assembly Res. A13–1, ICAO Doc. 8167 (A13–P/2) (1961).

[28] Convention, Art. 50(a).

major geographic areas of the world are represented on the
Council.[29] To comply with this requirement, the ICAO Assembly
has developed a complex set of rules that provides for a three-stage
election process.[30]

The Council is "a permanent body responsible to the
Assembly," [31] and can be described as being the governing board of
the Organization.[32] It has a multitude of functions, both
mandatory [33] and permissive,[34] of a legislative, judicial, and administrative character.[35] The Council's legislative functions include the
adoption of various ICAO air navigation and air transport regulations that are described in Part II of this book. The judicial functions of the Council are exemplified by its power to adjudicate
disputes between the Contracting States relating to the interpretation and application of the Convention.[36] The Council's many administrative functions encompass, among other things, the administration of the finances of the Organization, the appointment of the
Secretary General, the execution of Assembly directives, and the
supervision of international agreements for the joint financing of air
navigation facilities and services.

The chief executive officer of the Council is the President of the
Council. He is elected by the Council for a term of three years, and
may be reelected.[37] Whereas the Council, as we have seen, is composed of Contracting States whose delegates sit on this body as
representatives of their governments, the President is an international official who may neither receive nor seek instructions from
any authority external to the Organization.[38] The duties of the
President of the Council are described in Article 51 of the Convention, which provides that he shall perform the following functions:

---

[29] Convention, Art. 50(b).

[30] See ICAO Assembly, Standing Rules of Procedure, Sec. IX, Doc. 7600/2
(1963). This election process is described in Mankiewicz, *Organisation de
l'Aviation Civile Internationale*, [1962] Annuaire Français de Droit International 675.

[31] Convention, Art. 50(a).

[32] See ICAO Secretariat, MEMORANDUM ON ICAO 13 (5th ed. 1966).

[33] See Convention, Art. 54.

[34] See Convention, Art. 55.

[35] See Mankiewicz, *Organisation Internationale de l'Aviation Civile*, [1956]
Annuaire Français de Droit International 643, 650–52.

[36] This topic is discussed in Part III of this book.

[37] Convention, Art. 51.

[38] See Convention, Art. 59.

"(a) convene meetings of the Council, the Air Transport Committee, and the Air Navigation Commission; (b) serve as representative of the Council; and (c) carry out on behalf of the Council the functions which the Council assigns to him."

Although the President of the Council does not have a vote in the Council, he has proved to be the one individual most influential in shaping the activities of the Organization. This is due in part to the pervasive authority which, under the Convention, is vested in the Council. Equally important is the fact that the position of Council President has to date been held by only two individuals—Dr. Edward Warner of the United States, and the incumbent, Mr. Walter Binaghi of Argentina—both of whom had distinguished aeronautical careers before joining the Council. Their recognized technical competence and long tenure has enabled each of them to exercise very considerable influence on the work of the Council, and through it on the policies pursued by the Organization as a whole.

Five subsidiary bodies assist the ICAO Assembly and Council to discharge the functions that the Convention assigns to them. Two of these bodies—the Air Navigation Commission [39] and the Air Transport Committee [40]—are expressly mentioned in the Convention, whereas the ICAO Legal Committee, the Committee on Joint Support of Air Navigation Services, and the Finance Committee were established by the ICAO Assembly.[41]

The Air Navigation Commission is composed of twelve individuals having "suitable qualifications and experience in the science and practice of aeronautics," who are appointed by the ICAO Council from a list of nominees submitted by the Contracting States.[42] The Commission can be described as a committee of experts which, in addition to advising the Council on technical questions relating to air navigation in general, is entrusted with the task of developing the international air navigation legislation that the Council is empowered to adopt.[43]

The Air Transport Committee was established under Article 54

[39] Convention, Arts. 56 and 57.
[40] Convention, Art. 54.
[41] See Assembly Res. A1-7 and Res. A1-58, ICAO Doc. 4411 (A1-P/45) (1947).
[42] Convention, Art. 56.
[43] Convention, Art. 57. For an extensive study of this body, see Sheffy, *The Air Navigation Commission of the International Civil Aviation Organization*, 25 J. Air L. & Com. 281 and 428 (1958).

(d) of the Convention. This provision requires the ICAO Council to "appoint and define the duties of an Air Transport Committee, which shall be chosen from among the representatives of the members of the Council, and which shall be responsible to it." Although the membership of the Committee is theoretically limited to twelve persons,[44] the Council usually makes arrangements enabling any Council Representative wishing to participate actively in its work to do so.[45] The Air Transport Committee advises the Council on the economic aspects of international air transport. It is also responsible for the development of ICAO facilitation legislation. These enactments seek to improve international air transport by requiring Member States to do away with national regulations and practices that impede the expeditious movement of air passengers and freight.

In its constitution the ICAO Legal Committee is described as "a permanent Committee of the Organization, constituted by the Assembly and responsible to the Council except as otherwise specified herein." [46] The Committee is "composed of legal experts designated as representatives of and by Contracting States" and is "open to participation by all Contracting States" [47] The main function of the Legal Committee is to study various problems of private international air law that affect international civil aviation and to draft air law conventions which address themselves to these problems. When requested by the ICAO Council or Assembly, the Legal Committee also reports to these bodies on questions of public international air law in general, as well as on matters concerning the interpretation of the Chicago Convention.[48]

The Committee on Joint Support of Air Navigation Services, whose membership consists of nine Council Representatives, advises the ICAO Council on problems relating to the technical and administrative demands that modern international civil aviation makes on air navigation facilities and services. The Committee also assists the

[44] See Rules of Procedure for Standing Committees of the Council, Sec. I, Action of the Council, 42d Sess., ICAO Doc. 8159 (C/931), p. 26 (1961).

[45] See, e.g., Action of the Council, 47th Sess. [1962], ICAO Doc. 8312 (C/942), p. 3 (1963).

[46] Assembly Res. A7–5, ICAO Doc. 7417 (A7–P/3) (1953); ICAO Legal Committee, Constitution, para. 1, Doc. 7669 (LC/139) (1956).

[47] Id., para. 1.

[48] Id., para. 2. See generally, Mankiewicz, The [ICAO] Legal Committee—Its Organization and Working Methods, 32 J. Air L. & Com. 94 (1966).

Council with the administration of a number of international agreements which establish a multinational system for the joint financing of certain air navigation facilities serving the busy North Atlantic air routes.[49]

In discharging its responsibility to "administer the finances of the Organization," [50] the Council is assisted by a Finance Committee. This body was established by the Assembly which also assigned to the Finance Committee various functions relating to the implementation of the ICAO Financial Regulations.[51] The Finance Committee has the smallest membership of any of the permanent subsidiary organs of the Organization, being composed of seven Council Representatives.

The staff-work of the Organization, whose headquarters are located in Montreal, Canada, is performed by the ICAO Secretariat which consists of some 600 international civil servants of whom more than one-third are in the professional or higher service categories.[52] The Secretariat is directed by the ICAO Secretary General who is appointed by the Council. Although the Convention in Article 54(h) describes the Secretary General as "a chief executive officer," there is little doubt that as a practical matter this designation applies more readily to the President of the Council.[53] Given the functions which he performs, the Secretary General may be described as being the chief administrative officer of the Organization.[54]

Functionally, the ICAO Secretariat is organized along jurisdictional lines similar to those established for the subsidiary organs of the Organization. It consists of five departments: the Air Navigation Bureau, the Air Transport Bureau, the Legal Bureau, the Technical Assistance Bureau, and the Bureau of Administration and Services. Some of these Bureaus are in turn subdivided into various

---

[49] The activities of the Organization in the joint support field are described in ICAO Secretariat, MEMORANDUM ON ICAO 31–36 (5th ed. 1966). See also, Schenkman, *op. cit. supra* note 1, at 184–87.

[50] Convention, Art. 54(f).

[51] Assembly Res. A1–58, ICAO Doc. 4411 (A1–P/45) (1947); Schenkman, *op. cit. supra* note 1, at 187–90.

[52] See Annual Report of the Council to the Assembly for 1967, ICAO Doc. 8724 (A16–P/3), p. 133 (1968).

[53] Erler, *op. cit. supra* note 1, at 30.

[54] See also, Mankiewicz, *supra* note 34, at 653–54.

sections, units or branches. Each Bureau is headed by a Director who reports directly to the Secretary General. The ICAO Secretariat also maintains six Regional Offices. Located in Paris, Cairo, Bangkok, Lima, Mexico City, and Dakar, the Regional Offices report to the ICAO Air Navigation Bureau. Their main function is to assist the Contracting States with the implementation of ICAO Regional Air Navigation Plans.[55]

[55] See Erler, *op. cit. supra* note 1, at 31–32.

Part I

Membership in ICAO and Related Problems

INTRODUCTION

Few other aspects of the practice of an international organization tell us as much about the role of law in the organization's decision-making process as does the manner in which it has over the years resolved its membership problems. The legal questions that arise in connection with the admission of states to membership, with their expulsion, suspension, or withdrawal from the organization, often require extensive interpretation of its constitutive instrument, and thus account for a substantial part of the constitutional practice of many international organizations. Membership disputes tend, moreover, to be either the product of or the vehicle for advancing the different ideological views that divide the members of the organization. Although the will of the ideologically dominant force within the organization usually prevails, the manner in which this will is asserted probably differs from organization to organization, depending upon the functions of the organization, its *modus operandi,* the various economic, political, or social stakes which the Member States may have in the smooth operation of the organization, and many other factors.

Many of the same legal and political considerations that apply to membership disputes in large measure also affect the outcome of other constitutional disputes. It is therefore not surprising that an organization's approach to membership questions tends to be rather characteristic of the manner in which it deals with constitutional problems generally. The membership practice of an international organization accordingly provides a useful introduction to the methodology and character of its decision-making process.

The study which follows is designed to determine how the International Civil Aviation Organization has resolved its membership problems, and how it might resolve other problems that could arise

13

in the future.[1] The resulting answers should, it is hoped, indicate whether the practice of the Organization evinces certain methodological patterns characteristic of ICAO's approach to constitutional questions generally.

ACQUISITION OF MEMBERSHIP

General Membership Problems

In addition to the clearly implied stipulation that membership in the International Civil Aviation Organization is open to sovereign states only,[2] the Convention on International Civil Aviation distinguishes between states that may join the Organization either by ratifying[3] or adhering[4] to the Convention, and former enemy states which are subject to a special admissions procedure.[5] But once a state has become a member of ICAO, it is entitled to all the rights and privileges of membership without any distinction based on the admissions procedure that applied to it.

MEMBERSHIP BY RATIFICATION OF THE CONVENTION

The acquisition of ICAO membership by ratification of the Convention is reserved to the signatory states.[6] As self-explanatory as this classification appears to be, it presents certain problems. The Convention was opened for signature at Chicago on December 7, 1944. It was not signed on that date by all states represented at the Chicago Conference, however; it fixes no cut-off date after which the Convention is no longer open for signature; and it does not identify the states which may become signatories. The entry into force of the Convention was conditioned on its being "ratified or

---

[1] For the most extensive study to date on ICAO membership problems, see Erler, RECHTSFRAGEN DER ICAO: DIE INTERNATIONALE LUFTFAHRTORGANISATION UND IHRE MITGLIEDSTAATEN 72–90 (1967). See also Jennings, *Some Aspects of International Air Law,* 75 Recueil des Cours 513, 564–66 (1949).

[2] See the discussion in the Council relating to the application of Trieste, ICAO Council, 3rd Sess., Doc. 5302 (C/657), p. 2 (1948). See also Erler, *op. cit. supra* note 1, at 72.

[3] Convention, Art. 91.

[4] Convention, Art. 92.

[5] Convention, Art. 93.

[6] Convention, Art. 91(a).

adhered to by twenty-six States."[7] Adherence to as well as ratification of the Convention is possible after it has entered into force.[8] Furthermore, states that were invited to the Chicago Conference[9] could join ICAO by "adhering" to the Convention, which is "open for adherence by members of the United Nations and States associated with them, and States which remained neutral during the present world conflict,"[10] because only states meeting this description were invited to the Chicago Conference.[11] The confusion between ratification and adherence is further compounded by the fact that in moving the deletion from the draft Convention of a provision fixing a time limit for the signature of the Convention, the chairman of the Chicago Conference explained that this action was designed to "leave it open for any State to *adhere* to this Convention at any time." (Emphasis added.)[12]

It is therefore possible that any state which is not subject to the special admissions procedure to be discussed below could join ICAO either by depositing an instrument of adherence, if it has not previously signed the Convention, or by signing it and then depositing an instrument of ratification. It is difficult to say whether this was the intention of those who drafted the Convention, or whether they wished to reserve the right of signature and ratification to the states that attended the Chicago Conference. ICAO has, moreover, not as yet had to rule on this question,[13] which might conceivably arise if

[7] Convention, Art. 91(b).

[8] Convention, Arts. 91(b) and 92(b).

[9] The Chicago Conference was attended by 52 states—wartime allies, states associated with them, and neutral states—as well as by the Danish and Thai Ministers to Washington who were invited to attend in their personal capacities. The U.S.S.R. was invited but did not attend. For a list of these states, see International Civil Aviation Conference, FINAL ACT AND RELATED DOCUMENTS [hereinafter cited as FINAL ACT], p. 3 (1945); 61 Stat. 1180, T.I.A.S. No. 1591, 15 U.N.T.S. 295 (1948).

[10] Convention, Art. 92(a).

[11] See 1 PROCEEDINGS OF THE INTERNATIONAL CIVIL AVIATION CONFERENCE (CHICAGO, ILLINOIS, NOVEMBER 1–DECEMBER 7, 1944) [hereinafter cited as PROCEEDINGS], p. 13 (1948).

[12] *Id.* at 94.

[13] To date, only the states represented at the Chicago Conference have joined ICAO by ratification, whereas all others have done so by depositing an instrument of adherence. I have been able to find only two rather *sui generis* exceptions to this practice. The first involves Panama, which participated in the

the U.S.S.R., which was invited but did not attend the Chicago Conference, decided to join the Organization by ratifying the Convention.

MEMBERSHIP BY ADHERENCE TO THE CONVENTION

The states which may join ICAO by depositing an instrument of adherence to the Convention are described in Article 92(a) as "members of the United Nations and States associated with them, and States which remained neutral during the present world conflict." [14] Since the United Nations Organization was not in existence at the time the Convention was concluded, the reference in Article 92(a) to the "United Nations" was undoubtedly meant to describe the wartime United Nations. This interpretation finds support in the language of Article 64 of the Convention, under which ICAO concluded an agreement with the U.N. whereby ICAO acquired the status of a Specialized Agency of the U.N. [15] Article 64 of the Convention provides that "the Organization may, with respect to air matters within its competence directly affecting world security, by vote of the Assembly enter into appropriate arrangements with any general organization set up by the nations of the world to preserve peace." This "general organization set up by the nations of the world to preserve peace" rather than the "United Nations" is, furthermore, designated under Article 93 of the Convention as the body which must approve the application for ICAO membership by former enemy states.

Chicago Conference. Panama signed the Convention *ad referendum* and with a reservation. This reservation was not accepted and Panama did not become a Contracting Party until 1960, when it deposited an instrument of adherence which amounted to a withdrawal of the original reservation.

The other case involves Denmark and Thailand. They were not represented *qua* states at the Chicago Conference, but their accredited ministers to Washington were invited and participated in their personal capacities. Even though these representatives signed the Convention in their personal capacities only, both states subsequently ratified the Convention.

[14] Such membership takes effect on the thirtieth day following the receipt of the instrument of adherence by the U.S. Government, the depositary of the Convention. Convention, Art. 92(b).

[15] See Protocol concerning the Entry into Force of the Agreement between the United Nations and the International Civil Aviation Organization, 8 U.N.T.S. 316 (1947); Agreement Between the United Nations and the International Civil Aviation Organization, 8 U.N.T.S. 324 (1947). This Agreement came into force on 13 May 1947.

A recent decision by the ICAO Assembly indicates, however, that present membership in the United Nations Organization will be considered to satisfy the requirements for adherence laid down in Article 92(a). This result follows from the action taken by the ICAO Assembly with regard to Romania. On April 30, 1965, Romania, a former enemy state, deposited its instrument of adherence to the Convention with the U.S. Government. The Romanian note requested the U.S. Secretary of State to consider "this letter as the notification provided by Article 92(b) of the . . . Convention." [16] The U.S. Government forwarded the Romanian note to the Contracting States and advised the ICAO Secretary General that Romania had indicated that it planned to attend the 1965 ICAO Assembly as a Contracting State.[17] This information was transmitted to the Executive Committee of the Assembly where, without any discussion, "it was agreed that the delegation of Romania, when it arrived, would sit as the delegation of a Contracting State." [18] After reporting this decision to the Assembly, the President of the Assembly ruled that if a Romanian delegation arrived it would be seated as the delegation of a Contracting State.[19] Since the President's ruling was not challenged, the Assembly can be deemed to have interpreted Article 92(a) as providing that any member of the U.N. can join ICAO by merely adhering to the Convention, notwithstanding the fact that such state was neither neutral in the Second World War nor associated with the wartime United Nations.[20]

All the Contracting States which acquired statehood after the Second World War joined ICAO under the provisions of Article 92, and this despite the fact that some of them did not as yet belong to the U.N. or one of its specialized agencies when they deposited their instruments of adherence.[21] Here the Organization no doubt pro-

---

[16] The Romanian note is reprinted in ICAO Doc. A15–WP/112 (EX/18), p. 5 (1965).

[17] *Id.* at 1.

[18] ICAO Assembly, Report of the Executive Committee, 15th Sess., Doc. 8522 (A15–EX/43), p. 3 (1965).

[19] ICAO Assembly, 15th Sess., Doc. 8516 (A15–P/5), p. 119 (1965).

[20] For a view questioning the legality of the Assembly's action, see Mankiewicz, *L'Organisation de l'Aviation Civile Internationale*, [1965] Annuaire Français de Droit International 630.

[21] ICAO, *Memorandum of the Legal Officer of [the] Organization of July 5, 1962 (Application of the Chicago Convention to the newly independent States)*,

ceeded on the assumption that these new states qualified for membership on the ground that prior to their independence they were "associated" with "members of the United Nations."

MEMBERSHIP BY ADMISSION

The states which are subject to a special admissions procedure are described in Article 93 [22] as "States other than those provided for in Articles 91 and 92 (a)." This group accordingly includes all non-signatories of the Convention in addition to states that do not meet the conditions for adherence set forth in Article 92 (a). In view of the interpretation of Article 92 (a), adopted in the case of Romania, it would seem that Article 93 applies today only to former enemy states which have not as yet acquired membership in the U.N.

The basic feature of the procedure envisaged by Article 93 is that states subject to it cannot become Contracting Parties by merely signifying their adherence to the Convention. They may be "admitted to participate" in the Convention and thus to membership in the Organization by a four-fifths vote of the ICAO Assembly,[23] subject to any conditions that the Assembly may prescribe. The admission of these states must furthermore be approved by the United Nations [24] and assented to by "any State invaded or attacked during the present war by the State seeking admission." [25]

---

reprinted in International Law Ass'n, THE EFFECT OF INDEPENDENCE ON TREATIES: A HANDBOOK 331 (1965); ICAO Doc. C–WP/4031, p. 1 (1964).

[22] For the legislative history of this provision, see 2 PROCEEDINGS, pp. 1396–97; Bärmann, *Art. 93 des Abkommens von Chicago und das Völkerrecht*, 2 Zeitschrift für Luftrecht 1 (1953).

[23] As interpreted by the Assembly, the four-fifths vote shall be that of "the total number of Contracting States represented at the Assembly and qualified to vote at the time the vote is taken." It excludes the votes of states under suspension, of those which have previously signified their withdrawal or departure from the Assembly, and of the delegates whose credentials expressly deprive them of the right to participate in such a vote. ICAO Assembly, Standing Rules of Procedure, Rule 54, Doc. 7600/2 (1963).

[24] Convention, Art. 93, speaks of "any general international organization set up by the nations of the world to preserve peace." This function has been assumed by the United Nations. See Agreement between the United Nations and the International Civil Aviation Organization, Art. II, *supra* note 15.

[25] Convention, Art. 93. By "present war" is meant "the war of 1939–1945." Assembly Res. A1–9, ICAO Doc. 4411 (A1–P/45) (1947). This ruling was made after the admission of Italy, and thus did not affect the express understanding of the Chicago Conference that the phrase "present war" applied to the war waged against Ethiopia. See 1 PROCEEDINGS, p. 95.

The Assembly has not, for all practical purposes, availed itself of the power to prescribe conditions for the admission of states subject to the provisions of Article 93. Beyond conditioning admission upon the approval of the U.N. General Assembly and, where necessary, the assent of the states that had been invaded or attacked by the applicant, the ICAO Assembly has required no more than the deposit of an instrument of adherence to the Convention. Furthermore, it has in each instance stipulated that membership would take effect thirty days after compliance with these requirements.[26]

Article II of the Agreement between the U.N. and ICAO[27] establishes the procedure pursuant to which the U.N. will either approve or disapprove applications for ICAO membership by states described in Article 93.[28] After providing that such applications shall be immediately transmitted by the ICAO Secretariat to the U.N. General Assembly, Article II stipulates:

> The General Assembly may recommend the rejection of such application, and any such recommendation shall be accepted by the Organization. If no such recommendation is made by the General Assembly at the first session following receipt of the application, the application shall be decided upon by the Organization in accordance with the procedure established in Article 93 of the Convention.

To date, none of the applications submitted to the General Assembly have been rejected. Moreover, while the General Assembly is free under Article II to signify its approval by silence, it has in each case passed a resolution informing ICAO that it has no objection to the admission of the applicant state.[29] It is noteworthy, however,

---

[26] See, e.g., Assembly Res. A7-2, ICAO Doc. 7417 (A7-P/3) (1953) (Resolution relating to the admission of Japan).

[27] 8 U.N.T.S. 324 (1947).

[28] For a summary of this procedure, see U.N. Secretary-General, *Explanatory Memorandum*, U.N. Docs. A/2912 and A/2912/Corr. 1 (1955); ICAO Doc. C-WP/1265 (1952).

[29] Gen. Ass. Res. 121 (II) of 31 Oct. 1947, Gen. Ass. Off. Rec., 2d Sess., RESOLUTIONS, pp. 25–26, U.N. Doc. A/519 (1948) (Application of Italy); Gen. Ass. Res. 122 (II) of 1 Nov. 1947, Gen. Ass. Off. Rec., 2d Sess., RESOLUTIONS, p. 26, U.N. Doc. A/519 (1948) (Application of Austria); Gen. Ass. Res. 203 (III) of 18 Nov. 1948, Gen. Ass. Off. Rec., 3rd Sess., 1st pt., RESOLUTIONS, p. 43, U.N. Doc. A/810 (1948) (Application of Finland); Gen. Ass. Res. 697 (VII) of 6 Nov. 1952, Gen. Ass. Off. Rec., 7th Sess., RESOLUTIONS, p. 71, Supplement No. 20, U.N. Doc. A/2361 (1952) (Application of Japan); Gen. Ass. Res. 991 (X) of 25 Oct. 1955, Gen. Ass. Off. Rec., 10th Sess., RESOLUTIONS, p. 49, Supplement No. 19, U.N. Doc. A/3116 (1955) (Application of Fed. Rep. of Germany).

that when the General Assembly considered the application of the Federal Republic of Germany, the Representative of the U.S.S.R., supported by his Czechoslovak colleague, stated that his delegation would vote in favor of the application "in the expectation that, if a similar application is made by the German Democratic Republic, it will also be approved." [30] This statement was not challenged by any delegation. The German Democratic Republic has not as yet applied for ICAO membership.

Since the Convention was drafted in the expectation that all former Allied and Associated Powers would become members of ICAO, it is not surprising that the Convention conditions the admission of former enemy states on the assent of "any State invaded or attacked" by them. Because this expectation did not materialize— the U.S.S.R., for example, is not as yet a member of the Organization—the question presents itself whether the requisite assent must also be sought from non-Contracting States which were the victims of such aggression. A strict interpretation of the Convention would compel an affirmative reply because Article 93, unlike some other provisions of the Convention, does not distinguish between Contracting and non-Contracting States. [31] The Organization has in the past, however, consistently proceeded on the assumption that only the consent of Contracting States is necessary. An express ruling to this effect was apparently made by the Executive Committee of the ICAO Assembly when it considered Italy's request for admission to the Organization. [32] This interpretation has been followed in subsequent cases, notwithstanding the doubts expressed in the ICAO Council regarding its validity. [33] Thus, the assent of non-Contracting

---

[30] U.N. Gen. Ass. Off. Rec., 10th Sess., PLENARY MEETINGS 266 (1955).

[31] This view was advanced by the Canadian Representative on the ICAO Council who, in contesting the argument that "any State" under Article 93 meant "any Contracting State," pointed out that "Contracting States were referred as such everywhere else in the Convention." ICAO Council, 4th Sess., Doc. 5710 (C/681), p. 10 (1948).

[32] See ICAO Doc. C–WP/1256, Appendix A, p. 4 (1952), reporting that on May 13, 1947, the Executive Committee decided that " 'any State invaded or attacked during the present war by the State seeking admission,' should be interpreted to mean any Contracting State so invaded or attacked." See also, Statement by the U.S. Delegation in moving Italy's admission, ICAO Assembly, Proceedings of the First Session [1947], Doc. 7325 (C/852), pp. 88–89 (1952).

[33] See ICAO Council, 4th Sess., Doc. 5710 (C/681), p. 10 (1948).

States was not sought in the case of Finland,[34] Japan,[35] or the Federal Republic of Germany.

In admitting the Federal Republic of Germany to the Organization, the ICAO Assembly departed from its prior practice in that it did not expressly condition the admission of Germany on the assent of those Contracting States that had been invaded or attacked by it. Instead, in the resolution approving Germany's application, the Assembly merely conditioned its admission on the approval of the U.N. General Assembly and the deposit by the Federal Republic of its instrument of adherence.[36] This departure from past practice is attributable to a statement of the United States Delegate to the ICAO Assembly. He explained, in submitting the draft resolution for Germany's admission,[37] that "it is implicit in this Resolution that all of the conditions of the Convention applicable to the Assembly, its Member States and the Organization will have been satisfied when this Resolution is approved by a roll call vote of this Session of the Assembly." [38]

Three assumptions appear to be implicit in this statement. First, that only Contracting States which were invaded or attacked by Germany need give their assent to its admission. This interpretation is, as we have seen, in conformity with the practice of the Organization. Second, the Contracting States whose assent is required may be deemed to have signified it by not voting against the resolution proposing the admission of the Federal Republic. In the absence of any objections to this procedure it cannot be said to violate Article 93. Besides, this method for obtaining the requisite assents had

[34] In the case of Finland, where the assent of the U.S.S.R. should have been sought if Article 93 applied also to non-Contracting States, the preamble to the Assembly resolution admitting that state to ICAO membership expressed the view that "the condition of Article 93 of the Convention relating to the assent of any State invaded or attacked during the war of 1939–45 does not apply to the application of Finland." Assembly Res. A2–4, ICAO Doc. 5692 (A2–P/37) (1948).

[35] The Assembly approved Japan's application for membership by Assembly Res. A7–2, ICAO Doc. 7417 (A7–P/3) (1953). For documentation relating to Japan's admission, see especially ICAO Doc. A7–WP/21 (EX/7) (1953); ICAO Assembly, Report of the Executive Committee, 7th Sess., Doc. 7413 (A7–EX/1), p. 8 (1953).

[36] See Assembly Res. A9–1, ICAO Doc. 7595 (A9–P/12) (1955).

[37] ICAO Doc. A9–WP/27 (EX/15) (1955).

[38] ICAO Assembly, Report of the Executive Committee, 9th Sess., Doc. 7594 (A9–EX/25), p. 6 (1955).

already been used in connection with the admission of Japan.[39] The third assumption upon which the U.S. may have proceeded is less clear. On the one hand, the U.S. might be deemed to have asserted that under Article 93 a former enemy state may be admitted to membership in ICAO if its application is approved by the requisite four-fifths vote of the Assembly, even though one or more states whose assent is required under Article 93 voted against the resolution of admission. This interpretation would obviously be incompatible with the provisions of Article 93. It is possible to assume, on the other hand, that the United States, having canvassed all Contracting States whose assent was required, concluded that they would not vote against the admission of the Federal Republic.

On the basis of this information, which proved to be correct,[40] the U.S. could validly assert that the approval of its draft resolution by a roll call vote of the Assembly would satisfy "all of the conditions of the Convention applicable to the Assembly, its Member States and the Organization." It should be emphasized, however, that the Federal Republic could not legally have been admitted to ICAO if its application for membership had been vetoed by any one of the Contracting States that were invaded or attacked by Germany in World War II.

The admission of Austria to ICAO raised another interesting question relating to the interpretation of Article 93. When Austria applied for membership in September of 1947 [41] it had not as yet become a member of the U.N. Austria did not, furthermore, qualify for membership under Article 92(a) since it had been neither a member of the wartime United Nations, a state associated with them, nor a state that remained neutral in the Second World War. Austria could, as a result, become a member of the Organization only by admission pursuant to the provisions of Article 93. Its application would accordingly have to receive the requisite four-fifths vote of the ICAO Assembly and the approval of the U.N. General Assembly. But was the Austrian application also subject to

[39] See ICAO Assembly, 7th Sess., Doc. 7409 (A7–P/2), pp. 61–62 (1953).

[40] The resolution approving the application of the Federal Republic was adopted by 51 votes in favor and none against, with Israel abstaining; see ICAO Assembly, 9th Sess., Doc. 7596 (A9–P/13), pp. 45–46 (1955).

[41] The Austrian application is reproduced in ICAO Doc. 5224 (A2–P/8) (1948).

"the assent of any State invaded or attacked . . . by the State seeking admission"? The answer to this question turned upon Austria's status in the Second World War. That is to say, depending upon the interpretation adopted with regard to Germany's annexation of Austria, Austria might be characterized either as an aggressor or as a victim of German aggression.

In reviewing the documentation relating to Austria's application with the ICAO Council prior to its submission to the Assembly,[42] the President of the Council expressed the view that there was no need to seek the assent of states invaded or attacked by Austria, because the Allied Governments at the First Moscow Conference had declared that they regarded the German annexation of Austria as null and void. It was therefore "difficult to conceive how a victim of Nazi aggression could also be considered to be guilty as a sovereign State of having invaded another country."[43] The President's interpretation was accepted by the Council[44] and expressly affirmed by the Assembly. That is to say, in its resolution approving Austria's admission to ICAO, the Assembly ruled that "it is considered that the condition in Article 93 of the Convention relating to the assent of any State invaded or attacked during the 1939–45 war does not apply to the application of Austria."[45]

In retrospect, it is apparent that, notwithstanding the fears expressed by some commentators,[46] Article 93 has thus far not been used to block the admission of any former enemy state wishing to join ICAO. This result is no doubt attributable to the Organization's decision not to seek the assent of any non-Contracting State which had been invaded or attacked by these applicants. Although it is

---

[42] Austria's application was initially considered by the Council because, under Assembly Res. A1–9, ICAO Doc. 4411 (A1–P/45) (1947), if applications for admission under Article 93 are received by the Organization while the Assembly is not in session, "the Council may, in accordance with Article 93 . . . and pending submission of the application to the next Assembly in accordance with that Article, consult with the State or States invaded or attacked during the war of 1939–45 by the State seeking admission."

[43] ICAO Council, 3rd Sess., Doc. 5233 (C/646), p. 1 (1948).

[44] *Ibid.*

[45] Assembly Res. A2–3, ICAO Doc. 5692 (A2–P/37) (1948). While the same language appears in the resolution relating to the admission of Finland, see Assembly Res. A2–4, ICAO Doc. 5692 (A2–P/37) (1948), it was prompted by different considerations. See note 34 *supra.*

[46] See, *e.g.*, Jennings, *supra* note 1, at 565–66.

open to question whether this practice is strictly in keeping with the language of Article 93, it would have been absurd to give states unwilling to join the Organization a veto power over ICAO membership.

Special Membership Problems

RESERVATIONS TO THE CONVENTION

The Chicago Convention contains no clause relating to reservations, and is silent on the question whether a state which ratifies or adheres to the Convention with a reservation is entitled to ICAO membership.[47] This question has been considered, however, both by the ICAO Council and Assembly primarily because of an attempt by Yugoslavia to ratify the Convention with a reservation.

Yugoslavia deposited its instrument of ratification on February 15, 1954, with a reservation relating to Article 5 of the Convention. The U.S. Government, as depositary, thereupon requested all Contracting States to signify whether they accepted the Yugoslav reservation. Although no express determination was ever made that the acceptance of this reservation by all Member States was a condition precedent to Yugoslavia's admission to the Organization, the ICAO Council proceeded on this assumption and reported to the Assembly that "pending a decision on this point Yugoslavia cannot be considered a Contracting State." [48]

This position was challenged by France in the Executive Committee of the Assembly. While the French Delegate acknowledged that it was in conformity with international law and practice for the parties to an international convention to consult regarding the acceptability of a reservation contained in an instrument of ratifica-

---

[47] See, on this subject generally, International Law Commission, Draft Articles on the Law of Treaties, Arts. 16–20, U.N. Gen. Ass. Off. Rec., 21st Sess., Supplement No. 9, U.N. Doc. A/6309/Rev. 1 (1966); Anderson, *Reservations to Multilateral Conventions: A Re-Examination*, 13 Int'l & Comp. L.Q. 450 (1964); Bishop, *Reservations to Treaties*, 103 Recueil des Cours 245 (1961); U.N. Secretary-General, *Summary of the Practice of the Secretary-General as Depositary of Multilateral Agreements*, U.N. Doc. ST/LEG/7, pp. 31–40 (1959); Fitzmaurice, *Reservations to Multilateral Conventions*, 2 Int'l & Comp. L.Q. 1 (1953); U.N. Secretary-General, *Reservations to Multilateral Conventions*, U.N. Doc. A/1372 (1950).

[48] [1954] Report of the Council, ICAO Doc. 7564 (A9–P2), p. 55 (1955).

tion, he felt that such a procedure "might not be altogether appropriate when the reservation was to a treaty or convention establishing an international organization with an Assembly as its supreme decision-making body." The most objectionable aspect of this procedure was that it "gave any one Contracting State what amounted to a veto, as unanimous acceptance of the reservation was necessary before the State making it could become a member of the organization." The French authorities therefore believed that the approach adopted with regard to the Yugoslav reservation "did not correspond to the constitutional procedure usually applied in international organizations for deciding very important matters—a majority vote in the Assembly." [49]

Without addressing himself to the issue raised by his French colleague, the U.S. Delegate replied merely that the Yugoslav ratification could not be considered "as having been deposited until the reservation it contained had been accepted by all Contracting States." [50] Left unexplored also was the French suggestion that the ICAO Assembly should pass upon the acceptability of the reservation by a majority vote. Instead, in its next report to the Assembly, the Council simply noted that twenty-two states had signified their willingness to accept the Yugoslav reservation, that eight found it unacceptable, and that the remainder had not as yet been heard from. [51] Thus, without further discussion, the Yugoslav reservation was deemed to have been rejected on the ground that it had not been accepted by all Contracting States. Yugoslavia did not become a Contracting State until 1960, when it deposited a new instrument of ratification without any reservation. [52]

ICAO had previously taken a similar position on a Cuban reservation to Article 5 of the Convention. When a number of Contracting States refused to accept the Cuban reservation, [53] the U.S. De-

[49] ICAO Assembly, Executive Committee, 9th Sess., Doc. 7597 (A9–EX/MIN. 1–9), p. 71 (1955).

[50] Ibid.

[51] [1955] Report of the Council, ICAO Doc. 7636 (A10–P/3), p. 46 (1956).

[52] Notifying the Assembly that Yugoslavia had become a Contracting State, the ICAO Council recalled that "the Yugoslav instrument replaced one deposited six years earlier with a reservation on Article 5 which a number of Contracting States had declined to accept." [1960] Report of the Council, ICAO Doc. 8140 (A14–P/1), p. 65 (1961).

[53] [1947–1948] Report of the Council, ICAO Doc. 5221 (A2–P/5), p. 3 (1948).

partment of State, relying on "general concepts of international law and procedure," notified Cuba that the U.S. could not accept the Cuban instrument of ratification because ". . . the consent of all Governments parties to the Convention is required before a reservation of the nature of that submitted by Cuba may become effective and before Cuba may become a party to the Convention." [54] While neither the ICAO Assembly nor the Council explored the question whether the non-consenting states did in fact have the power to veto Cuba's membership in the Organization, Cuba was not considered to have become a Member State until 1949, when it deposited a new instrument of ratification without any reservation.[55]

While it is not clear exactly how many other states have in the past attempted to ratify the Convention with a reservation,[56] no reservations have to date been accepted.[57] This does not mean, of

[54] Quoted in Bishop, *supra* note 47, at 277–78, from the U.S. Department of State, *The Law of Treaties as Applied by the Government of the United States of America* 105–06 (transmitted to the United Nations by the Department of State on March 31, 1950, in mimeographed form).

[55] ICAO Council, 7th Sess., Doc. 6913 (C/802), p. 39 (1949). The assertion by Erler, *op. cit. supra* note 1, at 74, that Cuba merely withdrew its reservation is not borne out by the authority he cites.

[56] In its annual report to the Assembly the Council in 1949 noted that "certain States have ratified [the Convention] with a reservation on Article 5 of the Convention or propose to do so, but a number of Contracting States have refused to assent to the acceptance of ratifications so conditioned." [1949] Report of the Council, ICAO Doc. 6433 (A3–P/4), p. 2 (1949). It is not clear whether any other states in addition to Cuba *actually* made such a reservation, although it is possible that the Council's statement had reference also to a Panamanian reservation which, while not expressly mentioning any provisions of the Convention, seemed to apply to Article 5. This reservation was made by Panama when signing the Convention *ad referendum*. See ICAO Doc. 7300 (1952), where the signatures are reproduced. Panama did not become a member of ICAO until 1960, when it deposited an instrument of adherence. See also Erler, *op. cit. supra* note 1, at 75.

[57] In depositing his government's ratification of the Convention in 1947, the Czechoslovak Ambassador to the U.S. notified the Department of State that the Convention was ratified by his Government "on the assumption" that ICAO "will carry out fully the resolution passed by the United Nations Organization on December 12, 1946 concerning the exclusion of Franco Spain from cooperation with the United Nations." [1950] Report of the Council, ICAO Doc. 7148 (A5–P/1), p. 121 (1951). Since ICAO complied with this condition as soon as the first ICAO Assembly convened in 1947, see Assembly Res. A1–3, ICAO Doc. 4411 (A1–P/45) (1947), the reservation must be considered to have lapsed. It seems to have been accepted by the U.S. Government, however, since Czechoslovakia's ratification of the Convention became effective on March 1, 1947, *viz.*,

course, that reservations to the Convention are not permitted. The Organization's practice in the case of Cuba and Yugoslavia indicates, however, that a reservation will have to be accepted by all Contracting States before the state attaching it will gain membership in ICAO.

In theory, much can be said in favor of the French contention that one state should not have the power to veto a reservation to the Convention and thus exclude another state from membership in ICAO.[58] As a matter of fact, the International Law Commission in its Draft Articles on the Law of Treaties [59] takes a similar position. Article 17(3) thereof provides that "when a treaty is a constituent instrument of an international organization, the reservation requires the acceptance of the competent organ of that organization, unless the treaty otherwise provides." Since the ICAO Assembly is authorized to "deal with any matter within the sphere of action of the Organization not specifically assigned to the Council," [60] and since the powers of the Council do not extend to the question here under consideration,[61] the Assembly would be the "competent organ" within the meaning of Article 17(3) of the Draft Articles on the Law of Treaties. It is accordingly arguable that the Assembly has the power to promulgate rules for passing upon the acceptability of reservations for purposes of ICAO membership [62] without thereby

---

two months before ICAO complied with the U.N. resolution. In depositing its instrument of adherence to the Convention in 1960, Panama made a "reservation" to the Spanish translation of a word appearing in Article 2 of the unofficial Spanish text of the Convention. The U.S. accepted this instrument on the theory that, since "the National Assembly of Panama has approved the Convention as it appears in the English text . . . the reservation does not detract in any way from the obligations assumed by Panama with respect to the Convention." Report of the President of the Council, ICAO Doc. C–WP/3100, p. 1 (1960). This explanation was merely noted by the Council. ICAO Council, 39th Sess. [1960], Doc. 8057 (C/922), p. 22 (1961).

[58] See Reservations to the Convention on the Prevention and Punishment of the Crime of Genocide, International Court of Justice, [1951] I.C.J. Rep. 15, at 21–22 (advisory opinion).

[59] International Law Commission, Draft Articles on the Law of Treaties, U.N. Gen. Ass. Off. Rec., 21st Sess., Supplement No. 9, U.N. Doc. A/6309/Rev. 1 (1966).

[60] Convention, Art. 49(k).

[61] For the powers of the Council, see Convention, Arts. 54 and 55.

[62] A similar procedure was recently adopted by the Organization of American States. See First Special Inter-American Conference, Act of Washington, in

necessarily determining the effect of the reservation as between the Member States.[63]

Since the decision whether or not to accept a reservation, even if limited in its effect to ICAO membership, is of considerable importance, it should require the consent of more than the simple majority that usually determines Assembly action.[64] Here two possible solutions present themselves. The first would take its cue from the fact that the acceptance of a reservation can be viewed as a *pro tanto* amendment of the Convention. Since under Article 94(a) a two-thirds vote of the Assembly is needed for the adoption of an amendment to the Convention, a similar vote might be required for the acceptance of a reservation. Amendments to the Convention do not, however, enter into force until they have been ratified by no less than two-thirds of the total number of Contracting States.

The delay that ratification would thus entail, if it were made applicable to the acceptance of reservations, could be avoided by a second solution. Since the Assembly may, under Article 93, admit to ICAO membership any state that does not qualify for such membership merely by ratifying or adhering to the Convention, the Assembly might proceed under Article 93 in passing on the acceptability of reservations. In doing so, the Assembly could decide by a four-fifths vote whether, despite its reservation, the state in question should be admitted to ICAO membership.

This approach for dealing with reservations, whether it be based on Article 93 or Article 94(a), would have the advantage of preventing one or a small number of states from vetoing the admission of states wishing to adhere to the Convention with a reservation. At the same time, of course, it would require an assent large enough to

---

FINAL ACT OF THE CONFERENCE, p. 3, Doc. 31, Rev. 3, December 18, 1964, O.A.S. Official Records, OEA/Ser.E/XII.1. Pursuant to Article 2 of this Act

> the Council of the Organization . . . shall determine by the vote of two thirds of the member states whether it is appropriate that the Secretary General be authorized to permit the applicant state to sign the Charter of the Organization and to accept the deposit of the corresponding instrument of ratification.

No express provisions for such action by the OAS Council can be found in the Charter of the Organization of American States. See Thomas & Thomas, THE ORGANIZATION OF AMERICAN STATES 54–58 (1963).

[63] For the legal effect of reservations, see International Law Commission, Draft Articles of the Law of Treaties, Art. 19, *supra* note 59.

[64] See Convention, Art. 48(c).

ensure that a substantial part of the Organization's membership has a voice in passing on the acceptability of the reservation.[65] However, even assuming that this solution could be adopted without amending the Convention, it would probably not be wise at this late date to facilitate ICAO membership for states attaching reservations to the Convention. Since 116 states have thus far found it possible to adhere to the Convention without doing so, it is unlikely that the few states still remaining outside the Organization will be deterred from joining ICAO if denied the right to make reservations.[66]

NEW STATES

The membership status of "new states" in ICAO presents two separate problems.[67] The first has to do with the question whether

[65] A similar solution, albeit by a unanimous vote of the Assembly, was adopted by the World Health Organization in accepting a U.S. reservation. See W.H.O., First Assembly, Official Records, No. 13, pp. 77–80 (1948).

However, when India sought to make a reservation in ratifying the Convention on the Inter-Governmental Maritime Consultative Organization, the IMCO Assembly did not itself pass on the acceptability of the reservation. It requested the U.N. Secretary-General, the depositary of the IMCO Convention, "to circulate the document to member states of the Organization," but resolved ". . . that until the member states have had an opportunity of expressing their views, the representatives of India shall be free to take part, *without a vote*, in the proceedings of this Assembly." (Emphasis added.) IMCO/A.I/Resolution 5 (1959). Thereafter, India stated in the U.N. General Assembly that its reservation was merely a declaration. Informed of India's position by a resolution of the General Assembly, Resolution 1452A (XIV) of 7 Dec. 1959, Gen. Ass. Off. Rec., 14th Sess., RESOLUTIONS, p. 56, Supplement No. 16, U.N. Doc. A/4354 (1959), the IMCO Council "expressed the view that the Indian Declaration did not constitute an impediment to membership and . . . stated that India was a member of the Organization." Oral Report by IMCO Secretary-General, IMCO Assembly, 2d Sess., Doc. A.II/SR.1, p. 14 (1961). This decision was simply noted by the IMCO Assembly. *Ibid.* For the disposition by the U.N. General Assembly of the controversy relating to the Indian "reservation" to the IMCO Convention, see U.N. Gen. Ass. Off. Rec., 14th Sess., ANNEXES, Agenda Item 65 (1959). See also, Schachter, *Question of Treaty Reservations at the 1959 General Assembly,* 54 Am. J. Int'l L. 372 (1960).

[66] In this connection, see *The Union of Soviet Socialist Republics and the International Labour Organisation,* 37 I.L.O. Official Bulletin 229–31 (1954), reprinting the documentation relating to the U.S.S.R.'s attempt to attach a reservation to its ratification of the I.L.O. Constitution, the refusal of the I.L.O. Director-General to accept the reservation, and the withdrawal of the reservation by the U.S.S.R.

[67] For an excellent analysis of both problems see Mankiewicz, *Air Law Conventions and the New States,* 20 J. Air L. & Com. 52 (1963). See also Erler, *op. cit. supra* note 1, at 75–77; O'Connell, *Independence and Problems of State Succession, in* O'Brien, THE NEW NATIONS IN INTERNATIONAL LAW AND DIPLO-

those newly independent states to whose territory the Convention applied before they acquired statehood[68] automatically succeed to membership in ICAO. The second problem relates to the membership status of states created by the union of two or more Contracting States.

Newly Independent States

ICAO has consistently proceeded on the assumption that colonial territories formerly belonging to Contracting States do not automatically acquire ICAO membership upon gaining independence.[69] Thus, when the United Kingdom, for example, informed the ICAO Council in 1948 that Burma and Ceylon had been granted independence, the Council, after concluding that these states were "eligible under Article 92 of the Convention to acquire membership in ICAO by adhering to the Convention," decided that "it would be appropriate to communicate with the Governments concerned bringing their position to their attention and inviting their adherence."[70] A former ICAO Legal Officer justifies this practice on the ground that "the restrictions on the rights of a sovereign State as established by the international civil aviation code contained in the Chicago Convention, as well as the obligations attached to membership in ICAO, are of such nature that they cannot bind a State without its express consent."[71]

ICAO has also taken the position that newly independent states cannot become Contracting States automatically by simply signifying their readiness to assume the rights and obligations of their former sovereign under the Convention. Thus, when Pakistan

---

MACY 7 (1965); International Law Ass'n, THE EFFECT OF INDEPENDENCE ON TREATIES: A HANDBOOK (1965); U.N. Secretary-General, *Summary of Practice of the Secretary-General as Depositary of Multilateral Agreements,* U.N. Doc. ST/LEG/7, pp. 47–64 (1959).

[68] Convention, Art. 2 describes the territory of a state as being "the land areas and territorial waters adjacent thereto under the sovereignty, suzerainty, protection or mandate of such State."

[69] ICAO, *Memorandum of the Legal Officer of [the] Organization of July 5, 1962 (Application of the Chicago Convention to the newly independent States),* reprinted in International Law Ass'n, THE EFFECT OF INDEPENDENCE ON TREATIES: A HANDBOOK, 331 (1965).

[70] ICAO Council, 3rd Sess., Doc. 5110 (C/635), p. 2 (1948). See also, ICAO Council, 52d Sess., Doc. 8423 (C/951), p. 28 (1964).

[71] Mankiewicz, *supra* note 67, at 55.

gained independence following the partition of India it informed the Organization that Pakistan considered itself bound by the Convention. Despite the fact that the Government of India had ratified the Convention prior to the partition, the ICAO Council advised the Government of Pakistan that to achieve the status of a Contracting State, Pakistan would have to comply with the provisions of Article 92 by formally adhering to the Convention.[72] As a consequence of this ruling, Pakistan did not become a Member State until thirty days after depositing its instrument of adherence with the U.S. Government.[73]

Merging of Contracting States and Dissolution of Unions

The membership status of states created by the union of two or more Contracting States was considered by the Organization as a result of the union of Egypt and Syria.[74] Both states had previously ratified the Convention—Egypt in 1947 and Syria in 1949. After they established the United Arab Republic in 1958 the Foreign Minister of the U.A.R. advised ICAO that his Government considered itself bound by the obligations which Egypt and Syria had severally assumed under the Convention. The foreign minister simultaneously transmitted the credentials of the new U.A.R. Representative on the ICAO Council.[75] Since Egypt's term on the Council had not as yet expired, and since the Assembly was not in session, the President of the Council requested the Council to decide whether the U.A.R. was a member of ICAO and whether it could assume Egypt's seat on the Council.[76] The Council answered both questions in the affirmative. It noted, however, that this decision was "for matters within the competence of the Council," and without prejudice to "the right of the Assembly to determine for itself questions concerning the United Arab Republic in relation to the Organization." [77]

The Council made two assumptions which account for its guarded

---

[72] ICAO Council, 2d Sess., Doc. 4818 (C/605), p. 2 (1947).

[73] See ICAO Council, Proceedings of the Second Session [1947], Doc. 7248 (C/839), p. 70 (1952).

[74] For a discussion of this case, see Mankiewicz, *supra* note 67, at 56–57.

[75] For the various communications, see ICAO Doc. A11–WP/23 (P/4), and Enclosure I (1958).

[76] See ICAO Council, 33rd Sess., Doc. 7878 (C/905), p. 262 (1958).

[77] *Id.* at 261–62.

language.[78] The first related to the fact that the determination of a state's claim to Council membership is ultimately within the competence of the Assembly which, under Article 50 of the Convention, elects the Council. Accordingly, until the Assembly did have an opportunity to act on this matter, the Council considered itself authorized only to pass on the credentials presented by the U.A.R. Representative. The Council's second assumption was that the status of the U.A.R. as a Contracting Party was a question which the Member States themselves had to decide. As a matter of fact, the original draft resolution contained a clause to that effect.[79] It was withdrawn at the suggestion of one Council Representative, who thought it "dangerous . . . to remind Contracting States that they had a right to decide this matter for themselves." He acknowledged that they had this right, but thought that "chaos would result if they exercised it." [80] The Council therefore decided simply to advise the Assembly of the steps it had taken,[81] thus leaving the final determination to the Assembly. Interestingly enough, the Assembly merely noted the Council's report without questioning the membership status of the U.A.R.[82]

Shortly after Syria withdrew from the U.A.R. in 1961, it advised the President of the ICAO Council that "Syria was reassuming its place in ICAO as a Contracting State separate from the United Arab Republic," and that "Syria abides by all the agreements, arrangements and obligations which existed between ICAO and the United Arab Republic at the moment of the constitution of the Syrian Arab Republic." [83] After receiving Syria's communication, the President of the Council transmitted the following note to the Council:

> In my memorandum . . . of 23 October I explained the situation and indicated that, unless views to the contrary were received before 1 November 1961, Syria would in the future be regarded as a Contracting State. No comments having been received by that date,

[78] *Id.* at 264–65.
[79] *Id.* at 263.
[80] *Id.* at 265.
[81] See ICAO Doc. A11–WP/23 (P/4), p. 2 (1958).
[82] See ICAO Assembly, Report of the Executive Committee, 11th Sess., Doc. 7887 (A11–EX/11), p. 11 (1958); ICAO Assembly, 11th Sess., Doc. 7886 (A11–P/11), p. 45 (1958).
[83] ICAO Doc. C–WP/3434, p. 2 (1961).

the Secretary General will now consider Syria as a Contracting State.[84]

The President's ruling was not challenged.[85] Syria accordingly reassumed its membership in ICAO, and was shortly thereafter assessed as a Contracting State.[86]

Two conclusions emerge from the disposition of the U.A.R. case. First, it is apparent that where two or more Contracting Parties unite, the new entity will be regarded as a Member State, provided only that it signifies to ICAO its willingness to assume the obligations which its component parts had severally accepted under the Convention. This does not necessarily mean that a Contracting State might not effectively challenge the status of the new entity as a Contracting Party on the ground that the latter has, as a practical matter, varied the obligations that its component parts had assumed under the Convention. Secondly, the U.A.R. case indicates that, upon the dissolution of the union, the state whose seat was vacated will be able to "reassume" its membership in ICAO without again having formally to accede to the Convention.

Here it may be asked whether the state's resumption of membership must be conditioned on its willingness to abide not only by its former obligations under the Convention but also by those which, with regard to the territory now under its sovereignty, had been assumed by the dissolved union. Syria, it will be recalled, signified its intention to be bound also by these latter obligations. Did it have to take this step? It is at least arguable that it is implicit in the notion of a state "reassuming" its membership that it never withdrew from the Convention, but that it merely delegated to another entity the duty of representing its interest and performing its obligations.[87] If that is so, the other Contracting States would have the

---

[84] *Ibid.*

[85] One Council Representative noted, however, that "it would have been a somewhat better statement" regarding Syria's position, "if it had been said . . . that 'Syria is now considered as a Contracting State' instead of 'the Secretary General will now consider Syria as a Contracting State.' " ICAO Council, 44th Sess. [1961], Doc. 8192 (C/934), p. 28 (1963).

[86] *Id.* at 180.

[87] In the case of Syria, ICAO seems to have proceeded on this theory. During the union of Egypt and Syria, the U.A.R. alone was listed as a Contracting State followed, however, by a reference to the dates of Syria's (1949) and Egypt's (1947) ratification of the Convention. See [1959] Report of the Council, ICAO

right to demand, as a condition for resuming ICAO membership, that the state in question accept the obligations which were assumed for it. This argument would, of course, lose its validity if it could be shown that the union had not been voluntarily entered into, since a state should not be held to obligations which were forced upon it.

As a practical matter, of course, the solution which ICAO might adopt will most likely depend upon one of two factors: the attitude of the Contracting States towards the union at the time of its establishment, or their willingness to recognize the existence of the re-emerging state. Political considerations will, in other words, determine the ultimate result. This is well illustrated by the problems which Malaysia encountered in the ICAO Council. In 1963, the Ministry of External Affairs of Malaysia notified the Organization [88] that the Federation of Malaysia considered itself, as constitutional successor to the Federation of Malaya, a Contracting State; and that it was the same entity with a different name.[89] Despite the fact that the Malaysian position presented no serious legal problems, the Indonesian and Philippine Representatives on the ICAO Council strenuously objected to a motion that the Contracting States be notified that the Federation of Malaysia, as successor to the Federation of Malaya, was a member of ICAO. Admitting frankly that they were motivated by political rather than legal considerations, these Representatives argued that the Federation of Malaysia should be regarded as a new state which, to acquire membership in the Organization, would have to deposit an instrument of adherence to the Convention.[90] This view did not prevail, however, and the Federation of Malaysia was ruled to be a Contracting State.[91] A

Doc. 8063 (A13–P/1), p. 95 (1960). Today Syria is again listed as a Member State which became a Contracting Party in 1949. This entry is followed by the margin notation: "From 21 February 1958 to 28 September 1961 Syria was part of the United Arab Republic." [1965] Report of the Council, ICAO Doc. 8572 (A16–P/1), p. 129 (1966).

[88] For the exchange of cables between ICAO and the Federation of Malaysia, see ICAO Doc. C–WP/3881 (1963).

[89] ICAO Council, 50th Sess. [1963], Doc. 8373 (C/948), p. 125 (1964).

[90] *Id.* at 125–26.

[91] *Id.* at 124. ICAO reached a similar decision in 1964 when Tanganyika, a Contracting State, formed a union with Zanzibar, a non-Contracting State. Informed of the establishment of this union, the Council simply instructed the ICAO Secretary General to notify all Contracting States that ". . . the United Republic was a Contracting State—in other words, a party to the Convention . . . and a member of ICAO, in place of the former Republic of Tanganyika." ICAO Council, 52d Sess., Doc. 8423 (C/951), p. 195 (1964).

contrary result would obviously have been reached if Indonesia and the Philippines had not been alone in their feud with Malaysia.

TERMINATION AND SUSPENSION OF MEMBERSHIP

Termination of Membership

A state's membership in ICAO can be terminated [92] by its denunciation of the Convention [93] or by its expulsion from the Organization. [94]

DENUNCIATION OF THE CONVENTION

Article 95 of the Convention permits a Contracting State to withdraw from the Organization by denouncing the Convention. Such denunciation takes effect one year after receipt of the notification of denunciation by the U.S. Government. The only state which has to date denounced the Convention is the Republic of China. [95] In 1952 Guatemala deposited a notice of denunciation but withdrew it before it had become effective. Guatemala's right to recall its denunciation was not challenged by ICAO. [96]

China's notice of denunciation was deposited on May 31, 1950. [97] The validity of this action was contested by some Contracting States on the ground that the Nationalist Government of China was not the rightful Government of China and thus lacked the power to denounce the Convention. [98] This view did not prevail, however.

[92] On this question generally, see Singh, TERMINATION OF MEMBERSHIP OF INTERNATIONAL ORGANISATIONS (1958).

[93] Convention, Art. 95.

[94] Convention, Arts. 93 bis and 94(b). Article 93 bis was added to the Convention by an amendment that was adopted by the ICAO Assembly on May 13, 1947. Assembly Res. A1–3, ICAO Doc. 4411 (A1–P/45) (1947). It entered into force on March 20, 1961. [1961] Report of the Council, ICAO Doc. 8219 (A14–P/4), p. 78 (1962).

[95] On the Chinese denunciation, see Schenkman, INTERNATIONAL CIVIL AVIATION ORGANIZATION 130–32 (1955).

[96] See ICAO Council, 19th Sess., Doc. 7390 (C/861), pp. 46–49 (1953). Guatemala's denunciation was motivated by financial considerations. It was withdrawn when a satisfactory settlement of its arrears had been worked out.

[97] [1950] Report of the Council, ICAO Doc. 7148 (A5–P/1), p. 79 (1951). China withdrew from the Organization, in the words of its Delegation, "primarily because of her difficulties in fulfilling her financial obligations." ICAO Assembly, 7th Sess., Doc. 7409 (A7–P/2), p. 35 (1953). But see, Schenkman, op. cit. supra note 95, at 131.

[98] See [1950] Report of the Council, ICAO Doc. 7148 (A5–P/1), p. 79 (1951).

Instead, while never expressly ruling on this question, the Assembly at least implicitly accepted the Chinese denunciation. This is apparent from the assessment policy it adopted with regard to China. In determining China's financial contribution for 1951, the Assembly had a choice of applying one of two possible assessment scales that had been prepared by the Contributions Working Group of the Assembly's Administration Commission. One of these scales showed what the amount of China's assessment would be for the full financial year; the second scale was limited to the five-month period ending May 31, 1951 [99]—the date on which China's denunciation, if valid, would become effective. This latter scale, while it had been adopted by the Administrative Commission over some objections,[100] was approved by the Assembly.[101] The ICAO Council thereupon concluded that "the Assembly took no action which would either constitute or imply a rejection of the [China's] notice of denunciation . . . and the denunciation will accordingly take effect . . . on 31 May 1951." [102] Adhering to this interpretation, the Council informed the Assembly in 1951 that "the membership of the Organization was reduced by one during the year, when the withdrawal of the Government of the Republic of China from the Convention on International Civil Aviation took effect on 31 May." [103]

The Republic of China re-ratified the Convention on December 2, 1953 and resumed its ICAO membership on January 1, 1954.[104] The

[99] See Final Report of the Administrative Commission, ICAO Assembly, Proceedings of the Fourth Session [1950], Doc. 7225 (C/834), p. 217 (1951).

[100] See ICAO Assembly, Administrative Commission, 4th Sess., Doc. A4–WP/297 (Ad./34), p. 111 (1950). A motion made by the United Kingdom, which would have resulted in the assessment of China for the full financial year, was defeated in the Administrative Commission by 21 votes, with 4 votes in favor of the motion and 3 abstentions. The Administrative Commission resolved, however, that its decisions relating to the assessment scales "do not prejudice, in any way whatsoever, any matter relating to the denunciation of the Chicago Convention by the Republic of China." Ibid.

[101] It served as the basis of the Assembly's assessment policy for the year 1951. See Assembly Res. A4–26, ICAO Doc. 7017 (A4–P/3) (1950); Final Report of the Administrative Commission, ICAO Assembly, Proceedings of the Fourth Session [1950], Doc. 7225 (C/834), pp. 217 and 237 (1951).

[102] [1950] Report of the Council, ICAO Doc. 7148 (A5–P/1), p. 79 (1951).

[103] [1951] Report of the Council, ICAO Doc. 7270 (A6–P/1), p. 69 (1952).

[104] See [1953] Report of the Council, ICAO Doc. 7456 (A8–P/2), p. 50 (1954); [1954] Report of the Council, ICAO Doc. 7564 (A9–P/2), p. 55 (1955).

seating and participation of its delegation in the 1954 Assembly was not challenged.[105] However, when in 1953 the Republic of China, with a view to re-entering the Organization, began negotiations to settle its financial arrears,[106] a number of Council Representatives again unsuccessfully contended that China had never ceased to be a Contracting State.[107] This view was not shared by the Assembly which, in approving an arrangement for the settlement of China's arrears, expressly predicated its resolution on the "event that China becomes again a party to the Convention." [108]

Schenkman, in his book on ICAO, states that shortly before the Republic of China denounced the Convention the People's Republic of China addressed a note to "officials of ICAO" which asked that "the members of the Chinese Nationalist Delegation be 'driven out.' " This note apparently also asserted that the People's Republic of China "was the 'only legal government representing the Chinese people.' " [109] However, since no reference to such a note appears in any document index published by ICAO or in its official records, it would appear that the People's Republic of China never formally challenged the right of Nationalist China to denounce the Convention. It also did not attempt to assume China's seat in the Organization during the absence of Nationalist China. One can, of course, do no more than speculate on the reasons why Communist China failed to take these steps. It might have been unwilling, for military reasons, to assume the obligations incumbent upon Contracting States under the Convention, or it may well have believed that its attempts to join the Organization would be unsuccessful.

Be that as it may, the People's Republic of China, and those states which sought to challenge the legality of the Chinese denunciation, were strategically in a disadvantageous position. This resulted from the fact that the U.S. Government is the depositary of the Convention. If the depositary had been a state that recognized the People's Republic, it might well have refused to accept the Republic of China's denunciation or its subsequent re-ratification of the Con-

[105] See ICAO Assembly, 8th Sess., Doc. 7505 (A8–P/10), p. 16 (1954).

[106] These arrears covered the period between July 1, 1948, and May 31, 1951.

[107] See ICAO Council, 19th Sess., Doc. 7390 (C/861), pp. 49–53 (1953).

[108] Assembly Res. A7–3, ICAO Doc. 7417 (A7–P/3) (1953).

[109] Schenkman, op. cit. supra note 95, at 131. Schenkman attributes this information to Interavia, Air Letters, Geneva, No. 1917, June 6, 1950, p. 3, and No. 1973, June 8, 1950, p. 3.

vention. Formal action would then have been necessary to overrule the depository. Instead, the U.S. presented ICAO with what amounted to a *fait accompli* because, while quite a number of states might have been prepared to question the authority of the Republic of China to denounce or re-ratify the Convention, few were prepared to do so by challenging the Government of the United States.[110] Although the outcome may eventually have been the same, regardless of the political views of the depository, this case nevertheless casts serious doubts on the wisdom of designating a state rather than an international organization as the depository of a constitutive instrument.[111]

EXPULSION

A state can be expelled from ICAO [112] if it fails to ratify certain amendments to the Convention,[113] or if the U.N. General Assembly recommends its expulsion.[114]

Expulsion for Failure to Ratify Amendments to the Convention

Article 94(b) of the Convention stipulates that the ICAO Assembly in its resolution adopting an amendment to the Convention ". . . may provide that any State which has not ratified [the amendment] within a specified period after the amendment has come into

---

[110] Following China's re-ratification of the Convention, unsuccessful periodic attempts have been made to unseat this Government. See ICAO Assembly, 10th Sess., Doc. 7708 (A10–P/17), p. 8 (1956); ICAO Assembly, 12th Sess., Doc. 7996 (A12–P/2), pp. 29–30 (1959); ICAO Assembly, 13th (Extraordinary) Sess., Doc. 8167 (A13–P/2), pp. 23–24 (1961); ICAO Assembly, 14th Sess., Doc. 8269 (A14–P/21), pp. 57–59, and 97–99 (1962); ICAO Assembly, 15th Sess., Doc. 8516 (A15–P/5), pp. 63–65 (1965).

[111] The International Law Commission recognized this problem by providing in Article 71(2) of its Draft Articles on the Law of Treaties that "the functions of a depositary of a Treaty are international in character and the depositary is under an obligation to act impartially in their performance." This provision was prompted in part by a desire to prevent politically motivated abuses by the depositary. Rosenne, *The Depositary of International Treaties*, 61 Am. J. Int'l L. 923, 933–34 (1967).

[112] On this topic generally, see Sohn, *Expulsion or Forced Withdrawal from an International Organization*, 77 Harv. L. Rev. 1381 (1964); Singh, *op. cit. supra* note 92.

[113] Convention, Art. 94(b).

[114] Convention, Art. 93 *bis*(a).

force shall thereupon cease to be a member of the Organization and a party to the Convention." The Assembly may only take this action "if in its opinion the amendment is of such a nature as to justify this course." Under Article 94(a), an amendment which has been approved by the Assembly must be ratified by at least two-thirds of the total number of the Contracting States. The amendment comes into force when this requirement has been complied with, but solely "in respect of States which have ratified such amendment." Since an amendment to the Convention thus enters into force only *inter se* the parties that have ratified it, Article 94(b) gives the Organization the power to compel the ratification of those amendments whose acceptance by all Contracting States it deems absolutely necessary.

The provisions of Article 94(b) have to date not been invoked by the Assembly.[115] The Convention, unlike the constitutions of some other international organizations, does not distinguish between "organizational" and "substantive" amendments. One might therefore have assumed that the Assembly, in order to prevent creating two constitutive instruments, would have had recourse to Article 94(b) when adopting amendments relating to the internal structure or operation of the Organization. The Assembly has not availed itself of this opportunity, however, even though it has adopted a number of important organizational amendments over the years.[116] It may therefore be assumed that the Assembly will not invoke Article 94(b) unless the amendment in question involves a fundamental change of the entire Convention scheme.

Expulsion by Recommendation of the United Nations

When the Convention entered into force it contained no provision other than Article 94(b) relating to the expulsion or exclusion of a Contracting State from the Organization. As soon as the first ICAO Assembly convened in 1947, it had to rectify this situation. The Assembly was compelled to do so because the U.N. General Assembly refused to grant ICAO the status of a specialized agency unless the Organization complied "with any decision of the General Assem-

[115] For the Organization's amendment practice, see ICAO Doc. C–WP/3456 (Annex I), pp. 7–28 (1961). This topic is dealt with in Part IV *infra*.

[116] See, *e.g.*, Assembly Res. A13–1, ICAO Doc. 8167 (A13–P/2) (1961), amending Article 50(a) to permit an increase in the membership of the ICAO Council.

bly regarding Franco Spain." [117] The decision in question—a General Assembly recommendation—provided that

> the Franco Government of Spain be debarred from membership in international agencies established by or brought into relationship with the United Nations, and from participation in conferences or other activities which may be arranged by the United Nations or by these agencies, until a new and acceptable government is formed in Spain.[118]

From a legal point of view, it was by no means easy for ICAO to comply with the conditions imposed by the U.N. General Assembly because Spain had already ratified the Convention. The ICAO Assembly might conceivably have invalidated the U.S. Government's acceptance of the Spanish instrument of ratification.[119] The Assembly did not take this step, however. Instead, it proceeded on the assumption that Spain had become a Contracting State and that an amendment to the Convention was necessary to comply with the condition imposed by the General Assembly.

After considering various schemes that might meet the exigencies of the situation, among them one limited only to Spain's exclusion from the Organization,[120] the Assembly approved an amendment that is general in scope and permits both the expulsion and suspension of Member States.[121] This amendment, designated as Article 93 *bis*, contains two provisions relating to expulsion. The first provides for the automatic termination of a state's membership in ICAO whenever the U.N. General Assembly recommends that its government "be debarred from membership in international agencies established by or brought into relationship with the United Nations."

[117] Gen. Ass. Res. 50 (I) of 14 Dec. 1946, Gen. Ass. Off. Rec., 1st Sess., 2d pt. RESOLUTIONS, p. 78, U.N. Doc. A/64/Add. 1 (1947). For a discussion of the relevant U.N. action relating to Spain, see Sohn, *supra* note 112, at 1401–04.

[118] U.N. Gen. Ass. Rec. 39 (I) of 12 Dec. 1946, Gen. Ass. Off. Rec., 1st Sess., 2d pt., RESOLUTIONS, pp. 63–64, U.N. Doc. A/64/Add. 1 (1947).

[119] Sohn, *supra* note 112, at 1402–03. The effective date of Spain's ratification preceded the first meeting of the Assembly by two months and the establishment of ICAO by one month. It is, therefore, by no means clear that the Assembly had the power to reject Spain's ratification at this late date, especially since it was Spain's ratification among others which had brought the Organization into being.

[120] The various possibilities were outlined for the Assembly in ICAO Doc. 4013 (A1–CP/1), pp. 4–6 (1947).

[121] See Assembly Res. A1–3, ICAO Doc. 4411 (A1–P/45) (1947).

The second provision contemplates the automatic expulsion of states that have been expelled from membership in the United Nations, "unless the General Assembly of the United Nations attaches to its act of expulsion a recommendation to the contrary." A state which has been expelled under Article 93 *bis* may be readmitted to ICAO membership if the U.N. General Assembly gives its assent, and if the state's application is approved by a majority of the ICAO Council.

The adoption of Article 93 *bis* by the Assembly[122] did not in theory achieve the expulsion of Spain.[123] This resulted from the fact that under Article 94(a) of the Convention an amendment approved by the Assembly does not come into force until it has been ratified by at least two-thirds of the total number of Contracting States, and then only "in respect of States which have ratified such amendment." Mindful of the delay that ratification would entail and of the legal problems inherent in the language of Article 94(a), a committee of the Assembly prepared a draft resolution stipulating that "the Assembly declares its wish that the present government of Spain, during the period until the amendment comes into force, should not participate in this Assembly or in conferences and other activities which may be arranged by ICAO."[124] This draft resolution was not put to a vote, however, because Spain informed the Assembly that if the Organization decided to exclude Spain, "we could hardly accept the role of an unwelcome guest."[125]

The haste with which Article 93 *bis* was adopted no doubt accounts for the questions it presents. Thus it is not clear whether the expulsion of a state under this provision also terminates its status as a Contracting Party to the Convention. Article 93 *bis* merely speaks of cessation of ICAO membership. If one proceeds on the assumption that adherence to the Convention and membership in the Organization are inseparable, one will have to conclude that the expul-

---

[122] Article 93 *bis* was adopted by a vote of 27 to 3, with 2 states abstaining, and 2 being absent. For the Assembly debate relating to this amendment, see ICAO Assembly, Proceedings of the First Session [1947], Doc. 7325 (C/852), pp. 82–87 (1952).

[123] See Cheng, THE LAW OF INTERNATIONAL AIR TRANSPORT, 34–37 (1962).

[124] ICAO Assembly, Commission No. 1, Doc. 4077 (A1–CP/15), p. 2 (1947).

[125] Statement by the Spanish Delegation, ICAO Assembly, Proceedings of the First Session [1947], Doc. 7325 (C/852), p. 127, at 128 (1952).

sion of a state under Article 93 *bis* also terminates its rights and obligations as a Contracting Party.[126]

While the Organization might adopt this view, two considerations can be advanced against it. The first has to do with the fact that Article 94(b)—the only other provision dealing with expulsion—expressly stipulates that a state to which it is applied "shall . . . cease to be a member of the Organization and *a party to the Convention.*" (Emphasis added.) It is at least arguable, therefore, that the absence of similar language in Article 93 *bis* may evince an intention to leave the expelled state's status as a Contracting Party unaffected. This argument gains some support from the second consideration, which has to do with the fact that the readmission of an expelled state is not conditioned on its re-accession to the Convention. For if a state's expulsion under Article 93 *bis* amounts also to a forced denunciation of the Convention, one might have assumed that readmission would have been expressly subjected to re-accession.[127]

The expulsion of Spain offers no useful precedent for determining how the Organization would resolve this question. Spain resumed its ICAO membership before Article 93 *bis* entered into force,[128] and thus never formally lost its status either as a Contracting Party or as a Member State. When the U.N. General Assembly on November 4, 1950, revoked its 1946 recommendation relating to Spain,[129] the ICAO Council on December 6, 1950, merely "noted with approval the action taken by the President of the Council to re-establish normal relations between ICAO and the Government of Spain, and expressed its satisfaction that this had been done." [130]

The application of Article 93 *bis* is further complicated by a second problem which is closely related to the one just discussed. It

---

[126] See Jenks, *Some Constitutional Problems of International Organizations,* 22 Brit. Yb. Int'l L. 11, 25 (1945), who asserts that "the effect of expulsion is to release a State from its obligations towards other States under the constitution of the organization from which it is expelled."

[127] This omission can, of course, be cured by the ICAO Council. If it decided to interpret an expulsion under Article 93 *bis* to be a forced denunciation of the Convention it would no doubt be free, in processing an application for readmission, to require the state in question to re-adhere to the Convention.

[128] Article 93 *bis* entered into force on March 20, 1961.

[129] Gen. Ass. Res. 386 (V) of 4 Nov. 1950, Gen. Ass. Off. Rec., 5th Sess., RESOLUTIONS, pp. 16–17, Supplement No. 20, U.N. Doc. A/1775 (1950).

[130] ICAO Council, Proceedings of the Eleventh Session, 2d pt. [1950], Doc. 7188 (C/828), p. 60 (1953).

has to do with the fact that, even though this amendment has now entered into force, it has still not been ratified by a substantial number of Contracting States. Since an amendment to the Convention upon its entry into force only binds those states that have ratified it,[131] it is by no means clear what the status of an expelled state is in relation to the states that have not ratified Article 93 *bis*. Theoretically the amendment is binding only *inter se* the parties that have ratified it. It would follow therefrom that an expelled state would remain a Contracting Party vis-à-vis some states, even though it did not enjoy this status in relation to others. And if the expelled state itself never ratified Article 93 *bis,* it might have to be regarded as a Contracting State with regard to all other states.[132] Past ICAO practice indicates, however, that the Organization might proceed on the assumption that the entry into force of Article 93 *bis* binds the Organization as such.[133] While this approach does not affect the *inter se* rights of the Contracting States, it would mean that ICAO would consider the "expelled" state to have ceased to be a member of the Organization.[134]

A third problem presented by Article 93 *bis* relates to the action which the U.N. General Assembly must take to effect a state's expulsion from ICAO. It will be recalled that under Article 93 *bis* (a)(2), a state which has been expelled from the U.N. automatically loses its membership in ICAO unless the General Assembly makes a recommendation to the contrary. While this provision is self-explanatory, the same is not true of Article 93 *bis*(a)(1). It provides for the automatic expulsion of a state "whose government the General Assembly of the United Nations has recommended be debarred from membership in international agencies established by or brought into relationship with the United Nations." If the General Assembly adopts a general recommendation applicable to all spe-

---

[131] Convention, Art. 94(a).

[132] See ICAO Doc. C–WP/3456 (Annex I), p. 21 (1961). This problem could have been avoided in part had the Assembly invoked Article 94(b) in adopting this amendment. The Contracting States would thus have had to choose between ratification or loss of ICAO membership. The Assembly did not take this step, however.

[133] This approach was adopted, for example, following the entry into force of the amendment to Article 50(a), which expanded the membership of the ICAO Council. See ICAO Assembly, 14th Sess., Doc. 8269 (A14–P/21), p. 59 (1962).

[134] This problem is fully explored in Part IV *infra*.

cialized agencies, Article 93 *bis*(a)(1) would clearly be applicable. But what if the General Assembly merely singles out ICAO? The language of Article 93 *bis*(a)(1) can be read as conditioning the application of its provisions upon a General Assembly recommendation that is general in nature. It could thus be argued that a General Assembly recommendation seeking to debar a state only from membership in ICAO is outside the scope of Article 93 *bis*(a)(1), and would therefore not be capable of effecting the state's expulsion.

This question gains considerable importance in connection with some U.N. General Assembly action relating to South Africa and Portugal. On November 6, 1962, the General Assembly in paragraph 4(e) of Resolution 1761 (XVII) [135] "requested" all Member States to refuse "landing and passage facilities to aircraft belonging to the Government of South Africa and companies registered under the laws of South Africa." On December 21, 1965, it took similar action with regard to Portugal by "urging" all U.N. Member States in paragraph 7(d) of Resolution 2107 (XX) [136] "to refuse landing and transit facilities to all aircraft belonging to or in the service of the Government of Portugal and to companies registered under the laws of Portugal." This resolution prompted the ICAO Secretary General, in a letter addressed to the U.N. Secretary-General,

> to point out that, in so far as concerns States members both of the United Nations and of the International Civil Aviation Organization, this request is inconsistent with the terms of the Convention on International Civil Aviation . . . as was also General Assembly resolution 1761 (XVII) dealing with South African aircraft, in particular with article 5.[137]

Under Article 5 of the Convention each Contracting State, subject to certain conditions, accords to aircraft not engaged in scheduled international air services belonging to another Contracting State the right "to make flights into or in transit non-stop across its territory and to make stops for non-traffic purposes without the necessity of obtaining prior permission."

[135] Gen. Ass. Off. Rec., 17th Sess., RESOLUTIONS, pp. 9–10, Supplement No. 17, U.N. Doc. A/5217 (1962).
[136] Gen. Ass. Off. Rec., 20th Sess., RESOLUTIONS, pp. 62–63, Supplement No. 14, U.N. Doc. A/6014 (1965).
[137] ICAO Secretary General, Letter of 30 March 1966, U.N. Doc. A/6294 (1966), reprinted in 4 Int'l Legal Materials 486–87 (1966).

If the expulsion of a state from ICAO under Article 93 *bis* has the effect also of terminating that state's status as a party to the Convention, the General Assembly would have the power to accomplish its policy towards South Africa and Portugal, notwithstanding the provisions of Article 5, by recommending that they be debarred from membership in all the specialized agencies. Given the current political climate in the U.N., such action is not inconceivable. It is more likely that, at least initially, piece-meal expulsion of these states from international organizations might—for political reasons —command greater support in the U.N. than would their total ostracism. The General Assembly might therefore seek to debar South Africa and Portugal from some specialized agencies. Since Article 5 of the Convention poses a legal problem for any ICAO Member State wishing to abide by the aforementioned General Assembly resolutions, the General Assembly might attempt to implement its policy by seeking to debar South Africa and Portugal from ICAO alone.

As previously indicated, it is by no means clear whether a recommendation limited only to the expulsion of these states from ICAO would meet the requirements of Article 93 *bis*(a)(1). As a practical matter, however, the Organization would in all likelihood honor any such General Assembly request. This is apparent from the fact that in the 1965 ICAO Assembly a proposed amendment to the Convention,[138] which was designed to permit the suspension or exclusion from ICAO of any state practicing "a policy of apartheid and racial discrimination," was supported by a considerable number of states. Although the amendment failed to receive the requisite two-thirds vote of the Assembly and was thus not adopted,[139] many states claimed that they voted against it or abstained only because they believed that any move to oust South Africa from ICAO should be initiated by the General Assembly.[140] It may thus be assumed that

---

[138] This draft resolution is reprinted in ICAO Assembly, Report of the Executive Committee, 15th Sess., Doc. 8522 (A15–EX/43), pp. 30–31 (1965).

[139] The proposed amendment received 42 affirmative votes, 30 negative votes; 15 states abstained, and 13 were absent. ICAO Assembly, 15th Sess., Doc. 8516 (A15–P/5), p. 142 (1965).

[140] For the debates relating to this proposed amendment, see ICAO Assembly, Executive Committee, 15th Sess., Doc. A15–WP/213 (MIN–EX/1–13), pp. 55–68, 82–107 (1965); ICAO Assembly, 15th Sess., Doc. 8516 (A15–P/5), pp. 137–43 (1965).

the requisite number of votes can be mustered in the Assembly to interpret the provisions of Article 93 *bis*(a)(1) so as to implement a General Assembly request for the expulsion of these states from ICAO, even in the absence of a similar General Assembly recommendation addressed to other specialized agencies.[141]

Suspension of Membership and Voting Rights

A state's membership or right to vote in ICAO may be suspended under three different circumstances. First, the ICAO Assembly *may* suspend a Contracting State's right to vote in the Assembly and Council, if that state "fails to discharge within a reasonable period its financial obligations to the Organization."[142] Second, the Assembly *must* impose this sanction whenever a state has failed to comply with the provisions of Chapter XVIII of the Convention, which deals with the settlement of disputes arising under the Convention.[143] Finally, a state may be suspended from membership in the Organization under Article 93 *bis*(c), which applies to Contracting States "suspended from the exercise of the rights and privileges of membership in the United Nations."

SUSPENSION FOR FAILURE TO DISCHARGE
FINANCIAL OBLIGATIONS

Article 62 of the Convention empowers the Assembly to suspend a state's voting power in the Council and Assembly for failing to discharge its financial obligations to the Organization. This provision has been extensively interpreted, because ICAO has from its very inception been plagued by problems relating to the inability or refusal of some states to pay their assessments.[144] While these problems are in large measure attributable to *bona fide* financial difficulties which some countries have encountered, others can be attributed to political considerations.

The dispute between Poland and ICAO is a striking example of a case falling in the latter category. Poland was a participant at the

---

[141] *But see,* Jenks, *Due Process of Law in International Organizations,* 19 Int'l Org. 163 (1965).
[142] Convention, Art. 62.
[143] Convention, Art. 88.
[144] See generally on this subject, ICAO Doc. C–WP/3924, Appendix B (1964).

Chicago Conference and the first state to ratify the Convention,[145] but the government which took these steps was the Polish Government-in-Exile, the so-called "London" Government. Since it did not succeed to power upon the liberation of Poland, the Secretary General of the Provisional International Civil Aviation Organization approached the newly established Polish Government in Warsaw requesting payment of Poland's PICAO assessments. He received the following cable in reply: "Payments of contributions are not being considered because PICAO Agreements not yet officially accepted by Provisional Government of National Unity of Poland." [146] Thereafter, requests by ICAO for clarification of Poland's position remained unanswered. It was clear, nevertheless, that the Polish authorities in Warsaw took the position that Poland was not bound by the "London" Government's ratification of the Convention. This attitude was underscored by the fact that Poland sent only an observer to the first ICAO Assembly. Thereafter, on June 8, 1948, Poland sought to deposit an instrument of adherence with the U.S. Government, which the latter refused to accept on the ground that Poland had already ratified the Convention.[147] Successive ICAO Assemblies sustained the U.S. Government's position in that they suspended Poland's voting power for non-payment of arrears predating Poland's 1948 attempt to adhere to the Convention.[148]

After the second ICAO Assembly suspended Poland's voting power in 1948,[149] the Polish Government severed its already limited relations with ICAO by discontinuing its earlier practice of sending an observer to the meetings of the ICAO Assembly. This stalemate continued until 1957. In May of that year the U.S. Government

[145] The Polish instrument of ratification was deposited with the U.S. Government on April 6, 1945.

[146] ICAO Assembly, Commission No. 1, Doc. 4131 (A1–CP/25), p. 1 (1947).

[147] The Polish note, addressed to the U.S. Department of State, is dated June 8, 1948. U.S. Department of State, File No. 26/28/48. This note was rejected by the Department of State on August 6, 1948. Poland challenged the position taken by the United States and requested the U.S. Government to reconsider its position. See Polish note of August 10, 1948, U.S. Department of State, File No. 26/52/48. This note was rejected by the Department of State on September 2, 1948. See also, ICAO Council, 8th Sess. [1949], Doc. 6922 (C/803), p. 203 (1950).

[148] See, e.g., Assembly Res. A3–6, ICAO Doc. 6459 (A3–P/28) (1949).

[149] Assembly Res. A2–1, ICAO Doc. 5692 (A2–P/37) (1948).

received a cryptic note from the Government of Poland, declaring that Poland "has adhered without qualification to the Convention . . . and has become a member of the International Civil Aviation Organization."[150] In response to a Swiss request for clarification, the U.S. Department of State replied that "the Department is of the view that the Polish note of May 9, 1957, . . . does not affect the legal status of Poland with respect to the Convention, or prejudice the position which the Department has consistently maintained. . . ."[151] The U.S. thus interpreted the Polish note as an expression of Poland's willingness to resume membership in the Organization.

That this view was shared by the Organization is apparent from the settlement that was reached regarding Poland's financial arrears. Poland initiated negotiations to this end in 1957.[152] At its 1958 session the Assembly approved a Polish proposal for the settlement of its arrears and restored Poland's voting powers.[153] This settlement was a compromise to the extent that the Organization agreed to accept only a fraction of the full amount owed by Poland. However, by recognizing its indebtedness to ICAO for the period antedating its attempted adherence to the Convention in 1948, Poland must be deemed to have acknowledged the validity of the earlier ratification of the Convention by the "London" Government.[154]

The political implications inherent in ICAO's dispute with Poland distinguish this case from those involving states that have simply defaulted on their financial obligations. These cases do, nevertheless, present considerable problems of their own, which may in large measure be attributed to the language of Article 62. It provides that "the Assembly may suspend the voting power in the Assembly and in the Council of any contracting State that fails to discharge within a reasonable period its financial obligations to the Organization." Article 62 thus leaves the Organization wide discretion both in

---

[150] This note is dated May 9, 1957. U.S. Department of State, File No. 45/25/57.

[151] U.S. Department of State note to Switzerland dated June 28, 1957 (no file number given).

[152] See Actions of the Council, 33rd Sess., ICAO Doc. 7895 (C/908), p. 29 (1958).

[153] Assembly Res. A11–1, Doc. 7888 (A11–P/12) (1958).

[154] ICAO has always listed the date of Poland's ratification of the Convention as being April 6, 1945. See, e.g., [1965] Report of the Council, ICAO Doc. 8572 (A16–P/1), p. 129 (1966).

determining what constitutes "a reasonable period," and how to deal with states subject to serious financial difficulties. Besides, it is also not clear what other sanctions, if any, the Assembly may impose in addition to those that Article 62 expressly provides for. Over the years, the answers to these questions have gradually emerged from the Organization's application of Article 62.

Thus the third ICAO Assembly, in suspending the voting powers of a number of states, first expressed the view "that two years is a reasonable period in which to permit a State to discharge its financial obligations." [155] Implicit in this assertion, however, was the assumption that the states involved had made no attempt to negotiate a settlement of their outstanding indebtedness. We find the first clear articulation of this principle in a 1951 resolution. Here the Assembly resolved that the voting power of certain defaulting states "which have not presented proposals for the settlement of such obligations before this Assembly should be suspended. . . ." [156] In other words, the Assembly was prepared to apply Article 62 with considerable liberality in order not to penalize states that had shown a desire to settle their arrears but had encountered financial difficulties in doing so.[157]

By 1954 the Assembly concluded that a clear-cut policy statement relating to this problem was needed because the previous resolutions had created a certain amount of confusion.[158] Such a statement was formulated in 1955 [159] and has been followed since then. It articulates two basic principles. The first is that "only States in arrears for an amount equal to or in excess of the total amount assessed for the two preceding financial years may have their voting power suspended." The second principle limits the first to the extent that the state in question will be able to avoid suspension if it can meet one of the following three conditions: (a) it has concluded and is abiding by an agreement with the ICAO Council relating to its arrears,

---

[155] Assembly Res. A3–6, ICAO Doc. 6459 (A3–P/28) (1949).

[156] Assembly Res. A5–2, ICAO Doc. 7173 (A5–P/3) (1951). This notion was implicit also in Assembly Res. A4–2, ICAO Doc. 7017 (A4–P/3) (1950).

[157] See, in this connection, Assembly Res. A7–1, ICAO Doc. 7417 (A7–P/3) (1953), relating to the status of Bolivia and El Salvador.

[158] See Assembly Res. A8–8, ICAO Doc. 7499 (A8–P/9) (1954).

[159] Assembly Res. A9–6, ICAO Doc. 7595 (A9–P/12) (1955). For the Assembly debates relating to the adoption of this resolution, see ICAO Assembly, 9th Sess., Doc. 7596 (A9–P/13), pp. 50–53 (1955).

(b) the Assembly "decides that failure to pay is due to circumstances beyond the State's control," or (c) the state has demonstrated to the Assembly a willingness to reach an equitable settlement relating to its financial obligations. Thus, no state should encounter—or has encountered—any serious difficulties in retaining its vote so long as its default is the result of *bona fide* economic hardship.

The Convention is silent on the question whether the Assembly, in addition to suspending a recalcitrant state's voting power in the Assembly and Council, may impose other sanctions as well. The practice of the Assembly indicates, however, that it has assumed that it does have this power. The third Assembly, for example, suspended the voting power of certain states not only in the Council and the Assembly but also in their subsidiary bodies.[160] Subsequent Assembly resolutions, after reiterating that the suspension applied also to subsidiary bodies, go further and authorize the Council also to deprive states under voting suspension of "such part of the general services furnished to Contracting States as it may find reasonable to suspend." [161]

In determining whether the Assembly has the right to impose these additional sanctions, the answer is easy with regard to the disfranchisement of a state in the various subsidiary bodies of the Assembly and the Council. Although Article 62 does not mention these subsidiary bodies, the terms "Council" and "Assembly" certainly do encompass, in an institutional sense, their subsidiary bodies as well. As far as concerns the withholding of general services— which include mainly documents and various other informational materials—this action is neither expressly nor implicitly authorized by Article 62.[162] However, the funds necessary to underwrite the cost of these general services come from the General Fund of the Organization, which consists of the contributions of the Member

---

[160] Assembly Res. A3–6, ICAO Doc. 6459 (A3–P/28) (1949). Only Regional Air Navigation Meetings were excluded from the application of this resolution.

[161] Assembly Res. A4–2, ICAO Doc. 7017 (A4–P/3) (1950). See, to the same effect, Assembly Res. A5–2, ICAO Doc. 7173 (A2–P/3) (1951); Assembly Res. A6–2, ICAO Doc. 7315 (A6–P/3) (1952); Assembly Res. A7–1, ICAO Doc. 7417 (A7–P/3) (1953); Assembly Res. A8–7, ICAO Doc. 7499 (A8–P/9) (1954).

[162] For a discussion of the various sanctions that might be invoked, see ICAO Docs. C–WP/1184 (1952), and C–WP/1193 (1952).

States. It is thus arguable that the Assembly's authority to fix ICAO's budget [163] carries with it the power to determine that the Organization's General Fund not be used to furnish general services to states which have not contributed to the Fund.[164]

If the Assembly has fully disfranchised a state and has authorized the Council to withhold from it any part of the general services, it has for all practical purposes suspended that state from membership in the Organization. The suspension would be complete but for the state's right to attend and be heard at the various meetings and conferences of the Organization. It is difficult to say how significant this right is, although it may be assumed that some states may attach considerable importance to it. This raises the question whether the Assembly has the constitutional power, if all other pressures fail, to bar such a state from taking its seat at any or all ICAO conferences and meetings. The ICAO Council considered this problem on one occasion, albeit in a somewhat different form.

The subject came up in the context of a suggestion that those states which showed no willingness at all to pay their assessments be placed in an "inactive membership category." [165] The Council's Finance Committee which first considered this suggestion had some doubts about its legality,[166] and the Council, apparently sharing these doubts, did not act on it.[167] Inactive membership—whatever that term denotes—presumably would have meant a state's exclusion from all ICAO activities, and thus has relevance to the questions here under consideration. In theory there may well be a difference between the formal designation of a state as an "inactive member" and its *ad hoc* exclusion from participation in the various bodies of the Organization. The former, it can be argued, would be unconstitutional because it creates a legal status neither expressly nor implicitly provided for in the Convention. The latter might be permissible, for it can be characterized as a disciplinary measure which every parliamentary body may have the inherent power to impose, in order to prevent its authority from being openly flouted.

---

[163] Convention, Art. 61.

[164] *But see* Cheng, *op. cit. supra* note 123, at 34, who expresses some doubts as to the constitutionality of this sanction.

[165] See ICAO Docs. C–WP/1184, p. 7 (1952), and C–WP/1193, p. 7 (1952).

[166] ICAO Doc. C–WP/1184, p. 8 (1952).

[167] See ICAO Council, 16th Sess., Doc. 7291 (C/845), pp. 80–92 (1952).

SUSPENSION FOR FAILURE TO DISCHARGE OBLIGATIONS
UNDER CHAPTER XVIII OF THE CONVENTION

Article 88 of the Convention provides that "the Assembly shall
suspend the voting power in the Assembly and in the Council of any
contracting State that is found in default under the provisions of
this Chapter." The reference here is to Chapter XVIII which comprises Articles 84 through 88 of the Convention. These provisions
establish a machinery for the adjudication of disputes between the
Contracting States relating to the interpretation and application of
the Convention and its Annexes. Since this topic is discussed in
detail in Part III of this book, it should merely be noted here that
ICAO has not as yet been called upon to apply the provisions of
Article 88.

SUSPENSION AT THE REQUEST OF THE UNITED NATIONS

Article 93 *bis*(c) of the Convention provides that:

> Members of the Organization which are suspended from the exer-
> cise of the rights and privileges of membership in the United Nations
> shall, upon the request of the latter, be suspended from the rights and
> privileges of membership in this Organization.

It is difficult to read this provision without wondering whether its
draftsmen really intended the consequences that its language compels.[168]

These doubts arise because, under Article 93 *bis*(c), the U.N.
cannot obtain the suspension of a state from ICAO unless the U.N.
itself has suspended the state in question. It would seem, furthermore, that a state which does not belong to the U.N. is immune from
suspension because it cannot, of course, be suspended from membership in the U.N. These consequences are difficult to reconcile with
the provisions of Article 93 *bis*(a), which empowers the U.N.
General Assembly to obtain the expulsion of a state from ICAO by

---

[168] The sparse legislative history relating to Article 93 *bis*(c) would indicate
that it was something of an afterthought and never received the attention that
was given to the other provisions of Article 93 *bis*. A vague reference to
suspension appears in the first draft of the proposed amendment. See ICAO Doc.
4013 (A1–CP/1), Add. III (1947). The present form of Article 93 *bis*(c)
appears in a revised draft. See ICAO Doc. 4077 (A1–CP/15), p. 2 (1947).

merely recommending that such steps be taken. In some cases Article 93 *bis*(c) might thus compel the U.N. to demand a state's expulsion from ICAO for no other reason than that it lacks the power to invoke the less drastic sanction of suspension.

Article 93 *bis*(c) presents a number of other problems that will have to be resolved when the occasion for its application arises. Thus, while under Article 93 *bis*(a) the expulsion of a state from ICAO is automatic once the U.N. General Assembly requests it, Article 93 *bis*(c) does not speak of an automatic suspension. It is therefore not clear whether the suspension envisaged by this provision is self-executing [169] or whether it requires implementation by ICAO before it becomes effective. Since Article 93 *bis*(c) makes compliance with the U.N.'s request mandatory, and since it does not specify what ICAO body is to effectuate the suspension, the Organization may be expected to interpret this provision as making the request of the U.N. self-executing. This would mean that the state in question would be deemed to have been suspended as soon as the request has been received by ICAO.[170]

Article 93 *bis*(c) does not specify what U.N. organ is competent to request the suspension envisaged by this provision. It may be assumed, however, that the appropriate recommendation will have to come from the General Assembly which has the power under Article 5 of the U.N. Charter, subject to a recommendation of the Security Council, to suspend a state from membership in the U.N.

Article 93 *bis*(c) does not indicate, moreover, how and under what circumstances the suspension can be revoked. Once the U.N. has reinstated the state in question, the legal basis for its suspension by ICAO has disappeared. Resumption of full ICAO membership might thus follow automatically upon the state's reinstatement by the U.N. It is also possible to read Article 93 *bis*(c) as empowering

---

[169] *But see* Cheng, *op. cit. supra* note 123, at 34, who asserts that Article 93 *bis*(c) envisages an automatic suspension.

[170] A contrary interpretation would necessitate a determination as to which ICAO body has the power to implement the suspension. While this subject matter no doubt falls within the jurisdiction of the ICAO Assembly, considerable delay in the implementation of the suspension would result because the Assembly meets only every three years. To prevent such delay the Assembly might have to delegate to the ICAO Council or the Secretary General the power to comply with the U.N. request in the event that it be received while the Assembly is not in session.

the U.N. to bring about the revocation of a state's ICAO suspension, even though the state remains under suspension in the U.N. Pursuant to Article 93 *bis*(c), the suspension of a state by the U.N. will only result in its suspension by ICAO if the suspension is requested by the U.N. The power to request a state's suspension may thus carry with it the implied power to request its revocation. If, furthermore, we are correct in our previous assumption that the request for a state's suspension under Article 93 *bis*(c) will have to come from the General Assembly, the power to withdraw this request would also seem to belong to the General Assembly. Thus, while only the Security Council has the power to reinstate a state which has been suspended from the exercise of its rights and privileges as a Member of the U.N.,[171] the General Assembly could obtain its reinstatement by ICAO. And this notwithstanding the fact that the Security Council has not restored the state's membership rights in the U.N. A state's suspension under Article 93 *bis*(c) may accordingly be lifted either when the Security Council restores the state to its membership rights in the U.N., or when the General Assembly revokes its request for the state's suspension by the ICAO.

CONCLUSION

For a substantial part of its existence ICAO has been able to remain aloof from the ideological conflicts that have had such a disruptive effect on the work of some other international organizations. This has been due, in part at least, to the highly technical character of the functions entrusted to ICAO as well as to the relative political homogeneity of its membership.

ICAO has thus not had to cope with membership problems in an atmosphere torn by ideological strife. True, the disfranchisement of Poland, the handling of Yugoslavia's reservation, and the issue raised by Nationalist China's withdrawal and subsequent readmission to the Organization, all attest to the fact that ICAO did not remain immune to the Cold War. What is significant, however, is that even these problems never gave rise to the acrimony that the same or like cases provoked in other international organizations. The disposition of these cases by ICAO has tended to be similar to the manner in which a social club deals with an unpleasant affair:

[171] U.N. Charter, Art. 5.

discreetly, with a minimum of disruption and recrimination, and a tendency to decide no more than absolutely necessary.

ICAO debates on membership problems reveal, moreover, a strong desire on the part of many delegates to move on to other agenda items. This attitude seems to have been motivated by the fear that embroilment in political controversy would seriously affect the ability of the Organization to perform its technical functions, and a conviction that the resolution of political questions should be left to other international bodies. The institutional climate which these readily observable attitudes have created is highly amenable to compromise solutions, and quite hostile to any attempt to exploit membership problems for propagandistic purposes. ICAO has as a result tended either to adopt the legally most unobjectionable solution or, where that proved to be impractical or unacceptable, to leave the matter formally unresolved.

This situation may well be changing. The rapid increase in ICAO's membership has brought into the Organization many states whose immediate interest in the technical aspects of international air navigation is negligible, because they have not as yet developed an air transport or aviation industry of their own. Since these states do not have significant economic or administrative stakes in the smooth operation of the Organization, it is doubtful whether they can be counted upon to put the interests of international civil aviation above the attainment of some immediate political goal. In the future, politically sensitive membership problems might therefore not be disposed of as harmoniously as in earlier years. On the other hand, it is quite possible that the *modus operandi* of the past which, incidentally, is characteristic of the Organization's approach to other constitutional problems, has established an institutional climate for the resolution of constitutional issues that will not be significantly affected by a change in the Organization's membership.

Part II

ICAO Technical Legislation

INTRODUCTION

The manner in which the International Civil Aviation Organization has exercised its regulatory functions in matters relating to the safety of international air navigation and the facilitation of international air transport provides a fascinating example of international law-making. The study which follows explores this facet of the Organization's activities.

The legislative functions of ICAO are in large measure confined to highly technical problems of a non-political character. In exercising them the Organization has consequently not had to contend with any of the post-war ideological differences that have impeded effective international law-making on politically sensitive issues.

ICAO's regulatory activities, furthermore, leave little room for serious policy disagreements. Its legislative goals are largely determined by technical advances in the aviation field. The requirements for compliance with ICAO regulations, moreover, are sufficiently flexible to accommodate the economic and technical problems which any of its Member States might face. All this makes for a consensus-oriented legislative process whose regulatory product is geared to the technical requirements of modern aviation without unduly straining the economic, administrative, and technical resources of a constituency that embraces the most advanced industrial nations of the world, as well as the most underdeveloped ones. While it may readily be assumed that such compromise legislation does not meet the optimum demands of the aeronautically advanced states, it cannot but improve world-wide air navigation standards, and thus benefits international aviation generally.

It is impossible, of course, for a lawyer with no aeronautical training to pass judgment on the content of ICAO legislation or on its technical quality and efficacy. What a lawyer can do, however, is to analyze the Organization's legislative process with a view to

57

ascertaining how it actually works, and what legal consequences may be deemed to result from the action that is being taken.

The task which such a study entails seems easier than it actually is, for the Organization has done little to clarify the operation of its legislative process. As a result, one has to struggle through a seemingly never-ending maze of widely dispersed technical documents in the hope—quite often unrealized—of finding some information of legal significance. The arduousness of this task no doubt accounts for the fact that much of what has been written about ICAO's legislative process bears little resemblance to the actual practice of the Organization. The legislative process of the Organization has over the years, furthermore, moved further and further away from the governing provisions of the Chicago Convention. These were for the most part poorly drafted, and thus required extensive interpretative improvisations which have been accomplished in large measure without any formal or express legal rulings.

The gradual transformation of the legislative system established by the Chicago Convention that these improvisations brought about has been acquiesced to by the Member States through their representatives, many of whom are aeronautical experts who do not seem to have, or care to have, a clear understanding of what the legal rights and obligations of their governments are under the Convention. Whether such a *modus operandi* could exist within the framework of an international organization which deals with more controversial issues than does ICAO, or whose enforcement powers are more substantial, may well be doubted. This does not detract from the fact that ICAO's legislative experience indicates that a sufficiently flexible system of international regulatory activity is, in at least some technical areas, by no means doomed to failure.

INTERNATIONAL STANDARDS AND RECOMMENDED PRACTICES (SARPS)

General Characterization

The most important legislative function performed by ICAO consists of the formulation and adoption of International Standards and Recommended Practices (SARPS).[1] The Organization's authority

---

[1] On this subject, Erler, RECHTSFRAGEN DER ICAO: DIE INTERNATIONALE ZIVILLUFTFAHRT ORGANISATION UND IHRE MITGLIEDSTAATEN 112–28 (1967)

to adopt SARPS derives from Article 37 of the Convention. It reads as follows:

Each contracting State undertakes to collaborate in securing the highest practicable degree of uniformity in regulations, standards, procedures, and organization in relation to aircraft, personnel, airways and auxiliary services in all matters in which such uniformity will facilitate and improve air navigation. To this end the International Civil Aviation Organization shall adopt and amend from time to time, as may be necessary, international standards and recommended practices and procedures dealing with:

(a) Communications systems and air navigation aids, including ground marking;

(b) Characteristics of airports and landing areas;

(c) Rules of the air and air traffic control practices;

(d) Licensing of operating and mechanical personnel;

(e) Airworthiness of aircraft;

(f) Registration and identification of aircraft;

(g) Collection and exchange of meteorological information;

(h) Log books;

(i) Aeronautical maps and charts;

(j) Customs and immigration procedures;

(k) Aircraft in distress and investigation of accidents;

and such other matters concerned with the safety, regularity, and efficiency of air navigation as may from time to time appear appropriate.

The international standards and recommended practices which ICAO is empowered to adopt under Article 37 are, "for conven-

---

[hereinafter cited as Erler]; see Mateesco Matte, TRAITÉ DE DROIT AÉRIEN-AÉRONATIQUE 225-28 (2d ed. 1964); Cheng, THE LAW OF INTERNATIONAL AIR TRANSPORT 63-71 (1962) [hereinafter cited as Cheng]; Sheffy, *The Air Navigation Commission of the International Civil Aviation Organization,* 25 J. Air L. & Com. 281 and 428 (1958); Le Goff, *Les Annexes Techniques à la Convention de Chicago,* 19 Revue Générale de l'Air 146 (1956); Mankiewicz, *L'adoption des annexes à la Convention de Chicago par le Conseil de l'Organisation de l'Aviation Civile Internationale,* in Brandt, BEITRÄGE ZUM INTERNATIONALEN LUFTRECHT 82 (Festschrift zu Ehren von Alex Meyer) (1954) [hereinafter cited as Mankiewicz]; Ros, *Le Pouvoir Législatif International de l'O.A.C.I. et ses Modalités,* 16 Revue Générale de l'Air 25 (1953); Pépin, *ICAO and Other Agencies Dealing with Air Regulations,* 19 J. Air L. & Com. 152 (1952); Malintoppi, *La Fonction "Normatif" de l'O.A.C.I.,* 13 Revue Générale de l'Air 1050 (1950).

ience," designated as "Annexes" to the Convention.[2] To date the Organization has promulgated 15 such Annexes dealing with the following subjects: Personnel Licensing (Annex 1); Rules of the Air (Annex 2); Meteorology (Annex 3); Aeronautical Charts (Annex 4); Units of Measurement to be used in Air-Ground Communications (Annex 5); Operation of Aircraft, International Commercial Air Transport (Annex 6); Aircraft Nationality and Registration Marks (Annex 7); Airworthiness of Aircraft (Annex 8); Facilitation of International Air Transport (Annex 9); Aeronautical Telecommunications (Annex 10); Air Traffic Services (Annex 11); Search and Rescue (Annex 12); Aircraft Accident Inquiry (Annex 13); Aerodromes (Annex 14); and Aeronautical Information Services (Annex 15). Since their initial adoption in the period between 1948 and 1953, each Annex has been amended more or less extensively to meet the growing needs of international civil aviation.[3]

The Convention does not define "International Standards" or "Recommended Practices." The requisite definitions were formulated by ICAO Assembly in 1947 "for use by the Organization in relation to air navigation matters." [4] The Assembly, as the preamble to Resolution A1–31 indicates, took this step to provide the Contracting States and their representatives to ICAO meetings with "a uniform understanding of the obligations of the Contracting States under the Convention with respect to International Standards and Recommended Practices to be adopted and amended from time to time. . . ." Resolution A1–31 defines a "Standard" as

> any specification for physical characteristics, configuration, materiel, performance, personnel, or procedure, the uniform application of which is recognized as *necessary* for the safety or regularity of international air navigation and to which Member States *will conform* in accordance with the Convention; in the event of impossibility of compliance, notification to the Council is compulsory under Article 38 of the Convention. (Emphasis added.)

The same resolution describes a "Recommended Practice" as

---

[2] Convention, Art. 54(1).

[3] An up-to-date list of the various Annexes and amendments thereto, together with the dates of their adoption, can be found in [1967] Report of the Council, ICAO Doc. 8724 (A16–P/3), pp. 143–47 (1968).

[4] Assembly Res. A1–31, ICAO Doc. 4411 (A1–P/45) (1947).

any specification for physical characteristics, configuration, materiel, performance, personnel, or procedure, the uniform application of which is recognized as *desirable* in the interest of safety, regularity, or efficiency of international air navigation, and to which Member States *will endeavour to conform* in accordance with the Convention. (Emphasis added.)

These definitions remain in force today.[5]

Since the foregoing resolution applied only to "air navigation matters," corresponding definitions for SARPS relating to air transport had to be supplied by the ICAO Council when it adopted Annex 9, which deals with the facilitation of international air transport. These definitions read as follows:

> *Standards:* Any specification, the uniform observance of which has been recognized as practicable and as *necessary* to facilitate and improve some aspect of international air navigation, which has been adopted by the Council pursuant to Article 54(1) of the Convention, and in respect of which *non-compliance must be notified* by States to the Council in accordance with Article 38. (Emphasis added.)
>
> *Recommended Practice:* Any specification, the observance of which has been recognized as generally practicable and as *highly desirable* to facilitate and improve some aspect of international air navigation, which has been adopted by the Council pursuant to Article 54(1) of the Convention, and to which Contracting States *will endeavour to conform* in accordance with the Convention. (Emphasis added.) [6]

The Air Transport Committee, in recommending these definitions for adoption by the Council, noted that

> the nature of the FAL provisions appeared to require that the Standards and Recommended Practices be based on the general concept of 'uniformity [which] will facilitate and improve air navigation' as stated in the opening words of Article 37, rather than on the more specific items of 'safety, regularity and efficiency' mentioned towards the conclusion of Article 37.[7]

---

[5] Assembly Res. A15–8, Appendix E, ICAO Doc. 8528 (A15–P/6) (1965).

[6] ICAO, STANDARDS AND RECOMMENDED PRACTICES: FACILITATION OF INTERNATIONAL AIR TRANSPORT (ANNEX 9), p. 7 (1949). These definitions have been retained unchanged in all subsequent editions of Annex 9.

[7] Fourth Report to the Council by the Chairman of the Air Transport Committee, reprinted in ICAO Council, 6th Sess., Doc. 6764 (C/780), Annex A, p. 26 (1949).

The Development, Adoption, and Amendment of Annexes

The task of developing and formulating ICAO Annexes and amendments thereto is entrusted to the Air Navigation Commission,[8] which is responsible for the air navigation SARPS, and to the Air Transport Committee for SARPS dealing with the facilitation of international air transport. Each of these bodies in turn coordinates the activities [9] of various sub-committees—known as divisions—and international conferences established or convened by them to help formulate and review different SARPS.[10]

The first sets of ICAO Technical Annexes were in large measure prepared by the various divisions of the Air Navigation Commission. Their functions have been increasingly taken over in recent years by air navigation conferences and special expert panels, convened by the Air Navigation Commission to consider overlapping technical problems encountered in the development and application of SARPS.

It is now the practice for an air navigation conference to be convened whenever it is necessary to resolve a number of interrelated questions falling within more than one technical field, although sometimes it is more expedient to make use of a joint divisional meeting for this purpose. A Division Meeting is used whenever a task is

---

[8] The first sets of ICAO Air Navigation Annexes were largely developed by the PICAO Air Navigation Committee, which was continued in existence on an interim basis during the first two years after ICAO was established, when the Air Navigation Commission was formally constituted. See Assembly Res. A1-7, ICAO Doc. 4411 (A1-P/45) (1947); Assembly Res. A2-8, ICAO Doc. 5692 (A2-P/37) (1958). For a thorough study of the functions and activities of the Air Navigation Commission as well as its predecessor, the Air Navigation Committee, see Sheffy, *supra* note 1, *passim*. See also, Rules of Procedure of the Air Navigation Commission, ICAO Doc. 8229 (AN/876) (1962).

[9] See Development and Coordination of Technical Annexes to the Convention, ICAO Doc. 7215 (AN/858), p. 5 (1951).

[10] In the air navigation field, the following eleven distinct divisions have from time to time participated in the development and formulation of SARPS: Aerodromes, Air Routes and Ground Aids Div.; Accident Investigation Div.; Airworthiness Div.; Aeronautical Information Services Div.; Communications Div.; Aeronautical Charts Div.; Meteorology Div.; Operations Div.; Personnel Licensing Div.; Rules of the Air and Air Traffic Services Div.; and Search and Rescue Div. Rules of Procedure for the Conduct of Air Navigation Meetings and Directives to Divisional-Type Air Navigation Meetings, ICAO Doc. 8143 (AN/873), p. V (1961). The Facilitation Division of the Air Transport Committee is responsible for SARPS in the facilitation field.

confined to its particular technical field. A Special Meeting is used whenever a task of limited scope relating to a particular subject affects more than one technical field.[11]

All Contracting States have a voice in the formulation and development of SARPS at two different stages of the drafting process.[12] First, each Contracting State is free to participate in the divisional meetings and conferences, where it has an opportunity to initiate and help develop proposals for SARPS. Second, all proposals for SARPS, or amendments thereto, must be submitted to the Contracting States for their comments after they have been reviewed by the Air Navigation Commission or the Air Transport Committee.[13] These comments are carefully analyzed by the Air Navigation Commission or the Air Transport Committee before the final draft for the SARPS proposals is submitted to the Council.[14] This consultative process reduces the likelihood that any SARPS will be adopted to which a significant number of the Contracting States is opposed.[15]

The power to adopt the international standards and recommended practices comprising an Annex, as well as the adoption of any amendments thereto, rests with the ICAO Council.[16] Under Article 90(a) of the Convention, the adoption of an Annex requires "the vote of two-thirds of the Council at a meeting called for that purpose." The Council has interpreted the phrase "vote of two-thirds of the Council" to the effect that the vote ". . . required under Article 90 for the adoption of an Annex should be interpreted as the vote of two-thirds of the total membership of the Council. In

[11] Rules of Procedure for the Conduct of Air Navigation Meetings and Directives to Divisional-Type Air Navigation Meetings, ICAO Doc. 8143 (AN/873), p. VI (1961). In the facilitation field, corresponding functions are performed by the periodic sessions of the Facilitation Division.

[12] Erler 121.

[13] See Rules of Procedure for the Conduct of Air Navigation Meetings and Directives to Divisional-Type Air Navigation Meetings, ICAO Doc. 8143 (AN/873), p. 6 (1961). The Contracting States are traditionally given a period of three months within which to review these proposals and to submit their comments. See Assembly Res. A15–8, Appendix E, ICAO Doc. 8528 (A15–P/6) (1965).

[14] See Rules of Procedure for the Conduct of Air Navigation Meetings and Directives and Directives to Divisional-Type Air Navigation Meetings, ICAO Doc. 8143 (AN/873), p. 6 (1961); ICAO Assembly, Report of the Economic Commission, 14th Sess., Doc. 8286 (A14–EC/38), Annex III, pp. 79–80 (1962).

[15] See Mankiewicz 88 n.23.

[16] Convention, Arts. 54(l) and 54(m).

other words, fourteen affirmative votes would be needed for the adoption of an Annex." [17] While this interpretation has been consistently adhered to, it should be noted that at the time it was rendered the Council had a membership of 21 states. It has since been expanded to 27.[18] Today, accordingly, the adoption of an Annex to the Convention requires 18 affirmative votes.

Article 54(1), which deals with the adoption of Annexes, makes no reference to the adoption of amendments thereto. This subject is dealt with in Article 54(m) which directs the Council to "consider recommendations of the Air Navigation Commission for amendment of the Annexes and take action in accordance with the provisions of Chapter XX." Chapter XX consists of a single provision: Article 90. The language of Article 90(a) relevant here provides:

> The adoption by the Council of the Annexes described in Article 54, subparagraph (1), shall require the vote of two-thirds of the Council. . . . Any such Annex or any amendment to an Annex shall become effective within three months after its submission to the contracting States.

Since Article 90(a) speaks only of Article 54(1) when referring to the two-thirds-vote requirement, it is at least arguable that the adoption of amendments to Annexes requires no more than a simple majority vote of the Council, and that a special meeting does not have to be called for the adoption of amendments.[19] The reference in Article 54(m) to Chapter XX (Article 90) would have to be understood, if one accepts this view, as applying merely to the effective date and entry into force of such amendments—the other topics with which Article 90 also deals. Considering, however, that an amendment to an Annex may amount to a complete revision of the Annex in all but form,[20] it is obvious that the requirement of a two-thirds vote applicable to Annexes could be easily circumvented if this view were to be accepted. It is therefore not surprising that

[17] ICAO Council, Proceedings of the 3rd Sess. [1948], Doc. 7310 (C/846), p. 27 (1952).

[18] See Assembly Res. A13–1, ICAO Doc. 8167 (A13–P/2) (1961), amending Article 50(a) of the Convention. This amendment entered into force on 17 July 1962.

[19] Cheng 65–66.

[20] The legality of such a revision by amendment has been recognized by the Council. See ICAO Council, 14th Sess., Doc. 7216 (C/832), pp. 156–58 (1951).

the ICAO Council has from its inception proceeded on the assumption that the adoption of an amendment to an Annex is governed by the same voting requirements that apply to Annexes.[21] There has been some confusion on this question in past discussions of this subject because an early ruling of the Council was erroneously reported and accordingly misinterpreted.[22] In the report of the action taken by the Council during its third session the following statement appears: "The Council agreed at its 22nd Meeting that, in adopting an Annex or amendments thereto . . . (b) amendments to the Annexes should be carried or lost by a simple majority of those present and voting." [23] What this report does not record is that at the time this ruling was made no Annexes had as yet been adopted. The ruling was made shortly before the Council began to vote on the first ICAO Annexes,[24] and was designed solely to clarify the voting procedure applicable to amendments to the *draft* Annexes proposed for adoption by the Air Navigation Commission.[25] In other words, the Council's ruling had nothing to do with the voting requirements applicable to the adoption of amendments to existing Annexes, which have always been subject to the rules governing the adoption of Annexes proper.[26]

---

[21] Thus, when the ICAO Council considered the adoption of the first seven amendments to Annex 11, one of the proposed amendments was declared to have been "lost" even though it received 12 affirmative votes. ICAO Council, 14th Sess., Doc. 7216 (C/832), p. 174 (1951). At that time the Council consisted of 21 Members. More recently, a proposed amendment to Annex 10 "failed to receive the necessary two-thirds vote of the Council required under Article 90(a) of the Convention for the adoption of an amendment to an Annex. . . ." Action of the Council, 48th Sess., ICAO Doc. 8351 (C/946), p. 16 (1963).

[22] See Cheng 65 n.5; Carroz, *International Legislation on Air Navigation over the High Seas*, 26 J. Air L. & Com. 158, 165 n.27 (1959).

[23] ICAO Council, Proceedings of the 3rd Sess. [1948], Doc. 7310 (C/846), p. 27 (1952).

[24] See ICAO Council, 3rd Sess., Doc. 5701 (C/672), pp. 11–12 (1948).

[25] This is readily apparent from the context of the Council discussion. *Id.* at 11–13; Erler 125.

[26] The Council's ruling relating to the procedure applicable to the vote on amendments to the first draft Annexes proposed by the Air Navigation Commission was necessitated by the fact that these draft Annexes were based on PICAO Standards and Recommended Practices, whose continued application by the Contracting States had been formally recommended by the ICAO Council pending the adoption of the ICAO Annexes. ICAO Council, Proceedings of the 1st Sess. [1947], Doc. 6808 (C/791), pp. 33–34 (1949). Some Council Representatives felt that these draft Annexes, because they were based on the PICAO

The Entry into Force of an Annex or Amendment

THE RIGHT OF DISAPPROVAL

The adoption by the ICAO Council of an Annex or amendment thereto is merely the first stage in the legislative process leading to its formal enactment. The legislative power of the Council, as far as these regulatory acts are concerned, is subject to a veto of the Member States. Article 90(a) of the Convention accordingly provides that after its adoption by the Council

> any such Annex or any amendment of an Annex shall become effective within three months after its submission to the contracting States or at the end of such longer period of time as the Council may prescribe, unless in the meantime a majority of the contracting States register their disapproval with the Council.

In other words, an Annex or amendment to it adopted by the Council becomes effective only after the expiration of the period set for the notification of disapproval,[27] provided that a majority of Contracting States has in the meantime not registered such disapproval.

The language of Article 90(a) is silent on the question whether a state, in exercising its right of disapproval, has an option between (1) a disapproval of an Annex or amendment in its entirety, and (2) a disapproval limited to certain parts thereof. The ICAO Council considered this question in 1948 on a motion of the U.S. Representative, who urged that the Member States be given this option so as not to force them to veto an entire Annex merely because they could not accept some of the standards or recommended practices set out in the Annex.[28] This motion was opposed by the Canadian Representative who contended that Article 90, because it did not expressly provide for the disapproval of the Annex "or any part

---

Standards and Recommended Practices, had acquired a semi-official status and should therefore be treated with greater respect than other drafts emanating from the Air Navigation Commission. See Statement by Admiral Smith, U.S. Council Representative, ICAO Council, 3rd Sess., Doc. 5701 (C/672), pp. 12–13 (1948).

[27] The usual period allowed by the Council for the registration of disapprovals has ranged in the past from three and a half months to four and a half months. ICAO Doc. AN–WP/2743, p. 5 (1963).

[28] ICAO Council, 3rd Sess., Doc. 5159 (C/641), p. 11 (1948).

thereof," intentionally foreclosed the right of partial disapproval.[29] Drawn into the debate, the Chairman of the Air Navigation Commission explained that in his Commission "it had been recognized that to allow disapproval by States of parts of an Annex might disrupt the operations of the Annex so completely that it would be virtually of no effect." [30]

Apparently unpersuaded by the policy considerations advanced by the Air Navigation Commission, but troubled by the Canadian argument, the Council requested a ruling from the Legal Bureau on the constitutionality of the U.S. proposal. Following receipt of this opinion, which was totally unresponsive to the question that had been asked and merely opposed giving the Member States the right of partial disapproval on the ground that "the complete Annex might in certain cases become entirely unworkable," [31] the Council, by a vote of nine to six, ruled that the Contracting States had the option to disapprove of an Annex either in whole or in part.[32] This ruling has been consistently adhered to, both with regard to Annexes [33] and amendments thereto.[34] Thus, for example, the Council's "Revised Form of Resolution of Adoption of an Annex" [35] contains the following clause in paragraph 2, wherein the Council

> PRESCRIBES 1 September 1954 [hypothetical date] as the date upon which the standards and recommended practices shall become effective, except for any standard or recommended practice *or any part thereof* in respect of which a majority of the contracting States have registered their disapproval with the Council before that date. (Emphasis added.)

---

[29] *Ibid.*

[30] Statement by Mr. Graham, *id.* at 12. As a matter of fact, the draft standard form for the adoption of Annexes recommended to the Council by the Air Navigation Commission made no provisions for the disapproval of certain parts of an Annex. See ICAO Doc. 5108 (AN/583), pp. 3–4 (1948).

[31] ICAO Doc. C–Draft/473, p. 9 (1948).

[32] ICAO Council, 3rd Sess., Doc. 5290 (C/656), p. 7 (1948).

[33] See Standard Form Resolution for the Adoption of Annexes, ICAO Council, Proceedings of the 3rd Sess. [1948], Doc. 7310 (C/846), pp. 24–25 (1952); Revised Form of Resolution of Adoption of an Annex, ICAO Council, 18th Sess., Doc. 7361 (C/858), Appendix A, p. 199 (1953).

[34] See, *e.g.*, Resolution adopting Amendment No. 1 to the International Standards and Recommended Practices for Rules of the Air (Annex 2), ICAO Council, 14th Sess. [1951], Doc. 7216 (C/832), pp. 152–53 (1952).

[35] ICAO Council, 18th Sess., Doc. 7361 (C/858), Appendix A, p. 199 (1953).

To date no Annex or any part thereof has ever been disapproved by the requisite majority of the Contracting States. As a matter of fact, after the 15 original Annexes had been promulgated, the Organization was able to report that "the maximum number of disapprovals notified in relation to any one International Standard [contained in these Annexes] was 8." [36]

A number of reasons account for this phenomenon. The compromise-oriented consultative process which precedes the adoption of an Annex or amendment thereto no doubt reduces the likelihood that the Council will adopt an Annex which it knows to be unacceptable to a large number of Contracting States.[37] Equally important in explaining the very small number of disapprovals is the fact that the Member States, as we shall see, are in large measure free not to comply with the provisions of an Annex. Without necessarily underestimating the importance of these two considerations, it is well to keep in mind that the Council's decision to permit partial disapproval of an Annex is a significant factor in reducing even further the likelihood that a majority of the Member States will exercise the veto power. To the extent that the states avail themselves of the right of partial disapproval, those parts of an Annex found unacceptable by each of them will also have to be disapproved by a majority of the Contracting States to prevent their enactment. The probability that this will happen is quite small, given ICAO's heterogeneous (in terms of technical development) membership. Thus, by permitting partial disapprovals, the Council has obviously watered down the veto power which Article 90(a) vests in the Contracting States.

The Council's practice of stipulating in the resolution of adoption that only those parts of an Annex or amendment thereto which have not been disapproved shall become applicable,[38] no doubt assumes that the standards or recommended practices prescribed in the Annex are separable. It will be remembered, however, that the Air Navigation Commission initially opposed the right of partial disap-

---

[36] ICAO Doc. A7–WP/27 (TE/3), p. 2 (1953).

[37] Mankiewicz 87–88.

[38] See Revised Form of Resolution of Adoption of an Annex, para. 3, ICAO Council, 18th Sess., Doc. 7361 (C/858), Appendix A, p. 199 (1953); Council Resolution adopting Amendment 41 to Annex 10, para. 3, Action of the Council, ICAO Doc. 8352 (C/947), p. 11 (1963).

proval on the ground that its exercise "might disrupt the operation of the Annex so completely that it would be virtually of no effect."[39] The Council has not had to face this problem to date, nor has it established a procedure designed to cope with a case in which one or more partial disapprovals have substantially distorted the underlying policy of the Annex. It may be assumed, however, that in a case of this type the Council would rule that the particular Annex or amendment thereto has been disapproved in its entirety.

THE PROMULGATION OF AN ANNEX

After providing in Article 90(a) when an Annex or amendment thereto "shall become effective," the Convention prescribes in Article 90(b) that "the Council shall immediately notify all contracting States of the coming into force of any Annex or amendment thereto." But the Convention does not tell us when an Annex or amendment thereto is deemed to have "come into force" within the meaning of Article 90(b).

At least three interpretations of Article 90(b) are possible.[40] Its language might signify, on the one hand, that an Annex which has become effective under Article 90(a) requires a further legislative act before it is deemed to have been formally enacted. On the other hand, "coming into force" could be a synonym for the expression "become effective" used in Article 90(a). Thus understood, Article 90(b) would have to be read as providing that "the Council shall immediately notify all contracting States of the becoming effective of an Annex or amendment thereto." Another construction is possible, namely, that "coming into force" was used in Article 90(b) to describe not one but two distinct concepts traditionally associated with this phrase: "to be enacted," as well as "to become applicable." This would mean that Article 90(b) might be read as providing that "the Council shall immediately notify all contracting States of [a] the enactment (becoming effective) of an Annex or amendment thereto and [b] the date on which it shall become applicable (come into force)."

How has this issue been resolved in the practice of the Organiza-

---

[39] Statement by Mr. Graham, Chairman of the Air Navigation Commission, ICAO Council, 3rd Sess., Doc. 5159 (C/641), p. 12 (1948).

[40] The legislative history relating to this clause of the Convention is inconclusive at best.

tion? In 1948 the ICAO Council interpreted Article 90, albeit only by implication, when it promulgated the "Standard Form Resolution for the Adoption of Annexes."[41] Paragraph 2 of this resolution fixes "D plus 120" (120 days following the adoption of the Annex) as the period within which the Contracting States must register their disapproval of the Annex. Paragraph 3 provides that "if on the said (*D plus 120*) a majority of the Contracting States have not registered their disapproval of the said Annex, it shall then become effective." The "coming into force" of the Annex is dealt with in paragraphs 6 and 7. The former stipulates that "the said Annex . . . shall come into force and be implemented on (*D plus 365*)," whereas paragraph 7 provides in part that "the becoming effective of the said Annex shall forthwith be notified to each Contracting State, and each State shall also, at the same time, be notified: (a) of the said date upon which the said Annex shall come into force."

This resolution indicates that in 1948 the Council assumed that an Annex which had "become effective" pursuant to the provisions of Article 90(a) had been formally enacted. The language employed in paragraphs 6 and 7 of the resolution shows that the Council assumed that the phrase "come into force" found in Article 90(b) had a dual meaning. To the extent that paragraph 7 of the form resolution provides for the immediate notification of "the becoming effective of the said Annex," although Article 90(b) prescribes that such notice be given upon "the coming into force" of the Annex, the Council must be deemed to have assumed that "coming into force" was synonymous with "become effective." The manner in which the phrase "come into force" is used in paragraph 6 ("the said Annex . . . shall come into force and be implemented on *D plus 365*") and in paragraph 7(a), indicates that in this context it refers to the date on which an Annex is to become applicable.[42] Accordingly, if one attempted to redraft Article 90(b) as it was understood by the Council in 1948, we would come up with the following provision: "The Council shall immediately notify all Contracting States of the

[41] ICAO Council, Proceedings of the 3rd Sess. [1948], Doc. 7310 (C/846), pp. 24–25 (1952). The Council adhered to this form resolution with minor variations in adopting fourteen of the original fifteen Annexes.

[42] The words "and be implemented" in paragraph 7 of the resolution added nothing beyond what was already implicit in the use of the phrase "come into force." See Statement by the President of the Council, ICAO Council, 13th Sess. [1951], Doc. 7177 (C/828), pp. 70–71 (1952).

becoming effective (enactment) of an Annex or amendment thereto and of the date on which the said Annex or amendment thereto shall become applicable (come into force)."

In 1951, while the Council was considering the adoption of Annex 14 (Aerodromes), the Representative of Brazil challenged the use of the phrase "shall come into force and be implemented" found in paragraph 6 of the Standard Form Resolution for the Adoption of Annexes. Relying on Articles 38, 54, and 90 of the Convention, he expressed the view that if "implementation" meant "carrying out the provisions of the Annex," the Council was acting contrary to the "spirit of the Convention" by fixing an implementation date "because of the heavy burden it would place on States if they had to implement the Standards with respect to all their airports on one specified date." If, on the other hand, the term "be implemented" was used merely to indicate when the Annex was to "come into force," this should be explained in the Foreword to the Annex to prevent misunderstanding by the Contracting States.[43] Since a number of Council Representatives agreed with their Brazilian colleague that some Contracting States had no clear understanding of their obligations under the Convention, and that this confusion was compounded by the language used in the Standard Form Resolution, the Council requested the Air Navigation Commission to look into this matter.[44]

After studying the issue raised by the Brazilian Representative,[45] the Air Navigation Commission proposed to the Council that the phrase "come into force and be implemented" be deleted from the Standard Form Resolution and that "shall be applied" be substituted for it. The Commission suggested this change on the ground that, since "some doubts prevailed as to the exact meaning of 'come into force' as used in Article 90 of the Convention," it was "better not to attempt [an] interpretation but to exclude this expression."[46]

In the ensuing debate, the U.K. Representative challenged the Commission's proposal, as well as the opinion of the ICAO Legal Bureau, that the phrases "coming into force" found in Article 90(b) and "become effective" used in Article 90(a) meant one and the

[43] ICAO Council, 13th Sess. [1951], Doc. 7177 (C/828), p. 70 (1952).
[44] Id. at 66.
[45] See ICAO Doc. C–WP/1319 (1953).
[46] ICAO Council, 17th Sess. [1952], Doc. 7328 (C/853), p. 168 (1953).

same thing. The U.K. Representative took the position that an Annex which had "become effective" was equivalent to a law that had been duly promulgated. To him the phrase "coming into force" referred to the date on which the Annex was to become applicable. The U.K. Representative found the Air Navigation Commission's proposal to substitute "be applied" for "coming into force" unacceptable, for the reason that it was synonymous with "be implemented." In his opinion, the addition of this latter phrase in the resolution of adoption had confused the Contracting States and was legally untenable. "Where the Council had gone wrong in the past," he emphasized, "was in confusing the functions of Council, adoption and promulgation, and the actions of Contracting States, compliance or the notification of differences." [47] He accordingly urged that

> No term should be used in the resolution which could possibly cause confusion between the functions of Council and the actions of States. Therefore the words "shall be applied" were inappropriate and he could see no reason to depart from the terms of the Convention, though he would not object in principle to "shall be applicable" or "shall be operative." [48]

The President of the Council and a number of other Representatives took the position that, conceptually, "coming into force" and "become effective" meant one and the same thing. In their opinion Article 90(b) imposed upon the Council the obligation merely to notify the Contracting States of the event envisaged in Article 90(a): the "becoming effective" of the Annex. It followed therefrom that an Annex must be deemed to have "come into force" as soon as it had "become effective," although the Council was free to fix a different applicability date for the various Annexes or parts thereof. Since to these Representatives the applicability date had nothing to do with the "coming into force" of the Annex, they urged that this phrase be deleted from the resolution of adoption.[49] But when the President of the Council, before adjourning the meeting, asked for an informal vote on the proposal of the Air Navigation Commission, the count indicated that nine Representatives favored the retention

[47] *Id.* at 169.
[48] *Ibid.*
[49] *Id.* at 170–72.

of the phrase "come into force," six opted for "be applicable," whereas "be applied" received no support.[50]

At the next Council meeting the Chairman of the Air Navigation Commission, in commenting on two draft resolutions prepared by the Secretariat,[51] emphasized that his Commission believed that the use of the expression "coming into force" resulted in unnecessarily complicated resolutions of adoption whenever more than one applicability date was envisaged for the different sets of SARPS that were included in the Annex. He therefore favored the phrase "shall be applicable" because it avoided this problem and because, in his opinion, it meant the same thing as "come into force." [52]

This view eventually prevailed, but not before yet another study was made by a Council Working Group,[53] which recommended that the resolution of adoption should refer only to the date on which the Annex is to "become effective," that the expression "come into force" not be used at all, and that the proper place for the dates specifying when an Annex or certain parts thereof were to become applicable was in the text of the Annex itself. Since some Council Representatives found this last suggestion unacceptable, the Representative of Argentina proposed that the resolution of adoption contain a clause to the effect "that those Standards and Recommended Practices that have become effective shall become applicable in accordance with Chapter . . . [Chapter on Applicability] of the Annex (as amended)." [54] This clause, the Argentine Representative explained, was prompted by the following considerations:

> The Council would note that he had not used the expression "come into force." This was deliberate, with the object of avoiding an interpretation of Article 90 which used both "come into force" and "become effective." The Director of the Legal Bureau [M. Pépin], an eminent jurist, had stated categorically that the two expressions did not have the same meaning. Certain equally eminent jurists on the Council held a precisely opposite view, and another member of the

---

[50] Id. at 172.
[51] See ICAO Doc. C–WP/1335 (1952).
[52] ICAO Council, 17th Sess. [1952], Doc. 7328 (C/853), p. 181 (1953).
[53] See ICAO Docs. C–WP/1380 (1953) and C–WP/1411 (1953). See also ICAO Doc. C–WP/1414 (1953) containing an opinion by the ICAO Legal Bureau.
[54] ICAO Council, 18th Sess., Doc. 7361 (C/858), p. 162 (1953).

Legal Bureau had advised the [Air Navigation] Commission in the same sense six months ago. The fact that "come into force" was used in Article 90 did not mean that it had to be used in the resolution of adoption, and since there was a difference of opinion about its meaning, the wise course seemed to be not to use it.[55]

After approving the Argentine proposal, the Council passed the "Revised Form of Resolution of Adoption of an Annex." [56] This resolution, which has remained in effect since its adoption in 1953, provides in part:

THE COUNCIL

Acting in accordance with the Convention on International Civil Aviation, and particularly with the provisions of Articles 37, 54 and 90 thereof

1. HEREBY ADOPTS on 28 April 1954 [hypothetical date] the international standards and recommended practices contained in the document entitled "International Standards and Recommended Practices . . . ," which for convenience are designated as Annex . . . to the Convention;

2. PRESCRIBES 1 September 1954 as the date upon which the standards and recommended practices shall become effective, except for any standard or recommended practice or any part thereof in respect of which a majority of the contracting States have registered their disapproval with the Council before that date;

3. RESOLVES that those standards and recommended practices that have become effective shall become applicable in accordance with Chapter . . . [Chapter on Applicability] of the Annex (as amended);

4. DIRECTS the Secretary General on behalf of the Council:
(i) to notify each contracting State immediately of the above action and immediately after 1 September 1954 of those parts of the standards and recommended practices that have become effective; . . .

An analysis of this resolution and the debates leading to its adoption indicates, first of all, that the Council has always proceeded on the assumption that an Annex, which has "become effective" in accordance with the provisions of Article 90(a), has ac-

[55] *Id.* at 162–63.
[56] *Id.* at 199, Appendix A.

quired the status of a duly enacted legislative act. As such it can no longer be withdrawn or modified by the Council without recourse to the formal amendment process prescribed in Article 90(a).[57] Furthermore, by settling on "shall become applicable" in its Revised Resolution of Adoption instead of retaining "shall come into force and be implemented," the Council clearly intended to dispel the erroneous assumption that the Contracting States were under an obligation to implement an Annex as soon as it had entered into force. It is also obvious that the language of paragraph 4(i) of the Revised Resolution of Adoption is predicated on the assumption that the expressions "become effective" and "coming into force" are synonymous, for this clause requires the ICAO Secretary General on behalf of the Council to notify the Contracting States that an Annex has "become effective," whereas Article 90(b) provides that such notice be given upon the "coming into force" of an Annex.[58]

It must be remembered, however, that those Council Representatives who argued that "become effective" and "coming into force" were not synonymous asserted that the latter expression corresponded to "shall become applicable." Paragraph 3 of the Revised Resolution of Adoption embodies this interpretation of Article 90(b), for it provides "that those standards and recommended practices that have become effective shall become applicable in accordance with Chapter . . .[Chapter on Applicability] of the Annex (as amended)." How can paragraphs 3 and 4(i) of the Revised Resolution of Adoption be reconciled with the conflicting interpretations of Article 90(b) that were advanced in the Council? The most satisfactory answer would seem to be that the Council never really departed from the interpretation of Article 90(b) upon which it based the 1948 Standard Form Resolution.

At that time the Council understood Article 90(b) to provide that "the Council shall immediately notify all contracting States of the becoming effective (enactment) of an Annex or amendment thereto and of the date on which the said Annex or amendment thereto shall come into force (become applicable)." The text of the Revised Resolution of Adoption, as well as the debates preceding its adop-

---

[57] See in this connection, the discussion and action of the Council relating to the annulment of an error in Amendment No. 10 to Annex 10, ICAO Council, 17th Sess. [1952], Doc. 7328 (C/853), pp. 208–10 (1953).

[58] See Mankiewicz 89–90.

tion, are entirely consistent with the Council's 1948 construction of Article 90(b).[59] True, the Revised Resolution excludes some of the objectionable language found in the 1948 Standard Form Resolution, which created the erroneous impression that the Contracting States must implement an Annex as soon as it has come into force. Moreover, by substituting "shall become applicable" for "shall come into force," the Council obviously desired to avoid awkwardly worded resolutions of adoption. But that is all.

If this conclusion is valid, it would follow that until the standards prescribed in an Annex have "come into force" or, to use the Council's present language, until they have "become applicable," they do not create legal obligations as far as the Member States are concerned. Thus, when the Convention speaks, for example, of "minimum standards which may be established from time to time pursuant to this Convention," [60] it is obvious that these standards do not bind the Member States until they have become applicable. The same is true of the obligation which the Contracting States have assumed in Article 38, wherein they undertake to conform their domestic legislation and practices to the provisions of an international standard or to notify the Organization of existing differences. Theoretically, this obligation does not arise until the particular standard has become applicable.

Compliance with International Standards and Recommended Practices

With some exceptions to be discussed below, the Contracting States have no legal obligation to implement or to comply with the provisions of a duly promulgated Annex or amendment thereto, unless they find it "practicable" to do so.[61] This conclusion is supported both by the language of the Convention as well as by the practice of the Organization. With regard to the standards promulgated by the Organization for the purpose of facilitating interna-

---

[59] The commentators who have discussed this problem uniformly hold that the Council's interpretation of Article 90(b) embodied in the Revised Resolution of Adoption is a reversal of its 1948 position. See, e.g., Erler 127–28; Mankiewicz 89–90. This conclusion results from a misunderstanding of what the Council presumably decided in 1948 and is, in my opinion, not borne out by the text of the Revised Resolution of Adoption nor by the legislative history relating to it.

[60] See, e.g., Convention, Art. 33.

[61] See Convention Arts. 22, 23, 28, 37 and 38; Erler 132–34.

tional air transport, a Contracting State merely undertakes to give effect to these regulations "so far as it may find [it] practicable." [62] The requirement for compliance with the air navigation standards established by ICAO is equally limited to the steps which a Contracting State "may find practicable" to take.[63] The obligation that these states have assumed in Article 37 of the Convention, which enpowers the Organization to adopt SARPS, furthermore consists merely of an undertaking "to collaborate in securing the *highest practicable degree* of uniformity in regulations, standards, procedures, and organization in relation to aircraft, personnel, airways, and auxiliary services in all matters in which such uniformity will facilitate and improve air navigation." (Emphasis added.)

That the standards prescribed in an Annex are not binding legislative enactments as that concept is traditionally understood is also apparent from the language of Article 38 of the Convention, which reads as follows:

> Any State which finds it impracticable to comply in all respects with any such international standard or procedure [which the Organization may adopt under Article 37], or to bring its own regulations or practices into full accord with any international standard or procedure after amendment of the latter, or which deems it necessary to adopt regulations or practices differing in any particular respect from those established by an international standard, shall give immediate notification to the International Civil Aviation Organization of the differences between its own practice and that established by the international standard. In the case of amendments to international standards, any State which does not make the appropriate amendments to its own regulations or practices shall give notice to the Council within sixty days of the adoption of the amendment to the international standard, or indicate the action which it proposes to take. In any such case, the Council shall make immediate notification to all other States of the difference which exists between one or more features of an international standard and the corresponding national practice of that State.

By necessary implication, Article 38 in effect provides that it is for each Contracting State to decide whether or not to comply with or

[62] Convention, Art. 23. See also, Convention, Art. 22.
[63] Convention, Art. 28.

give effect to an international standard,[64] for by requiring the notification of differences in all those cases in which a state might conceivably depart from the provisions of an international standard, Article 38 recognizes that the Contracting States are free not to adhere to these regulations. The same conclusion applies to recommended practices, because they are non-obligatory by definition.[65] It is true, of course, that the Contracting States have an obligation to act in good faith in determining what for them is "practicable."[66] Realistically speaking, however, that is no obligation at all, for a state can always find the necessary "practical" reasons to justify non-compliance with or deviations from international standards. Besides, since under the Convention the determination as to what is "practicable" is for each state to make, ICAO can neither question nor has it ever questioned the propriety of a Contracting State's decision with regard thereto.

Article 38 indicates, furthermore, that the Contracting States have retained the right to depart from the provisions of an existing standard *any time* they decide to do so, provided only that they notify the Organization accordingly.[67] This result follows from the

[64] The phrases "finds it impracticable" and "deems it necessary," which justify non-compliance under Article 38, indicate that the decision regarding the practicability or necessity of compliance or non-compliance is left to the determination of each individual state. That this was the intention of those who drafted the Convention is readily apparent from the remarks of Dr. Edward Warner. He made the following statement in presenting the report of the committee (Committee II) which drafted the provisions of the Convention relevant here:

> No Annex is specifically identified in the Convention; and there is no limit to the adoption by the Council of any Annexes which may in [the] future appear to be desirable. On the other hand, and in fact as a necessary consequence of that flexibility, *the Annexes are given no compulsory force.* It remains open to any State to adopt its own regulations in accordance with its own necessities. (Emphasis added.)

1 PROCEEDINGS OF THE INTERNATIONAL CIVIL AVIATION ORGANIZATION (CHICAGO, ILLINOIS, NOVEMBER 1–DECEMBER 7, 1944) [hereinafter cited as PROCEEDINGS], p. 92 (1948).

[65] See Assembly Res. A1–31, ICAO Doc. 4411 (A1–P/45) (1947); Assembly Res. A15–8, Appendix E, ICAO Doc. 8528 (A15–P/6) (1965).

[66] Erler 135–36.

[67] Cheng, *Centrifugal Tendencies in Air Law,* 10 Current Legal Problems 200, 205 (1957). *But see* Detter, LAW MAKING BY INTERNATIONAL ORGANIZATIONS

notification requirement prescribed in Article 38 for differences that arise whenever a state "deems it necessary to adopt regulations or practices differing in any particular respect from those established by an international standard," for if a state must give such notice whenever it enacts legislation in conflict with a standard to which it may or may not have adhered, it is at any time free to take this action so long as it complies with the necessary formalities.[68] The practice of the Organization fully supports this conclusion. Thus the ICAO Council not only requires the Contracting States to notify the Organization of the differences that will exist between their national practices and those prescribed in an international standard on the date on which the standard becomes applicable, but also "to keep the Organization currently informed of any further differences that may arise" after the standard has become applicable.[69] This language is obviously predicated on the assumption that the Contracting States retain the right to enact legislation in conflict with an existing standard whether or not they have previously adhered to it.

There are, however, certain exceptions to the freedom of action which the Member States enjoy.[70] The most important of these

251 (1965), who asserts, without citing any authority to support this view, that "practice shows that all Standards indicate a time-limit for reservations." There is no basis either in law or fact for this assertion.

[68] This conclusion applies also to amendments to standards, notwithstanding the second sentence of Article 38, which on superficial reading seems to convey the impression that unless a state gives the requisite notice within the prescribed 60-day period, it may no longer deviate from the amended standard. As a matter of fact, however, the second sentence of Article 38 is designed merely to indicate that a state, whose domestic practices are in accord with the provisions of a standard, has 60 days within which to notify the Organization whether it will conform its practices to the amendment of the standard. But even if this state enacts legislation to give effect to the amendment and thus files no differences within the required 60-day period, it may thereafter at any time deviate from the amended standard provided only that, in accordance with the provisions of the first sentence of Article 38, it notifies the Organization immediately of the steps it has taken.

[69] Revised Form Resolution of Adoption of an Annex, para. 4(ii), ICAO Council, 18th Sess., Doc. 7361 (C/858), Appendix A, p. 199 (1953). A slightly different wording is used in recent resolutions of adoption. See, e.g., Resolution Adopting Amendment 2 to Annex 13, para. 4(ii)(a), Action of the Council, 59th Sess., Doc. 8665 (C/970), p. 10, at 11 (1966), which requires the Contracting States "thereafter [after the standards have become applicable] to notify the Organization of any further differences that arise."

[70] See ICAO Doc. C–Draft/473, p. 7 (1948).

exceptions is laid down in Article 12 of the Convention. The others result from the provisions of Articles 33 and 34 of the Convention.

THE RULES OF THE AIR GOVERNING FLIGHTS OVER THE HIGH SEAS (ARTICLE 12)

Article 12 of the Convention [71] is entitled "Rules of the Air," and provides in part:

> Each contracting State undertakes to adopt measures to insure that every aircraft flying over or maneuvering within its territory and that every aircraft carrying its nationality mark, wherever such aircraft may be, shall comply with the rules and regulations relating to the flight and maneuver of aircraft there in force. . . . Over the high seas, the rules in force shall be those established under this Convention.

By stipulating that over the high seas the rules governing the flight and maneuver of aircraft "shall be those established under this Convention," Article 12 indicates that compliance with these rules is mandatory. The question that presents itself immediately is what is meant by "rules . . . established under this Convention." Read in its proper context, the "rules" of which Article 12 speaks are rules relating to the flight and maneuver of aircraft.[72] Since the Convention as such does not contain rules relating to the flight and maneuver of aircraft, the reference to "rules . . . established under this Convention," presumably refers to those rules which the Organization is empowered to establish. Article 37(c) of the Convention expressly authorizes the Organization to adopt international standards, recommended practices and procedures dealing, among other things, with "rules of the air." The reference in Article 12 to "rules . . . established under this Convention" thus points to the legislative measures which ICAO has the power to adopt under Article 37.[73]

Whether the phrase "rules . . . established under this Convention" refers to international standards as well as to recommended

---

[71] For a thorough analysis of Article 12, see Carroz, *supra* note 22. See also, Drion, *The Council of I.C.A.O. as International Legislator over the High Seas, in* STUDI IN ONORE DI ANTONIO AMBROSINI 323 (1957).

[72] Carroz, *supra* note 22, at 162–63; Drion, *supra* note 71, at 327; Erler 143.

[73] Carroz, *supra* note 22, at 160–61.

practices [74] is disputed in the literature. Dr. Carroz argues that only an international standard can be a "rule" within the meaning of Article 12. In his opinion, a recommended practice lacks by its very nature the mandatory character which the application of Article 12 presupposes.[75] Professor Drion contends, on the other hand, that the reference is to international standards as well as to recommended practices, because "a duty to notify deviations certainly cannot be a criterion by which certain rules are to be considered 'rules established under the Convention' and others are not." [76] Carroz' analysis seems more persuasive because a recommended practice by definition makes compliance optional,[77] whereas Article 12 refers to rules that must be observed.

The practice of the Organization on this question is unclear. In adopting Annex 2 (Rules of the Air) in 1948, the ICAO Council specified that this Annex established rules relating to the flight and

[74] The reference to "procedure" in Article 37 may be disregarded for two reasons. First, because the definition adopted by the ICAO Assembly for international standards and recommended practices includes "procedures." See Assembly Res. A1-31, ICAO Doc. 4411 (A1-P/45) (1947); Assembly Res. A15-8, Appendix E, ICAO Doc. 8528 (A15-P/6) (1965). Second, while the adoption and promulgation of international standards and recommended practices in form of Annexes is expressly provided for by the Convention—see Convention, Arts. 54(1) and 90—this is not true as far as "procedures" are concerned. The Procedures for Air Navigation Services (PANS), which are approved by the ICAO Council for world-wide application—see discussion *infra* pp. 115–17—were not envisaged by those who drafted the Chicago Convention. They thought of "procedures" as an integral part of international standards and recommended practices. See Statement by Sir Frederick Tymms, one of the draftsmen of the Convention, ICAO Council, 11th Sess., Doc. 7057 (C/817), p. 167 (1950); Carroz, *supra* note 22, at 165. This conclusion is supported by the lack of any reference to "procedures" in Articles 54(1) and 90 of the Convention.

[75] Carroz, *supra* note 22, at 166–68. This view is shared by Erler 142.

[76] Drion, *supra* note 71, at 326.

[77] See the definition adopted by the ICAO Assembly, Assembly Res. 1–31, ICAO Doc. 4411 (A1-P/45) (1947); Assembly Res. A15–8, Appendix E, ICAO Doc. 8528 (A15-P/6) (1965). The definition adopted by the Assembly is in conformity with the understanding of the draftsmen of the Convention. See Report of Committee II, 1 PROCEEDINGS, p. 700, at 708, where the Committee states: "A particular problem of status is that of recommended practice [*sic*]. The committee believes that in certain branches of regulatory action some subjects should be fully *standardized*, while upon others the internationally agreed documents should present only *recommendations implying no obligation*. . . ." (Emphasis added.)

maneuver of aircraft within the meaning of Article 12 and was mandatory over the high seas.[78] Although this Annex also contained two recommended practices, in addition to a large number of international standards,[79] these were apparently not of a type that could be applied over the high seas.[80] In 1951 the Council totally revised Annex 2.[81] The newly revised Annex contained no recommended practices, nor do the subsequent editions of Annex 2. A search of the relevant Council minutes fails to disclose whether the deletion of recommended practices was motivated by considerations relating to Article 12. It is accordingly unclear whether the "rules . . . established under this Convention" are considered by ICAO to refer to international standards as well as to recommended practices, or only to the former.

A more important problem that arises in analyzing Article 12 has to do with the question whether, under this provision, only the standards established in Annex 2 are mandatory over the high seas. The question can be put differently by asking whether Article 12 also applies to those standards which, while they relate to the flight and maneuver of aircraft, are incorporated in one of the other ICAO Annexes rather than in Annex 2. We know, of course, that in adopting Annex 2 the Council resolved "that the Rules of the Air Annex constitutes rules relating to the flight and maneuver of aircraft within the meaning of Article 12 of the Convention and [that] deviations from these rules may not be made insofar as they relate to flight over the high seas." [82] The Council debate preceding the adoption of the resolution containing this clause [83] clearly indicates that a number of Council Representatives proceeded on the assumption that Annex 2 did not exhaust the possible reach of Article 12. In their opinion, Article 12 applied to any rules relating to the flight

---

[78] Action of the Council, 3rd Sess. [1948], ICAO Doc. 7310 (C/846), p. 28 (1952).

[79] See ICAO, Standards and Recommended Practices: Rules of the Air (Annex 2), Rules 3.1.13.1 and 4.3.3.6 (1948).

[80] Carroz, *supra* note 22, at 168.

[81] See ICAO Council, 14th Sess. [1951], Doc. 7216 (C/832), pp. 156–58 (1952).

[82] Action of the Council, 3rd Sess. [1948], ICAO Doc. 7310 (C/846), p. 28 (1952). The complete resolution of adoption may be found in ICAO Council, 3rd Sess., Doc. 5701 (C/672), pp. 83–84 (1948).

[83] ICAO Council, 3rd Sess., Doc. 5701 (C/672), pp. 57–60 (1948).

and maneuver of aircraft regardless of the Annex in which these rules were established.[84] One cannot therefore conclude that the Council's decision with regard to Annex 2 constituted an implicit ruling that the scope of Article 12 was limited to the standards prescribed in that Annex.

To date the Council has not designated any but the Annex 2 rules as obligatory over the high seas under Article 12. Furthermore, since the adoption of the 1948 resolution relating to Annex 2, the Council only once considered the question whether to extend the application of Article 12 to rules relating to the flight and maneuver of aircraft found in other Annexes.[85] The Council considered this question in 1950 in connection with the adoption of Annex 11 (Standards and Recommended Practices for Air Traffic Services), when the U.K. Representative inquired "whether there was any reason why the Air Traffic Services Standards should not be mandatory over the high seas." [86] The Chief of the ICAO Legal Bureau replied that "a careful study of the Convention had convinced the Legal Bureau . . . that 'the rules and regulations relating to flight and manoeuvre of aircraft' were any rules that the Council designated as such and were not limited to the Rules of the Air as set out in Annex 2." [87] While the validity of this view was not challenged, the Council decided against making the rules prescribed in Annex 11 mandatory over the high seas.

Two reasons explain this decision. The first was advanced by the Chairman of the Air Navigation Commission. He pointed out that the Commission was opposed to making the rules of Annex 11 mandatory over the high seas because of the technical problems that would result whenever a State providing air traffic services decided to deviate from Annex 11. Such a State would then "have two sets of air traffic services regulations—one applicable to [the] airspace of its own territory, the other to the airspace over the high seas. . . ." [88] The second reason emerges from the statement of the U.S. Representative, who suggested that if the rules of Annex 11 were

---

[84] *Id.* at 57. See also, Carroz, *supra* note 22, at 168–70.
[85] See ICAO Council, 10th Sess. [1950], Doc. 7037 (C/814), pp. 29–30 (1951).
[86] *Id.* at 29.
[87] *Ibid.*
[88] *Ibid.*

made mandatory over the high seas they "might deter a State from supplying a much needed service in these areas, since . . . this service might have to be provided in accordance with rules differing in some respects from those applicable in its own territory." [89] These arguments prevailed. They may also explain why the Council has not seen fit to apply Article 12 to certain standards found in Annex 6 and Annex 12 which apparently also qualify as rules relating to the flight and maneuver of aircraft.[90] This notwithstanding, it is clear that the ICAO Council does have the power under Article 12 to designate as mandatory over the high seas a number of international standards which do not at present enjoy this status.[91]

One commentator has argued that, since the ICAO Council lacks the power to amend Article 12, its decision regarding the mandatory character of some rules does not relieve the Member States of the more extensive obligations they have assumed under Article 12.[92] The difficulty with this argument is that the Council's designation of certain rules relating to the flight and maneuver of aircraft as mandatory over the high seas, while not provided for in Article 12, has since 1948 come to be accepted as notice to the states that they may deviate from any rules which have not been so designated. Because the Member States and the Organization have acquiesced in this practice, Article 12 may now be read as requiring compliance over the high seas only with those rules which the ICAO Council has designated as obligatory.

The wisdom of the Council's policy cannot, of course, be fully assessed without a study of the economic and technical considerations that purport to justify it. It would seem, however, that the Council could achieve greater uniformity among the divergent national regulations relating to the flight and maneuver of aircraft by exercising more fully the powers it has under Article 12. Since the existence side-by-side of two different sets of rules cannot but cause

---

[89] *Ibid.*

[90] See Pépin, *The Law of the Air and the Articles Concerning the Law of the Sea Adopted by the International Law Commission at its Eighth Session,* U.N. Doc. A/CONF. 13/4, pp. 15–16 (1957).

[91] Thus Pépin, after commenting on the fact that the Council has only designated the rules of Annex 2 as mandatory over the high seas, emphasizes that "the documents of the Chicago Conference would seem to indicate that the authors of the Convention had more ambitious intentions." *Id.* at 15.

[92] Drion, *supra* note 71, at 328.

confusion and create air navigation hazards, might it not be assumed that many coastal states would make a greater effort to give domestic effect to those international standards which are obligatory over the high seas? Whether this assumption is valid might be tested by means of a study which sought to determine the extent to which there is greater qualitative domestic compliance with Annex 2 rules than with corresponding standards found in other Annexes.

THE JOURNEY LOG BOOK REQUIREMENT (ARTICLES 29 AND 34)

Article 29 of the Convention lists the various documents that must be carried by aircraft engaged in international air navigation. One of these documents is the journey log book.[93] This requirement is amplified in Article 34 which provides:

> There shall be maintained in respect of every aircraft engaged in international navigation a journey log book in which shall be entered particulars of the aircraft, its crew and of each journey, in such form as may be prescribed from time to time pursuant to this Convention.

It is thus clear that the Member States have recognized in Article 34 that the journey log book must conform to the format prescribed by the Organization. The power to adopt international standards and recommended practices relating to log books is vested in the ICAO Council.[94]

To date the Council has adopted only one international standard and one recommended practice dealing with journey log books.[95] These are found in Annex 6 (Operation of Aircraft [in] International Commercial Air Transport). The international standard prescribes that the pilot-in-command is responsible for the maintenance of the journey log book.[96] The recommended practice indicates what information the log book should contain.[97] Since a recommended practice is not mandatory, there is at present no prescribed log book format within the meaning of Article 34. This situation may be

---

[93] Convention, Art. 29(d).

[94] Convention, Arts. 37(h) and 54(1).

[95] For an analysis of ICAO practice relating to journey log books, see ICAO Doc. C–WP/3924, Appendix C, pp. 29–40 (1964).

[96] ICAO, INTERNATIONAL STANDARDS AND RECOMMENDED PRACTICES: OPERATION OF AIRCRAFT [IN] INTERNATIONAL AIR TRANSPORT, Standard 4.5.5. (5th ed. 1957).

[97] *Id.*, Recommended Practice 11.4.

attributed to the view of a substantial number of Contracting States that the log book requirement is obsolete.[98] Its obsolescence results from the fact that it largely duplicates the information found in other documents carried by aircraft, such as the simplified "General Declaration" prescribed in Annex 9 (Facilitation).[99] These considerations have prompted the ICAO Assembly to adopt a resolution, which provides that

> the General Declaration, when prepared so as to contain all the information required by Article 34 with respect to the journey log book, may be considered by contracting States to be an acceptable form of journey log book; and the carriage and maintenance of the General Declaration under such circumstances may be considered to fulfill the purposes of Articles 29 and 34 with respect to the journey log book.[100]

Thus, even though the log book is still prescribed in Annex 6 and required by some states [101] it is rapidly falling into disuse, but to the extent that the General Declaration performs the same functions as the log book, it might well be deemed mandatory under Article 34.

RECOGNITION OF CERTIFICATES AND LICENSES (ARTICLE 33)

Whereas under Article 12 of the Convention compliance with certain international standards is mandatory, Article 33 seeks to achieve a similar result indirectly. It attempts to do this by providing that the Member States must "recognize as valid" certificates of airworthiness and licenses issued or validated by the Contracting State where the aircraft is registered, "provided that the requirements under which such certificates or licenses were issued or rendered valid are equal to or above the minimum standards which may be established from time to time pursuant to this Convention." Since Member States are free to exclude from their territory aircraft and pilots having certificates or licenses that are not entitled to recognition under Article 33,[102] a state wishing to engage in international air

---

[98] See ICAO Doc. C–WP/3924, Appendix C, p. 33 (1964).

[99] See ICAO, INTERNATIONAL STANDARDS AND RECOMMENDED PRACTICES: FACILITATION (ANNEX 9), Chapter 2 (5th ed. 1964).

[100] Assembly Res. A10–36, ICAO Doc. 7707 (A10–P/16) (1956).

[101] An attempt to abolish this requirement by amendment of Annex 6 has so far failed because of the opposition of some Council Members. See ICAO Council, 29th Sess., Doc. 7739 (C/894), pp. 28–29 (1956).

[102] See Convention, Arts. 11, 31, 39, 40 and 41.

navigation cannot afford to follow less stringent certification or licensing practices than those prescribed by the applicable international standards. These international standards may be found in Annex 1 (Personnel Licensing) and Annex 8 (Airworthiness of Aircraft).

It should be noted, however, that ICAO did not establish a general airworthiness policy until 1957. When Annex 8 was adopted in 1949 [103] it prescribed airworthiness standards for only one category of aircraft. Certificates of airworthiness for aircraft falling in this category and complying with the applicable ICAO standards were accordingly entitled to recognition under Article 33.[104] But the absence of airworthiness standards governing other more important categories of aircraft significantly reduced the usefulness of Article 33.[105] This unsatisfactory situation was rectified in 1957 when the ICAO Council abandoned its attempt to establish airworthiness standards for various categories of aircraft. In their place the Council adopted an airworthiness policy [106] which, for the most part, lays down certain general airworthiness principles and objectives. The primary purpose of this policy is to compel the Contracting States to enact their own comprehensive airworthiness codes.[107]

[103] See Resolution of Adoption for Annex 8, ICAO Council, Proceedings of the 6th Sess. [1949], Doc. 6957 (C/807), pp. 31–34 (1950).

[104] See Resolution of Adoption, para. 7(c), *supra*, at 33; ICAO, STANDARDS AND RECOMMENDED PRACTICES: AIRWORTHINESS OF AIRCRAFT (ANNEX 8), p. 15 (1949).

[105] Anticipating this problem, and recognizing also that international standards relating to the licensing of airmen would have to be implemented over a period of years, the ICAO Assembly adopted a resolution in 1948 wherein it resolved, *inter alia,*

> That pending the coming into force of Standards respecting particular categories, classes or types of aircraft or classes of airmen, the Assembly strongly urges that Contracting States recognize, for the purpose of flight in or across their territories, certificates and licenses issued or rendered valid under national regulations by the State of registry of the aircraft concerned.

Assembly Res. A2–44, ICAO Doc. 5692 (A2–P/37) (1948). This policy was reaffirmed in 1965. See Assembly Res. A15–8, Appendix N, ICAO Doc. 8528 (A15–P/6) (1965).

[106] This policy change was accomplished by the adoption of Amendment 85 to Annex 8, and Amendment 139 to Annex 6. Action of the Council, 31st Sess. [1957], ICAO Doc. 7819 (C/902), pp. 20–22 (1958).

[107] See ICAO, INTERNATIONAL STANDARDS: AIRWORTHINESS OF AIRCRAFT (ANNEX 8), p. 7 (5th ed. 1962).

Annex 8 seeks to achieve this result by establishing the following international airworthiness standards:

> A Contracting State shall not issue or render valid a Certificate of Airworthiness for which it intends to claim recognition pursuant to Article 33 of the Convention on International Civil Aviation, unless the aircraft complies with a comprehensive and detailed national airworthiness code established for that class of aircraft by the State of Registry or by any other Contracting State. This national code shall be such that compliance with it will ensure compliance with:
>   (a) the Standards of Part II of this Annex; and
>   (b) where applicable, with the Standards of Part III of this Annex.[108]

Through incorporation by reference, national airworthiness codes which achieve the objectives set out in Annex 8 thus acquire the status of international standards. Certificates of airworthiness issued in compliance with these national airworthiness codes are now accordingly entitled to recognition by other Contracting States under Article 33, since they are deemed to conform to the "minimum standards . . . established . . . pursuant to this Convention." [109]

Notification of Differences

In Article 38 of the Convention [110] the Contracting States have assumed the obligation to notify the Organization of any differences between their own national practices and regulations and those prescribed in an international standard. Immediate notification by the state is provided for whenever a state does not conform to or departs from the practices or regulations "established" by an inter-

---

[108] ICAO, INTERNATIONAL STANDARDS: AIRWORTHINESS OF AIRCRAFT (ANNEX 8), Standard 2.2 (5th ed. 1962).

[109] In adopting Amendment 85 to Annex 8, which put into effect the new ICAO airworthiness policy, the Council resolved that "the Annex as hereby amended is to be regarded for the purpose of Article 33 of the Convention as defining the minimum standards established pursuant to the Convention." Resolution of Adoption, para. 4, Action of the Council, 31st Sess. [1957], ICAO Doc. 7819 (C/902), p. 20, at 21 (1958). No reference to Article 33 appears either in the resolution of adoption of Annex 1 (Personnel Licensing) or in the various resolutions adopting amendments thereto. This omission was apparently not intended to have any legal significance as far as Article 33 is concerned. See ICAO Council, 7th Sess., Doc. 6913 (C/802), p. 34 (1949).

[110] The text of Article 38 is reproduced on p. 77 *supra*.

national standard. This notice must be given within sixty days of the "adoption" of an amendment to an international standard whenever a Contracting State does not intend to conform its practices or regulations to the provisions of the amendment.

The ostensibly unambiguous language of Article 38 raises certain problems, because the terminology used in this provision does not correspond to the legislative scheme prescribed in Article 90 of the Convention for the adoption and promulgation of international standards. Whereas Article 38 provides for the notification of differences immediately after a standard has been "established," Article 90 speaks of the "becoming effective" and "coming into force" of an Annex. It is therefore by no means clear, on reading these two provisions, whether the Contracting States must give the notice required under Article 38 as soon as the Annex containing the international standards has become effective or as soon as it has come into force.

This textual discrepancy between Articles 38 and 90 is even more troublesome when one attempts to ascertain a state's obligation to notify differences resulting from a state's decision not to conform its national practices or regulations to the amendments of an international standard. Here Article 38 provides that such notice must be given within sixty days of the "adoption" of the amendment, whereas under Article 90 the adoption of an Annex or amendment thereto is merely the first step in the legislative process which eventually results in the promulgation of the standard. As we have seen, the regulatory material found in an amendment to an Annex does not become an international standard until it has been submitted to the Contracting States and not been disapproved by them within the three-month period provided for in Article 90. Since the sixty-day period prescribed in Article 38 begins upon "the adoption of the amendment to the international standard," the deadline for the notification of differences would expire thirty days before it would be known whether the amendment has in fact been promulgated. This would make very little sense.

The extremely poor draftsmanship which Articles 38 and 90 evince can probably be attributed to the fact that the framers of the Convention had initially assumed that the Annexes would be drafted at the Chicago Conference and would form an integral part of the Convention. Article XLV of the Canadian Revised Preliminary

Draft of an International Air Convention [111] thus provided that "the provisions of the present Convention are completed by the Annexes . . . which shall have the same effect and shall come into force at the same time as the Convention itself." Similarly, Article 1(3) of the United States Proposal for a Convention on Air Navigation stipulated that "the term 'Convention' shall mean this instrument of agreement and shall include the Annexes attached hereto." [112] However, because of lack of time, the attempt to adopt a final set of Annexes at Chicago was abandoned shortly before the Conference adjourned. [113] This decision necessitated last-minute textual adjustments which were probably not carefully examined. It should also be noted that under Article L of the Canadian Draft an amendment to an Annex was to be "binding on the member states as soon as it is *adopted* by the Assembly by at least two-thirds of the total possible votes." (Emphasis added.) [114] This may explain how the word "adoption" found its way into Article 38 of the Convention where, unlike in the Canadian Draft, it creates a contextual ambiguity.

The Organization has over the years gradually resolved these problems. When the first ICAO Assembly convened in 1947, its Technical Commission noted that Articles 38 and 90 were inconsistent and recommended a procedure to cope with it. [115] When this recommendation was inadvertently omitted from the Commission's report and thus not adopted by the Assembly, the ICAO Council implemented it by deciding to

> (1) Establish a date, normally ninety (90) days after the date of submission by the Council, after which States may no longer notify disapproval under Article 90;
>
> (2) Establish a further date by which International Standards and Recommended Practices shall be applied by Contracting States . . . ;
>
> (3) Establish a date prior to which States unable to comply are expected to give notification to that effect. This date shall be sufficiently in advance of the date set for application of the Standards to enable notification of non-compliance to reach ICAO from the States

---

[111] 1 PROCEEDINGS, p. 588.
[112] *Id.* at 555.
[113] See Resolution 11 (Draft Technical Annexes), 1 PROCEEDINGS, pp. 123–24.
[114] 1 PROCEEDINGS, p. 590.
[115] See ICAO Doc. 4487 (AN/511) (1947).

concerned, to be circulated by ICAO to other Contracting States, and to be circulated by Contracting States to those concerned.[116]

The Council restated this policy in its 1948 Standard Form Resolution for the Adoption of Annexes.[117]

The Standard Form prescribed that an Annex or amendment thereto shall "become effective" 120 days after its adoption by the Council (D plus 120) unless it had in the meantime been disapproved by a majority of the Contracting States. The Annex was to "come into force and be implemented" on D plus 365. With regard to the notification of differences, paragraph 7 of the Standard Form provided:

> (b) that on or before (*D plus 270*) each Contracting State should notify the Organization of any difference . . . which will exist on (*D plus 365*) between any of its own practices and those established by the said international standards contained in the said Annex, in order to enable the Organization to notify all Contracting States thereof,
>
> (c) that any difference which occurs after (*D plus 365*) shall be immediately notified to the Organization.[118]

In adopting this resolution, wherein it abandoned the ambiguous requirement for immediate notification of differences except for deviations arising after the entry into force of an international standard, the ICAO Council in effect rewrote Article 38 and thereby established a much more rational system for the notification of differences.

It should also be noted that the Standard Form did not provide for the notification of any differences between national regulations and the recommended practices set out in an Annex. This is in keeping with Article 38, which requires such notice only in case of deviations from international standards. By 1950 the Council had concluded, however, that the notice requirement should, in the interest of safety, be extended also to recommended practices. It therefore resolved that ". . . Contracting States be invited to notify the Organization of the differences between their national regulations and practices and any corresponding Recommended Practices con-

---

[116] Proceedings of the Council, 1st Sess. [1947], ICAO Doc. 6808 (C/791), pp. 34–36 (1949).

[117] Proceedings of the Council, 3rd Sess. [1948], ICAO Doc. 7310 (C/846), pp. 24–26 (1952).

[118] *Id.* at 26.

tained in an Annex when the knowledge of such differences is important for the safety of air navigation." [119] This language was incorporated almost verbatim in the "Revised Form of Resolution of Adoption of an Annex" adopted by the Council in 1953. [120]

The Revised Form has been used by the Council since its adoption in 1953. As far as concerns the notification of differences, the Revised Form does not change the basic procedure established in the 1948 Standard Form. It does, however, impose two additional reporting obligations on the Contracting States. We have already noted the first, which relates to the notification of differences from recommended practices. The second requires each Contracting State "to notify the Organization, before the dates on which the standards will become applicable, of the date or dates by which it will have complied with the provisions of the standards." [121] The reference in the Revised Form to the date on which the standard "will become applicable" points to the same event that was described in the Standard Form of 1948 as the date on which the Annex material "came into force." [122] Thus, in addition to requiring the Contracting States to notify differences within a period that expires before the date on which the standards "become applicable," as was the case in the Standard Form, the Revised Form also obliges the states to notify the Organization on what date they expect to comply with the standards in question. This new notification requirement, which was subsequently endorsed by the ICAO Assembly, [123] had been recommended by the Air Navigation Commission. [124] The Commission proposed this procedure on the ground that in planning ahead it was important for the Organization to know not only what differences would exist on the date fixed for the application of the standard, but also what action the states concerned intended to take in the future. [125]

While Article 38 distinguishes, for purposes of the notification of

[119] Proceedings of the Council, 11th Sess. [1950], ICAO Doc. 7188 (C/828), p. 32, at 33–34 (1953).

[120] Revised Form of Resolution of Adoption of an Annex, para. 4(iii), ICAO Council, 18th Sess., Doc. 7361 (C/858), Appendix A, p. 199 (1953).

[121] Revised Form of Resolution of Adoption of an Annex, para. 4(ii)(b) *supra.*

[122] See discussion on pp. 90–91 *supra.*

[123] Assembly Res. A10–29, ICAO Doc. 7707 (A10–P/16) (1956).

[124] See ICAO Doc. C–WP/1319, pp. 3–4 (1953).

[125] *Ibid.*

differences, between international standards and amendments to these standards, the ICAO Council has disregarded this distinction from the very beginning. Instead, the Council has applied the same rules to amendments that govern deviations from standards.[126] Two reasons no doubt account for this policy.[127] The first may be attributed to the previously discussed textual discrepancy between Articles 38 and 90. The second has to do with an internal inconsistency found in Article 38 itself. The first sentence of Article 38 requires immediate notification of differences whenever a state "finds it impracticable . . . to bring its own regulations or practices into full accord with any international standard . . . after amendment of the latter." The second sentence prescribes that "in the case of amendments to international standards" such notice be given within sixty days by any state which "does not make the appropriate amendments to its own regulations or practices." With one possible exception having no practical significance,[128] both sentences point to the same event. It is therefore not surprising that no distinction has been made in the reporting procedure for differences from amendments to standards and the standards themselves.

Prior to the adoption of the Revised Form Resolution, the Contracting States were asked to notify differences from "the international standards contained in the . . . amendments."[129] In 1952 the Air Navigation Commission proposed a change in this reporting method, because it had found that the notification of differences from amendments to Annexes "may affect compliance with the terms of the original Annex as previously notified by a State, for

---

[126] See, e.g., Resolution of Adoption of Amendments to Annex 6, Proceedings of the Council, 11th Sess., Part II [1950], ICAO Doc. 7188 (C/828), pp. 26–28 (1953).

[127] The Council has never expressly passed on this policy, although it has consistently adhered to it.

[128] The exception would come into play only in case of amendments which effect the revocation of a standard. Here one could argue that the obligation laid down in the first sentence of Article 38 does not apply, for it speaks of an "international standard . . . after amendment" and thus presumes the continued existence of the standard that has been amended. Here the second sentence of Article 38 would apply. From a practical standpoint this distinction is meaningless, however, because in both instances the failure of a state to conform its practices will result in notifiable differences of equal importance.

[129] See, e.g., Resolution of Adoption of Amendments to Annex 6, para. 6(b), Proceedings of the Council, 11th Sess., Part II [1950], ICAO Doc. 7188 (C/828), p. 26, at 28 (1953).

example, by eliminating certain differences that had previously existed."[130] The Commission accordingly urged "that after the Council has adopted an amendment to an Annex, States should be invited to notify, not differences from the Amendment as such, but differences from the Annex (or the Annex as previously amended) as amended by the amendment."[131] The Council accepted this recommendation and incorporated it in the Revised Form.[132]

NOTIFIABLE DIFFERENCES AND MANNER OF NOTIFICATION

In 1948 the ICAO Council formally stated that it

> understood that the "differences" to be notified pursuant to Article 38 should cover non-compliance in any respect with an international standard and any difference between any practice or regulation of a State and the practice established by an international standard, on all those subjects in respect of which ICAO may adopt standards under Article 37.[133]

It was soon recognized, however, that there was considerable confusion among the Contracting States regarding the type of differences that were to be reported, and that this in turn hampered the Organization's efforts to disseminate the relevant information. These considerations prompted the Council in 1950 to adopt the following guidelines for application by states when reporting differences: [134]

> (1) *Differences from International Standards Contained in Annexes to the Convention*
>
> (A) That Contracting States, when notifying ICAO of the differences between their national regulations and practices and the international Standards contained in Annexes in compliance with Article 38 of the Convention, be requested to give particular attention to those differences knowledge of which is essential to the safety or regularity of international air navigation;

---

[130] ICAO Doc. C–WP/1319, p. 3 (1952).

[131] *Ibid.*

[132] Revised Form of Resolution of Adoption of an Annex, para. 4(ii)(a), ICAO Council, 18th Sess., Doc. 7361 (C/858), Appendix A, p. 199 (1953).

[133] Standard Resolution of Adoption of an Annex, Preamble, Proceedings of the Council, 3rd Sess. [1948], ICAO Doc. 7310 (C/846), p. 24 (1952).

[134] Principles Governing the Reporting of "Differences" from ICAO Standards, Practices and Procedures, Proceedings of the Council, 11th Sess., Part II [1950], ICAO Doc. 7188 (C/828), pp. 32–34 (1953).

(B) That the following criteria, or such of them as are appropriate to a particular Annex, be brought to the attention of Contracting States to be used as a guide in determining reportable differences:

(i) When the national regulations of a Contracting State affect the operation of aircraft of other Contracting States in and above its territory

(a) by imposing an obligation within the scope of an Annex which is not covered by an ICAO Standard;

(b) by imposing an obligation different in character from that of the corresponding ICAO Standard;

(c) by being more exacting than the corresponding ICAO Standard;

(d) by being less protective than the corresponding ICAO Standard.

(ii) When the national regulations of a Contracting State applicable to its aircraft and their maintenance, as well as to aircrew personnel, engaged in international air operations over the territory of another Contracting State

(a) are different in character from that of the corresponding ICAO Standard;

(b) are less protective than the corresponding ICAO Standard.

(iii) When the facilities or services provided by a Contracting State for international air navigation

(a) impose an obligation or requirement for safety additional to any that may be imposed by the corresponding ICAO Standard;

(b) while not imposing an additional obligation differ in principle, type or system from the corresponding ICAO Standard;

(c) are less protective than the corresponding ICAO Standard.

(2) Differences from Recommended Practices

(A) That, although differences from Recommended Practices are not notifiable under Article 38 of the Convention, Contracting States be invited to notify the Organization of the differences between their national regulations and practices and any corresponding Recommended Practices contained in an Annex when the knowledge of such differences is important for the safety of air navigation;

(B) That, as a guide to determining the differences to be notified, States be invited to use the criteria in (1)(B) above, in so far as they are applicable.[135]

___

[135] An unnumbered footnote to these guidelines states that "the expression 'different in character' in [B](i)(b) and (ii)(a) would be applied to a national regulation which achieves by other means the same objective as that of the

After these guidelines were issued, each State Letter in which the Contracting States were informed of the adoption of SARPS was accompanied by a "Note on the notification of differences and form of notification." This Note was prepared by the Secretariat, and set out the reporting criteria laid down by the Council.[136]

The Organization soon found, however, that this reporting procedure imposed a very heavy administrative burden on the Contracting States and therefore significantly diminished compliance with the obligation to notify differences.[137] The administrative burdens resulted from the fact that the nine criteria of reportable differences prescribed by the Council applied to different types of standards, depending upon whether or not they fell into one of the three major categories under which the guidelines were classified. In order to comply with these guidelines in reporting differences, each state had to sort out the applicable criteria before it could apply them. Commenting on this problem, the Air Navigation Commission found it "understandable" that "in certain cases the application of this procedure may lead to some complexity." [138] These considerations prompted the ICAO Assembly to adopt a resolution in 1953, requesting that "the Council initiate a more effective and simplified programme with respect to the reporting by States of differences, pursuant to Article 38 of the Convention, to the end that the Organization may be better informed of the actual state of implementation among the Contracting States." [139] As a result of this resolution, the Air Navigation Commission in 1954 submitted to the Council a recommendation for the simplification of the reporting procedure that had been established in 1950. The Commission proposed that the State Letter transmitting newly adopted Annex material consist of: (1) the statement of the criteria for the notification of differences previously set out in the "Note on Notification of Differences and Form of Notification"; (2) an analysis of the types

corresponding ICAO Standard and so cannot be classified under (i)(c) or (d) and (ii)(b)." *Id.* at 33.

    [136] See ICAO Doc. C–WP/1663, p. 2 (1954).
    [137] See ICAO Assembly, Report of the Technical Commission, 7th Sess., Doc. 7416 (A7–TE/1), p. 5 (1953).
    [138] ICAO Doc. C–WP/1663, p. 2 (1954).
    [139] Assembly Res. A7–9, ICAO Doc. 7417 (A7–P/3) (1953).

of differences to be reported with respect to the particular SARPS that were being transmitted; and (3) a statement of the form in which notification of differences was desired.[140] The Council adopted these recommendations *in toto*.[141]

This procedure was followed until 1956, when it had to be further simplified in response to yet another resolution of the ICAO Assembly.[142] The "Note on the Notification of Differences," as formulated in 1956,[143] remains in force today. Its basic feature is that states now receive an analysis explaining how the newly adopted SARPS affect a particular Annex for the purpose of reporting differences. This analysis is specifically designed to permit the Contracting States to report their differences without having to consult the criteria of reportable differences established in 1950.[144] The 1950 criteria remain in effect, however, as guidelines for the ICAO Secretariat in analyzing and compiling the reported differences.

The new "Note" also contains an explanation of the underlying rationale for the notification of differences, and a request that the Contracting States notify the Organization of their "intent to comply with Standards on which no differences are reported." [145] These features were incorporated in the "Note" on the recommendation of the ICAO Assembly.[146] The Assembly's request was prompted by a report of its Technical Commission which, after noting that "some contracting States might not fully understand what was required in the matter of reporting of differences, particularly if they have only recently adhered to the ICAO Convention," strongly urged that all states be required to advise the Organization whether they intended to comply with the international standards on which they reported no differences, because "at present, failure to notify [differences]

---

[140] ICAO Doc. C–WP/1663, p. 2 (1954).
[141] Action of the Council, 21st Sess., ICAO Doc. 7884 (C/872), pp. 10–11 (1954).
[142] See Assembly Res. A10–29, ICAO Doc. 7707 (A10–P/16) (1956). See also, ICAO Assembly, Report of the Technical Commission, 10th Sess., Doc. 7711 (A10–TE/44), pp. 11–12 (1956).
[143] Action of the Council, 29th Sess. [1956], ICAO Doc. 7763 (C/896), pp. 16–17 (1957).
[144] *Ibid.*
[145] *Id.* at 16.
[146] Assembly Res. A10–29, ICAO Doc. 7707 (A10–P/16) (1956).

might justifiably, but probably erroneously, be taken to indicate that a State had no differences to report." [147]

LEGAL CONSEQUENCES OF FAILURE TO NOTIFY DIFFERENCES

ICAO's experience indicates that it is much easier to establish a procedure for the notification of differences than it is to get states to comply with it. Thus, in its 1955 report to the Assembly, the Council noted that the notification of differences by the Contracting States was "unfortunately still incomplete, although the situation is considerably better than it was a few years ago." [148] We can surmise what the situation was "a few years ago" by looking at the statistics which the Council supplied. In 1955, the year for which the statistics were compiled, the Organization had a membership of sixty-six states. During that period only seventeen states had filed reports with regard to Annex 6; fifteen with regard to Annex 12; sixteen with regard to Annex 13; and nineteen with regard to Annex 15. Complete reports had been received only for Annex 7 (Aircraft Nationality and Registration Marks). The second highest number of reports—with fifty-three states reporting—applied to Annex 5 (Dimensional Units to be used in Air-Ground Communications). [149]

There has, however, been a gradual improvement in the reporting practices of the Contracting States, due largely to a vigorous campaign by the ICAO Secretariat. [150] Even so, they are still rather unsatisfactory. The statistics available for the year 1965 indicate, for example, that out of 1,498 notifications (14 Annexes multiplied by 107 Contracting States) due by 1 January 1965, only 691 were received, resulting in a grand total of 46 per cent. [151] The data available for the year 1962 showed a 52 per cent reporting coverage. [152] The 1962 figures may be more representative of the normal state of affairs than those for 1965, because in the period between

---

[147] ICAO Assembly, Report of the Technical Commission, 10th Sess., Doc. 7711 (A10–TE/44), pp. 11–12 (1956).
[148] [1955] Report of the Council, ICAO Doc. 7636 (A10–P/3), p. 26 (1956).
[149] Ibid.
[150] See ICAO Doc. A12–WP/15 (TE/6), p. 2, and Appendices I–III (1959), for statistical information covering the years 1956, 1957 and 1958. See ICAO Doc. A15–WP/40 (TE/9), p. 8 (1965), for the years 1962 and 1965.
[151] ICAO Doc. A15–WP/40 (TE/9), p. 8 (1965).
[152] Id. at 8.

1962 and 1965 the membership of the Organization increased by seventeen states, resulting in a reporting lag. These statistics are probably less telling than is the fact that no information whatsoever is available for some states. Thus, almost every edition of the periodic Supplements to Annexes—the medium used by ICAO for the dissemination of differences reported by the Contracting States—lists a considerable number of states that have filed no reports at all. Admittedly, these are for the most part states where air transportation is nonexistent or almost nonexistent [153] and where, as a result, only the most rudimentary air navigation legislation may be in force. Nevertheless, this state of affairs cannot but affect air safety, since many of these states are at least overflown by aircraft engaged in international air transport.

As long as this situation persists, it is totally unrealistic to assert that a state's failure to notify any differences indicates that it has none to report. The practice of the Organization shows, furthermore, that ICAO no longer makes this assumption. In the early years of ICAO's existence the Council, when adopting an Annex or amendments thereto, often stipulated in the preamble to the resolution of adoption that each Contracting State "is presumed to have complied with the provisions of an Annex on the date on which it came into force unless, prior to that date, it has notified the Organization of any differences between its national regulations and practices and the international standards contained in the Annex." [154] By 1953 this clause had fallen into disuse.[155] Concurrently with this development, the Council began to request the Contracting States "to notify the Organization, before the dates on which the standards will become applicable, of the date or dates by which it will have complied with the provisions of the standards." [156] This step was motivated by the consideration, articulated in 1950 by a Working

[153] For a composite chart of the reporting practices of all Contracting States, see ICAO Doc. A15–WP/10 (TE/9), p. 9 (1965).

[154] See, e.g., Resolution of Adoption of Amendments to Annex 6, Proceedings of the Council, 11th Sess., Part II [1950], ICAO Doc. 7188 (C/828), pp. 26–28 (1953).

[155] See, e.g., Resolution of Adoption of Annex 15, Action of the Council, 19th Sess., ICAO Doc. 7408 (C/864), pp. 14–15 (1953).

[156] Revised Form of Resolution of Adoption of an Annex, ICAO Council, 18th Sess., Doc. 7361 (C/858), Appendix A, p. 199 (1953).

Group of the Air Navigation Commission, that the "presumption of compliance when no differences were reported was unsound, and that the lack of information regarding the extent of compliance . . . seriously handicapped the Organization in its efforts to disseminate differences effectively." [157]

It is thus readily apparent that ICAO itself no longer assumes that silence denotes compliance. Moreover, by formally requesting notification of compliance, the Organization may be deemed to have determined that no presumption of compliance attaches to the failure to notify differences under Article 38. This practice indicates that Article 38 has undergone a *de facto* amendment which has transformed what was intended to be a "contracting-out" provision into a hybrid procedure that has both "contracting-out" and "contracting-in" characteristics. In the light of these developments it is difficult to see how some distinguished commentators can seriously assert that "ICAO standards are in the nature of international agreements and that departures from standards made by individual States under Art. 38 are therefore in essence treaty reservations." [158]

One very important legal consequence of the transformation which Article 38 has undergone is that, as a general proposition, no state or pilot can justifiably rely on the absence of reported differences as indicia that a particular standard established in an Annex is in force in or being complied with by a state which has not filed the notice required by Article 38. It follows therefrom that the contention advanced by Dr. Cheng [159] is untenable when he asserts that, since "failure to give immediate notification of a non-compliance is a breach of the Convention," a Contracting State would "be liable to another contracting State if the latter, or one of its nationals, suffers damage as a result of a mistaken belief, induced by the lack of notification, that the former contracting State was complying with a given international standard." At present such reliance would be justified at most only when a state has advised the Organization by what date it will have complied with an Annex, or when it expressly

---

[157] ICAO Doc. AN–WP/419, p. 1 (1950).

[158] Alexandrowicz, *The Convention on Facilitation of International Maritime Traffic and International Technical Regulations: A Comparative Study*, 15 Int'l & Comp. L. Q. 621, 624 n.4 (1966). A similar view is expressed by Saba, *L'activité quasi-législative des institutions spécialisées des Nations Unies*, 111 Recueil des Cours 607, 678 (1964).

[159] Cheng, *supra* note 67, at 200, 205–06 (1957).

notifies the Organization that it has no differences to report. Given the many instances of incomplete reporting, it may well be doubted whether even the notification of some differences with regard to certain provisions of an Annex permits an assumption of compliance as to the remaining provisions.

It is true, of course, that the Organization does have the power to impose sanctions against states that fail to report notifiable differences,[160] but whether the threat of sanctions would achieve the desired result is most doubtful, because many of the delinquent states simply do not as yet have the technical and administrative personnel to fully discharge their obligations under Article 38.

Implementation of International Standards and Recommended Practices

In the early years of its existence, ICAO devoted the major part of its energies to the development and adoption of the SARPS comprising the various Annexes. Thereafter, the Organization's attention shifted to the task of updating the Annexes and bringing about their implementation by the Contracting States. While both tasks remain in the forefront of ICAO's endeavors, ever greater emphasis is being placed on implementation.[161] This development is undoubtedly due to the rapid expansion of international civil aviation and air travel, which have in turn increased the need for uniformity in air navigation regulations, services, facilities, and training.

The Organization's implementation achievements and the problems implementation presents have recently been explained by the Organization in the following terms:

> Implementation, or its lack, is a relative thing; a comparison between the existing air navigation facilities and services in 1946 and today shows that great improvements have been made, both in the installations serving aviation and in the operation and maintenance of these installations. Ever since 1956, when the imminence of large scale introduction of jet transports gave added impetus to implementation efforts, the increase in the facilities and services supporting the world's air routes has been notable. However, complete achievement

[160] See Convention, Arts. 54(j) and (k), as well as Arts. 84–88.
[161] See ICAO Secretariat, MEMORANDUM ON ICAO 20–22 (5th ed. 1966).

of the objective—the creation of a world-wide network of facilities and services installed and operated in accordance with ICAO standards, recommended practices and procedures, staffed and maintained by competent personnel, adequate to meet all justified requirements of international civil aviation without entailing disproportionate costs —is still some way off.[162]

The complete achievement of this objective is not only "still some way off." It is probably unattainable for some decades to come, given the ever increasing demands which modern aviation makes and will continue to make on the relatively limited economic, technical, and administrative resources available to ICAO and many of its Member States.

As understood by ICAO, implementation is a two-phase process. "The first comprises the administrative arrangements necessary to bring the Standards and associated Procedures into force nationally; the second consists of the practical arrangements necessary, such as the provision of facilities, personnel and equipment." [163] It may, accordingly, be useful to approach the problem of implementation by dealing with each of these aspects separately.

IMPLEMENTATION OF REGULATORY SARPS

The elimination of the multitude of conflicting national aeronautical regulations, through the domestic implementation of the regulatory SARPS prescribed in the Annexes, would be an immense step forward in facilitating international civil aviation. The achievement of this task is one of the fundamental aims of the Chicago Convention, wherein each Contracting State has undertaken "to collaborate in securing the highest practicable degree of uniformity in regulations . . . in all matters in which such uniformity will facilitate and improve air navigation." [164] Since its inception ICAO has sought to promote this goal.

The Domestic Status of Regulatory SARPS: The Policies of the ICAO Council and the Practice of the Contracting States

In 1948 the ICAO Council adopted a resolution urging the Contracting States "in complying with ICAO standards which are of a

[162] *Id.* at 21.
[163] ICAO Doc. A12–WP/15 (TE/6), p. 4 (1959).
[164] Convention, Art. 37.

regulatory character, to introduce the text of such standards into their national regulations, as nearly as possible, in the wording and arrangement employed by ICAO." [165] This resolution was predicated on the premise, enunciated in its preamble, that "many of the benefits of international standardization of practices and of regulatory requirements may be lost through diversity of form and arrangement in the publications through which they are promulgated in the various States."

By 1952, however, the Air Navigation Commission had concluded that the Contracting States were finding it difficult to give effect to this resolution.

> The Commission considers that there is merit in urging States to follow the procedure prescribed [by the resolution] in the case of an Annex such as Annex 2 (Rules of the Air), which is directly linked with the Convention. It is difficult, however, for all texts to be transposed into national laws or regulations since, while most standards are addressed to the Governments of States, others are, in effect, directives to individuals, to special sections of a State administration or to other agencies. At the time of promulgation of the early Annexes, the Council resolution was, doubtless, a useful guide to States, but with the adoption of further Annexes with their varied applications it would now appear to have become, to some extent, obsolescent.[166]

In a follow-up report the Air Navigation Commission indicated that "many States have found it constitutionally impracticable to draft the air navigation regulations in terms of the texts of ICAO Standards," and that these texts "are not always in a form suitable for incorporation in national regulations while others are not in themselves subjects for such regulation." [167] In the light of these findings, the Commission expressed the view that, in the interest of flexibility, the practice of simply reproducing the Council's resolution verbatim in the Foreword to each Annex should be abandoned. In its stead the Commission proposed that the Foreword, after explaining the Council's resolution, should indicate to which of the standards prescribed in the particular Annex the resolution was intended to apply

[165] ICAO Council, Proceedings of the 3rd Sess. [1948], Doc. 7310 (C/846), p. 26 (1952).

[166] ICAO Doc. C–WP/1318, pp. 2–3 (1952).

[167] ICAO Doc. C–WP/1399, p. 1 (1953).

or could be applied.[168] This approach has been adopted in the meantime. A typical Foreword to a recent edition of an Annex, after paraphrasing the Council's resolution, will now contain a sentence specifically adapted to the particular standard involved, which might read as follows: "With the exception of Chapter 3, the provisions of this Annex may be incorporated into national legislation without major textual changes." [169]

Since no country-by-country study relating to the manner and extent of the domestic legislative implementation of ICAO standards is available, it is difficult to determine what the actual practice of the Contracting States is.[170] In general, the domestic legislative implementation of SARPS appears to be effected in one of the following three ways:

> Some States embody the provisions of the Annexes . . . in their national legislation or regulations. Others issue the material as manuals or operating instructions for use in their installations, often under the authority of enabling legislation. Still others take a less formal approach and simply distribute the ICAO texts for use in their installations, with or without supplementary instructions tailored to local circumstances.[171]

The author's perusal of national aviation legislation [172] yields a similar conclusion.

[168] *Id.* at 2.

[169] ICAO, INTERNATIONAL STANDARDS AND RECOMMENDED PRACTICES: AERONAUTICAL INFORMATION SERVICES (ANNEX 15), Foreword, p. 6 (3rd ed. 1964).

[170] It is rather surprising that the Organization has not conducted a systematic study of this type, for it might reveal not only how the Contracting States implement the various Annexes but also what difficulties they have encountered in attempting to do so. The resultant findings could in turn provide the Organization with answers about how Annexes designed for domestic legislative implementation should be drafted. For example, while the legislative methods for the domestic implementation of Annex material doubtless vary because of the existing constitutional differences among the Contracting States, it is very likely that a study would reveal that these methods tend to fall into a limited number of categories or patterns of implementation. If this assumption is true, ICAO might achieve speedier and more effective legislative implementation of regulatory standards by drafting model legislation based on the Annex material, but varying in form depending upon the respective categories or patterns of implementation most commonly employed by the Contracting States.

[171] ICAO Doc. A15–WP/28 (TE/5), p. 2 (1965).

[172] English texts of national aviation legislation can be found in the U.S. Senate Committee on Commerce three-volume publication entitled AIR LAWS AND TREATIES OF THE WORLD (1965).

One of the most interesting national provisions is Article 71 of the Sudanese Air Act of 1960,[173] which provides:

On the coming into force of this Act, the provisions of the Annexes (as from time to time amended) of the Chicago Convention shall apply to the territory of the Sudan and to Sudanese civil aircraft within or outside Sudanese territory, and to foreign civil aircraft within Sudanese territory . . . as if the same were herein expressly included. Provided that in every case where the Republic of the Sudan has notified a difference under Article 38 of the said Convention, the provision or provisions to which that difference relates shall not apply, or shall apply as modified by that difference, as the case may be.

Another interesting provision is Article 2 of the Laotian Royal Decree of September 23, 1955, which provides that "in the matter of security of aeronautical navigation and air traffic, the Civil Aeronautics Administration applies the standards and recommendations given by the International Civil Aviation Organization, insofar as national requirements so permit." [174]

The aviation laws of a number of Contracting States confer domestic law status on various ICAO Annexes. Illustrative of this approach is the Civil Aviation Law of Libya, enacted on September 23, 1956, which requires that "between sunset and sunrise . . . all aircraft in flight or operating on the manoeuvering area of a land or water aerodrome, shall display the appropriate navigation lights specified in Appendix B to Annex 2 of the Chicago Convention." [175] While this treatment is more common with regard to Annex 2, it is not limited to it. Thus the El Salvador Law on Civil Aviation of December 20, 1955, stipulates in Article 88, for example, that "to have international character, an airport must be thus declared by the Executive Power . . . and it must fulfill all technical requirements specified in Annex No. 14 of the Convention on International Civil Aviation." [176]

---

[173] 2 AIR LAWS AND TREATIES OF THE WORLD 2306 (1965).

[174] *Id.* at 1603.

[175] *Id.* at 1693. Amendments to ICAO Annexes are incorporated into domestic regulations of this type by means of enabling legislation. See Article 44(2) of the Libyan Civil Aviation Law, which stipulates that "the Minister may make regulations amending the Schedule to this Law to the extent necessary to give effect to Annex 2 of the Chicago Convention as amended from time to time." *Id.* at 1686.

[176] 1 AIR LAWS AND TREATIES OF THE WORLD 654 (1965).

The aviation laws of a large number of Contracting States leave the enactment of aeronautical regulations to the executive branches of government. In these countries it is not uncommon to find enabling legislation containing express authorization for the promulgation of ICAO Annexes. Illustrative of this approach is the Australian Air Navigation Act of 1960, which in Section 26(1)(b) empowers the Governor-General to make regulations "for the purpose of carrying out and giving effect to the Chicago Convention . . .[and] any Annex to the Convention relating to international standards and recommended practices. . . ."[177] Similar language may be found in Section 8(1)(a) of the 1949 Civil Aviation Act of the United Kingdom,[178] under which the Air Navigation Order of 1960 was promulgated. The Air Navigation Order in turn implements the Convention, as well as some ICAO standards in the United Kingdom.[179] States following the regulatory approach of the United Kingdom and Australia do not, as a rule, give effect to ICAO standards through incorporation by reference. This method is not well suited for states which have to cope with highly complex aviation problems. In these states Annex material tends to be redrafted and often refined in conformity with the requirements of the domestic regulatory scheme. Incorporation by reference is not uncommon even in these states, however, for regulations governing flights over the high seas. Thus the United States provides that

> Each person operating a civil aircraft of U.S. registry outside of the United States shall—
> (1) When over the high seas, comply with Annex 2 (Rules of the Air) to the Convention on International Civil Aviation.[180]

Similar regulations can be found in a number of other countries.[181]

The extent to which the provisions of an Annex are directly applicable law in the courts of the Contracting States depends, of course, upon the domestic status which such Annexes enjoy. Two of three reported national court decisions on this subject reach opposing conclusions, and the third is inconclusive. Thus the Court of

[177] *Id.* at 78.
[178] 2 *id.* at 2604.
[179] See McNair, THE LAW OF THE AIR 380–81 (3rd ed. 1964).
[180] 14 C.F.R. § 91.1(b) (1967). See also, 14 C.F.R. § 135.3(b) (1967), which also incorporates Annex 2 by reference.
[181] See Erler 151.

Appeals of Dakar (French West Africa) held that Annex 9 (Facilitation) was directly applicable law which individuals could invoke in French territorial courts,[182] whereas the Belgian Supreme Court concluded in 1957 that without special implementing legislation the provisions of an Annex could not be relied upon in Belgian courts.[183] In a recent German decision, the Court of Appeal of Frankfurt assumed, without expressly deciding the question, that the provisions of Annexes 11 and 15 were directly applicable in the Federal Republic.[184]

The preceding survey of national court decisions and legislation indicates how some states implement regulatory SARPS. It does not tell us very much, however, about the extent to which the Contracting States are giving domestic effect to or complying with these international regulations. Many states whose aviation laws do not expressly mention ICAO Annexes may well give effect to them, and *vice versa*. What the practice of these states is cannot readily be determined so long as compliance with the requirement of Article 38 for the notification of differences is as inadequate as we found it to be. Accordingly, it is impossible to say with any degree of certainty what the state of implementation of regulatory Annex material really is.

Fostering the Domestic Implementation of Regulatory SARPS

Air Navigation SARPS. In fostering the domestic legislative implementation of regulatory air navigation SARPS, the Organization has gradually developed much more effective techniques than the periodic exhortations for implementation on which it initially relied. The need for such techniques became apparent when it was found that many of the newly emerging or developing nations which joined ICAO had either the most rudimentary aviation legislation on their books or none at all. To cope with this situation, and to assist these states in developing civil aviation, ICAO has utilized some of the funds made available to it under U.N. economic and technical

---

[182] Ministère Public c. Schreiber, 11 Rev. Français de Droit Aérien 355 (1957), 24 Int'l L. Rep. 54 (1961).

[183] État Belge c. Marquise de Croix de Maillie de la Tour Landry, [1958] Pasicrisie Belge, I, p. 88, 24 Int'l L. Rep. 9 (1961).

[184] Oberlandesgericht Frankfurt a.M., Judgment of 25 February 1965, 16 Zeitschrift für Luftrecht u. Weltraumrechtsfragen 185, 188 (1967).

development programs [185] to dispatch ICAO Technical Assistance Missions to various Contracting States. One of the tasks of these missions is to help the host states with the implementation of international standards and recommended practices.[186] Since the implementation of regulatory SARPS cannot be achieved without appropriate legislation, the ICAO experts have had to assist a large number of these states with the preparation of national aviation laws and regulations.[187] These activities have in turn enabled ICAO to influence the content and form of national aviation legislation so as to assure that the laws conform to the provisions of the Convention and regulatory Annex material.[188]

Another implementation problem encountered by the Organization results from the fact that aviation is not a static art. ICAO Annexes must therefore be amended frequently. This poses major administrative problems for many states whose aviation authorities are understaffed and simply cannot keep up with frequent Annex amendments. In 1965, for example, ICAO found that "perhaps 25% of ICAO Contracting States have been able to maintain the operating instructions at their installations essentially in step with the ICAO documents, another 25% are using instructions that are 1 to 3 years out of date and the remaining 50% are even further out of date." [189] This backlog has been attributed to "the frequent amendments to the ICAO documents," and to the fact that "in some cases a considerable part of an amendment may be of little or no practical concern to many [aviation] administrations because it covers techniques and practices actually employed only in areas where air traffic is very dense and sophisticated ground services are a necessity." [190] In dealing with these problems, the Organization must balance the obvious needs of the less developed nations for stability in Annex material against the rapidly changing demands of modern aviation with which other Contracting States have to cope. The

---

[185] On this subject generally, see ICAO Secretariat, MEMORANDUM ON ICAO 41–48 (5th ed. 1966).

[186] See ICAO Doc. A12–WP/7 (EX/5) (1959).

[187] ICAO Doc. A12–WP/15 (TE/6), p. 7 (1959). See also, Pépin, *Development of the National Legislation on Aviation since the Chicago Conference*, 24 J. Air L. & Com. 1 (1957).

[188] See, *e.g.*, ICAO Technical Assistance Bureau, TECHNICAL ASSISTANCE GUIDELINE NO. 5: AIR LAW AND REGULATIONS (1967).

[189] ICAO Doc. 15–WP/28 (TE/5), p. 2 (1965).

[190] *Ibid.*

dilemma which ICAO thus faces is that some states cannot keep up with the amendments and would like to see their number and frequency substantially reduced, whereas others find that the amendment process is too slow and tends to produce regulations which are obsolete by the time they are adopted.[191]

ICAO has not as yet found a way out of this dilemma, although it is slowly coming to grips with the problems it presents. Thus the ICAO Assembly has urged that "a programme for the application of amendments to SARPS . . . should be followed so that the relevant national regulations of contracting States will not require to be amended more frequently than at intervals of one year. . . ."[192] At the same time, the Assembly recommended that "States consider the practicability of modifying the internal processes by which they give effect to the provisions of SARPS . . . if such modification would expedite or simplify the processes or make them more effective."[193] The Organization is also exploring the possibility of developing two sets of SARPS: a simplified and stable set for areas with less exacting operational requirements, and a more complex set for areas demanding advanced techniques and frequent changes.[194] Since the ICAO Assembly has charged the Council with the task of exploring this possibility,[195] it may well be that in the years to come the Organization will move away from the concept of global SARPS, and seek instead to foster regional uniformity through SARPS or other legislation specifically tailored to the technical demands of various air navigation regions.

Facilitation SARPS. Facilitation SARPS (Annex 9) are designed to cut governmental red tape in processing the admission and departure of aircraft engaged in international civil aviation by streamlining the various formalities that tend unnecessarily to delay air travel and air transport.[196] Here, unlike in the case of air navigation SARPS where technical and economic problems impede implemen-

---

[191] See ICAO Assembly, Report of the Technical Commission, 15th Sess., Doc. 8524 (A15–TE/52), pp. 36–37 (1965).

[192] Assembly Res. A15–8, Appendix E, ICAO Doc. 8528 (A15–P/6) (1965).

[193] Assembly Res. A15–8, Appendix G, ICAO Doc. 8528 (A15–P/6) (1965).

[194] For a discussion of this proposal, see ICAO Doc. A15–WP/28 (TE/5), pp. 2–5 (1965); ICAO Assembly, Report of the Technical Commission, 15th Sess., Doc. 8524 (A15–TE/52), pp. 36–37 (1965).

[195] Assembly Res. A15–12, ICAO Doc. 8528 (A15–P/6) (1965).

[196] See Aims of ICAO in the Field of Facilitation, ICAO Doc. 7991 (C/906/2), p. 3 (2nd ed. 1965).

tation, the major obstacles are governmental inertia, administrative inefficiency, and bureaucratic inflexibility.[197] This does not necessarily mean that the task of obtaining widespread compliance by the Contracting States with the provisions of Annex 9 is, as a practical matter, any easier than in the case of other Annexes. All it means is that the problems are different and that, given the nature of these problems, what is needed to bring about compliance is patient and persistent prodding of the Contracting States by the Organization.

ICAO has done just that, in a variety of different ways. Thus, at almost every session of the ICAO Assembly a resolution is adopted which, after reminding the Contracting States that "Articles 22 and 23 of the Convention impose an obligation upon States to adopt all practicable measures to facilitate international air transport and to prevent unnecessary delays arising under immigration, quarantine, customs, and clearance laws," resolves that the Member State "should make renewed efforts to implement Annex 9 to the maximum extent possible." [198] These exhortations are supplemented by implementation efforts of a type similar to those reported for the year 1965:

> The Organization continued to keep in close touch with other international organizations having an interest in Facilitation and to encourage States to implement the provisions of Annex 9, mainly by correspondence but also, when circumstances permitted, by visits from FAL experts in the Secretariat. Field work was carried out in three South American countries in collaboration with the International Air Transport Association, and four African States were to be visited in January 1966.[199]

Probably the most interesting implementation tools used in the facilitation field are the National Facilitation Committees. These committees were initially established by a number of Contracting States on their own initiative. Impressed with the work which these committees were doing, the ICAO Assembly urged other states to constitute similar bodies after drawing their attention "to the successful results attained by a number of Contracting States through

---

[197] ICAO Assembly, Report of the Economic Commission, 14th Sess., Doc. 8286 (A14–EC/38), Annex III, pp. 86–87 (1962).

[198] See, e.g., ICAO Assembly, Res. A14–36, Doc. 8268 (A14–P/20) (1962).

[199] [1965] Report of the Council, ICAO Doc. 8572 (A16–P/1), p. 60 (1966).

the creation of Facilitation Committees for the purpose of coordinating efforts to implement Annex 9." [200] Since then, most Contracting States have established National Facilitation Committees.[201] The following excerpt from the report of the Assembly's Economic Commission is indicative of the importance which ICAO attaches to the work of these Committees and the role which they can perform:

> In many countries, National Facilitation Committees have proven valuable instruments [sic] in achieving a higher degree of implementation of Annex 9 and in promoting the FAL programme generally. In carrying out the obligation of a Contracting State under the Convention to comply with . . . the Annex 9 provisions, it usually falls to the aviation authorities to bring these matters to the attention of other governmental departments whose main interest lies elsewhere. The task is not easy when it entails convincing long-established agencies that controls which have been exercised for years over other forms of transport are unduly burdensome in the case of air transport.
>
> Special efforts are therefore required to demonstrate the specific needs of air transport and to obtain the sympathetic cooperation of these authorities. For this reason, the establishment of National Facilitation Committees has been repeatedly advocated because such committees bring together all the authorities concerned for discussion and solution of the problems.[202]

Since the National Facilitation Committees are advisory bodies, their effectiveness depends in large measure on the governmental authority of its individual members. It is for this reason that ICAO has urged the Contracting States to appoint senior governmental officials to these committees.[203] While it is difficult to say to what extent that has been done, it is clear that in some states National Facilitation Committees have been extremely effective in bringing about compliance with ICAO facilitation SARPS, whereas in other states they have not been utilized adequately or extensively enough.[204]

No information is available as to whether the general level of implementation is higher for Annex 9 provisions than it is with

[200] Assembly Res. A4–18, ICAO Doc. 7017 (A4–P/3) (1950).
[201] ICAO Assembly, Report of the Economic Commission, 14th Sess., Doc. 8286 (A14–EC/38), Annex III, p. 87 (1962).
[202] Id. at 86–87.
[203] Id. at 10.
[204] Id. at 87.

regard to air navigation SARPS. This lack of information is attributable to the fact that states are, as a rule, no less delinquent in reporting differences under Annex 9 than they are in the case of other ICAO Annexes.[205] On the whole, however, it would not be unreasonable to assume that ICAO's implementation efforts are probably more successful in the facilitation field than they are in the air navigation field. This conclusion is based on the general trend toward greater liberalization of national trade and travel restrictions in evidence today, which makes states more receptive to facilitation. It is also based on the fact that facilitation does not have to contend with the extremely difficult technical and economic problems that, more than anything else, impede the implementation of air navigation SARPS.

IMPLEMENTATION OF SARPS RELATING TO AIR NAVIGATION FACILITIES, PERSONNEL, AND EQUIPMENT

The extent to which the Contracting States can implement the technical specifications and procedures for air navigation facilities, equipment, and training of personnel prescribed in various ICAO Annexes depends in large measure on the economic resources and technical know-how that is available to them. As a result, many states simply cannot comply with these SARPS unless they are provided with massive economic and technical assistance designed to improve their air navigation facilities and equipment (such as airports, communications and meteorological stations, etc.), and to help them train operating personnel for aircraft and ground services.

Although ICAO lacks the funds to deal with this problem on the vast scale that would seem to be required, it has been able to make some progress.[206] Since 1951, the Organization has utilized the funds allocated to it under the U.N. Expanded Programme of Technical Assistance and the U.N. Special Fund to provide technical assist-

---

[205] See ICAO Secretariat, Supplement to Annex 9 (Fifth Edition), No. 6 (1/5/66), which indicates that no information at all had been received from more than one-third of the Contracting States. It also shows a very large number of reported differences.

[206] See generally, ICAO Doc. A12–WP/15 (TE/6) (1959); ICAO Doc. A15–WP/40 (TE/9) (1965).

ance to the Contracting States. With this money, amounting to approximately $35 million by 1966, "ICAO has given assistance over the years to some 80 countries involving more than 1,600 assignments by some 600 experts; the training of more than 6,500 students by ICAO instructors; and the award of more than 1,300 ICAO fellowships for study and training abroad." [207]

In addition to the ICAO Technical Assistance Missions which are dispatched to the Contracting States, the Organization also utilizes its six regional offices to assist the states to which they are accredited with implementation problems. These offices in turn supervise the activities of ICAO regional technical teams, whose task it is to study the implementation problems encountered in various air navigation areas and to recommend remedial measures.[208] These implementation endeavors and the contribution they have made have been described as follows:

> The regional offices, the special regional teams and also the technical assistance missions contribute very effectively [in] correcting failures in implementation of details of ICAO SARPS. . . . One of the main tasks of the regional offices is to seek improvement of details of implementation and operation of the recommended facilities, and this was the principal reason for establishing the special regional teams. Contacts by the regional office staff or by the regional teams often permit pointing out ways in which the operation or maintenance of the facilities could be improved. In this manner many of the deficiencies of non-implementation of details of ICAO specifications are taken care of.[209]

These activities are supplemented by the work of the ICAO Air Navigation Bureau, which prepares a multitude of technical manuals and instructional guides for distribution to the Contracting States.[210]

These implementation efforts are coordinated and supervised by the ICAO Council, and to some extent by the Standing Group on

---

[207] ICAO Secretariat, MEMORANDUM ON ICAO, p. 43 (5th ed. 1966).
[208] *Id.* at 22.
[209] ICAO Doc. A15–WP/40 (TE/9), p. 5 (1965). The activities of the regional offices for the year 1966 are summarized in [1966] Report of the Council, ICAO Doc. 8660 (A16–P/2), pp. 44–47 (1967).
[210] See ICAO Doc. C–WP/3912, p. 3 (1963).

Implementation,[211] in accordance with policy guidelines laid down by the ICAO Assembly. In its latest policy statement relating to the implementation of air navigation SARPS the Assembly, after calling on the Council to use all available means to foster and encourage implementation, "including the United Nations Programme of Technical Assistance, technical advice and expert assistance from the Regional Offices, and the Training Activities of the Air Navigation Bureau," resolved that

> primary emphasis be placed upon assisting States in the application of SARPS and PANS [Procedures for Air Navigation Services] in the fields of aerodromes and ground aids, communications, meteorology, air traffic services, aeronautical information services, and search and rescue, including the personnel licensing and training aspects of those fields.[212]

Whether this task can be accomplished with the limited resources presently available to the Organization may seriously be doubted. What is obviously needed is a well-financed long-term development program.[213]

OTHER FORMS OF ICAO TECHNICAL LEGISLATION

In addition to the international standards and recommended practices promulgated as Annexes to the Convention, ICAO issues other air navigation regulations.[214] These enactments are hierarchically

---

[211] The Standing Group on Implementation was established by the ICAO Council in 1960, Action of the Council, 40th Sess., ICAO Doc. 8097 (C/926), pp. 26–27 (1960), to continue on a permanent basis the work that had been carried on from 1956 to 1958 by the Special Panel on Implementation. While the main task of the Standing Group on Implementation is to foster the implementation of regional air navigation plans, it addresses itself also to the implementation of international standards and recommended practices which are related to regional plans.

[212] Assembly Res. A15–8, Appendix G, ICAO Doc. 8528 (A15–P/6) (1965).

[213] At the 1965 Session of the ICAO Assembly there was considerable support for a Malawi proposal calling for the establishment of an Aviation Development Fund to be administered by ICAO. See ICAO Assembly, Report of the Executive Committee, 15th Sess., Doc. 8522 (A15–EX/43), pp. 21–22 (1965). The Council's Standing Group on Implementation has in the meantime concluded that the establishment of such a Fund was not feasible, although it has suggested that the Council explore alternate methods of financing. Action of the Council, 59th Sess., ICAO Doc. 8665 (C/970), pp. 27–28 (1965).

[214] On this subject generally, see Erler 128–31; Sheffy, *supra* note 1, at 437–39.

inferior to the Annexes, and contain regulatory material that for one reason or another is not fit for inclusion in an Annex.

PANS and SUPPS

The most important of these enactments are the Procedures for Air Navigation Services (PANS). They are designed for "world-wide application" and consist, for the most part, of operating procedures that are

> regarded as not yet having attained a sufficient degree of maturity for adoption as International Standards and Recommended Practices, as well as material of a more permanent character which is considered too detailed for incorporation in an Annex, or is susceptible to frequent amendment, for which the processes of the Convention would be too cumbersome.[215]

The PANS presently in force deal with the following subjects: Aircraft Operations,[216] Rules of the Air and Air Traffic Services,[217] Meteorology,[218] and ICAO Abbreviations and Codes.[219]

The other type of regulations are the Regional Supplementary Procedures (SUPPS). As their name indicates, SUPPS establish operating procedures designed for application in specific air navigation regions.[220] Since PANS are intended for world-wide application, they do not contain procedures or specifications that regional operational requirements may demand. This need is met by the operating procedures laid down in SUPPS. They are specifically tailored to particular air navigation regions, and might accordingly be characterized as regional supplements to PANS.[221]

The Convention does not mention PANS or SUPPS by name, nor does it contain any provisions regulating their enactment.[222] They

---

[215] Rules of Procedure for the Conduct of Air Navigation Meetings and Directives to Divisional-Type Air Navigation Meetings, Part II, Rule 2.2.1, ICAO Doc. 8143 (AN/873) (1961).

[216] ICAO Doc. 8168 (OPS/611/2) (1967).

[217] ICAO Doc. 4444 (RAC/501/9) (1967).

[218] ICAO Doc. 7605 (MET/526/4) (1966).

[219] ICAO Doc. 8400/2 (1967).

[220] Regional Supplementary Procedures, Foreword, p. 7, ICAO Doc. 7030 (Amendment No. 114, 1967).

[221] ICAO Secretariat, MEMORANDUM ON ICAO, p. 19 (5th ed. 1966); Sheffy, *supra* note 1, at 438.

[222] See Carroz, *supra* note 22, at 164–65.

were initially conceived and developed by the PICAO Air Navigation Committee and were taken over by ICAO because they met a
need that the ICAO Annexes did not fully satisfy.[223] Since PANS
and SUPPS are regulations subordinate to the Annexes which they
are designed to supplement, ICAO's authority to promulgate them
can be implied from the Organization's general power to enact
SARPS,[224] as well as from the Council's power to "conduct research
into all aspects of . . . air navigation which are of international
importance, [to] communicate the results of its research to the
contracting States, and [to] facilitate the exchange of information
between contracting States on . . . air navigation matters." [225]

Given the function which the PANS and SUPPS perform, it
might have been possible through incorporation by reference to
elevate them to the status that the Annexes themselves enjoy.[226] The
ICAO Council has not followed this course, however, possibly because it might have complicated the already cumbersome process
that the enactment of Annexes entails. Instead, PANS and SUPPS
are simply approved by the Council for world-wide or regional
application, as the case may be.[227] While this adoption technique
assures considerable flexibility, it reduces the legal status of PANS
and SUPPS to that of ICAO Council recommendations having no
binding force.[228] The one significant consequence of this status is
that PANS and SUPPS relating to the Rules of the Air, because
they are not incorporated by reference into Annex 2, are not gov-

[223] For the history of PANS and SUPPS, see ICAO Doc. A4–WP/12 (TE/1)
(1950).
[224] Convention, Art. 37.
[225] Convention, Art. 55(c).
[226] Carroz, *supra* note 22, at 166.
[227] Rules of Procedure for the Conduct of Air Navigation Meetings and
Directives to Divisional-Type Air Navigation Meetings, Part II, Rule 2.2.1,
ICAO Doc. 8143 (AN/873) (1961); Regional Supplementary Procedures, Foreword, p. 7, ICAO Doc. 7030 (Amendment No. 114, 1967).
[228] Thus the Foreword to the Regional Supplementary Procedures, *supra*,
points out that PANS are *"recommended* to the Contracting States for world-
wide use, whilst the SUPPS are *recommended* to the Contracting States for
application in the region . . . to which they are relevant." (Emphasis added.)
Sheffy, *supra* note 1, at 437, asserts that "PANS obligate States to the extent
stated in Article 28 of the Convention." This position is untenable, if for no
other reason than that Article 28 speaks only of international standards and
recommended practices.

erned by Article 12 of the Convention and thus cannot be deemed to be obligatory over the high seas.[229]

Apart from this consequence, the non-obligatory character of PANS and SUPPS has no real practical significance. Since 1950, for example, the requirement for the notification of differences, which Article 38 prescribes for national deviations from international standards, has been applied not only to recommended practices but to PANS and SUPPS as well.[230] PANS have, moreover, been gradually assimilated to SARPS to the extent that the Assembly lumps these regulatory materials together in setting guidelines for their formulation [231] and implementation.[232] There is no reason to assume, furthermore, that the Contracting States distinguish between SARPS, PANS, and SUPPS when deciding whether or not to comply with these regulations.[233] The United States, for example, applies the same implementation criteria to PANS and SUPPS as it does to SARPS.[234]

The Relation Between SARPS, PANS, SUPPS, and Regional Plans

Viewed as a unit—as they must be for a proper understanding of the Organization's regulatory activities—ICAO Annexes, PANS, and SUPPS together make up an integrated international air navigation code. This code is supplemented by the Regional Air Naviga-

---

[229] Carroz, *supra* note 22, at 166. This conclusion is also borne out by the language found in the Foreword to the PANS on Rules of the Air and Air Traffic Services. See ICAO Doc. 4444 (RAC/501/9), p. ix (1967).

[230] See Principles Governing the Reporting of "Differences" from ICAO Standards, Practices and Procedures, ICAO Council, Proceedings of the 11th Sess., Part II [1950], Doc. 7188 (C/828), p. 32, at 34 (1953).

[231] See Assembly Res. A15–8, Appendix E, ICAO Doc. 8528 (A15–P/6) (1965).

[232] See Assembly Res. A15–8, Appendix G, ICAO Doc. 8528 (A15–P/6) (1965).

[233] See ICAO Doc. A15–WP/28 (TE/5), p. 2 (1965).

[234] See Interagency Group on International Aviation, *U.S. Policies Concerning SARPS, PANS, SUPPS, Regional Plans and Other ICAO Actions*, IGIA 6/IA, p. 9 (1962) (mimeo). One interesting U.S. aviation regulation provides that "each person operating a foreign civil aircraft overwater off the shores of the United States shall give flight notification or file a flight plan, in accordance with the Supplementary Procedures for the ICAO region concerned." 14 C.F.R. § 91.43(d) (1967).

tion Plans,[235] which are ICAO Council recommendations setting out the requirements for adequate air navigation facilities and services in the nine air navigation regions established by the Organization.[236] These plans are formulated at the respective Regional Air Navigation Meetings, and are approved by the Council under Article 69 of the Convention.[237] The interrelationship between these various regulatory materials, their structure, and functions are extremely well explained in the following paragraph of the Foreword to the PANS on Meteorology:

> Whereas the current edition of Annex 3 [Meteorology] contains the basic obligations of Contracting States for the provision of meteorological service for international air navigation, the PANS-MET provides the detailed procedures, the application of which is considered desirable for uniform fulfilment of the obligations stated in Annex 3. No reference has been made within the PANS-MET to the related basic obligation in Annex 3 which gives rise to a procedure. However, the sequence in the PANS-MET follows that of the Annex and [the] relationship between the two documents can readily be established. In numerous places reference will be found to regional air navigation agreements. Such regional air navigation agreements have been laid down in the Regional Supplementary Procedures—*Meteorology,* and the meteorological parts of regional plans. The world-wide provisions found in the PANS-MET, together with the procedural arrangements found in certain provisions of Annex 3 and the whole of Part 4 of the Supplementary Procedures, constitute a complete record of agreements reached between Contracting States for meteorological procedures to be observed.[238]

It is thus readily apparent that the ICAO Annexes, PANS, SUPPS, and Regional Air Navigation Plans constitute an integrated body of aviation legislation comparable both in structure and con-

[235] On ICAO Regional Air Navigation Plans, see Sheffy, *The Air Navigation Commission of the International Civil Aviation Organization (Part I),* 25 J. Air L. & Com. 281, 319–26 (1958).

[236] See generally, Rules of Procedure for the Conduct of Air Navigation Meetings and Directives to Regional Air Navigation Meetings, ICAO Doc. 8144 (AN/874) (1961).

[237] Article 69 of the Convention empowers the ICAO Council to make recommendations to the Contracting States, with a view toward improving air navigation facilities and services which "are not reasonably adequate for the safe, regular, efficient, and economical operation of international air services."

[238] ICAO Doc. 7605 (MET/526/4) (Amendment No. 12), p. 6 (1966).

tent to comprehensive domestic air navigation codes. Because of its technical complexity and legislative sophistication, this ICAO code is unique among international regulatory schemes.[239]

CONCLUSION

In assessing ICAO's law-making powers, most commentators conclude that the legislative scheme of the Chicago Convention is a retrograde step when compared to the system that had been established under the 1919 Paris Convention Relating to the Regulation of Aerial Navigation.[240] Two considerations are usually advanced in support of this conclusion. The first is that the technical annexes of the Paris Convention formed an integral part of and had the same force and effect as the Convention itself,[241] whereas ICAO Annexes do not enjoy this status. The second consideration is that the annexes to the Paris Convention could be amended by the International Commission for Air Navigation (ICAN) acting by a three-fourths vote of its total membership, and thereafter bound all Contracting States.[242] The Chicago Convention, on the other hand, permits a Contracting State to disregard the provisions of an ICAO Annex or amendment thereto whenever such state finds it "impracticable" to comply therewith.

The Chicago Convention would indeed compare unfavorably with the Paris Convention if the sole test for judging the efficacy of international regulatory schemes were the compulsory or non-compulsory character of their enactments. But this is simply not so, for this test tells us nothing about the extent to which such legislative acts are being complied with or about the function they perform. As

---

[239] On the legislative activities of other international organizations, see Detter, LAW MAKING BY INTERNATIONAL ORGANIZATIONS (1965); Alexandrowicz, *The Convention on Facilitation of International Maritime Traffic and International Technical Regulations: A Comparative Study*, 15 Int'l & Comp. L. Q. 621 (1966); Saba, *L'activité quasi-législative des institutions spécialisées des Nations Unies*, 111 Recueil des Cours 607 (1964).

[240] The Convention Relating to the Regulation of Aerial Navigation [hereinafter cited as Paris Convention] was signed at Paris on 13 October 1919, and came into force on 1 June 1922. The official text of the Paris Convention can be found in 11 L.N.T.S. 173 (1922). The Paris Convention, as subsequently amended, is also reproduced in 3 AIR LAWS AND TREATIES OF THE WORLD 3085 (1965).

[241] Paris Convention, Art. 39.

[242] Paris Convention, Art. 34.

a matter of fact, the non-binding character of ICAO Annexes probably accounts, more than anything else, for the advances the Organization has been able to make in the regulation of international air navigation.

Had the Chicago Convention adopted the legislative scheme of the Paris Convention, many states would have stayed out of ICAO, as was true in the case of ICAN, either because of domestic constitutional obstacles to the required delegation of legislative power or because they could not have committed the economic and technical resources that compliance with the Annexes would entail. The obligatory character of the Annexes would have made it extremely difficult, furthermore, to adopt any but the most insignificant amendments to the Annexes. Knowing that it would be bound to implement them, each state would scrutinize these amendments with great care and primarily in terms of its ability to comply with them. This in turn would have generated strong pressure to settle for less stringent technical requirements in order to obtain the passage of the amendment which, for that very reason, would have little practical significance.

The freedom of action which the Contracting States retain under the Chicago Convention makes it possible for them to forego the involvement and control of their foreign offices in the development and adoption of ICAO Annexes, and to leave these matters to their aeronautical authorities. This frees the ICAO legislative process of the legal, political, and economic complications that would otherwise drastically curtail its development. The administrative, technical, and economic problems of bringing about compliance with the Annexes remain, but they have been shifted to a different level where they no longer substantially affect the content and adoption of SARPS.

These problems must, of course, still be contended with on the implementation level, but since implementation is not mandatory, a state's failure to comply with an Annex does not produce dispute-like confrontations between that state and ICAO. The Contracting States are accordingly not on the defensive when dealing with ICAO, and this in turn permits them to explore freely their implementation problems with the Organization, to cooperate fully with ICAO technical missions, and to accept ICAO implementation assistance or advice. This collaborative climate, and the fact that the national aeronautical experts who have participated in the formulation of the Annex are often also responsible for its domestic implementation, makes for a natural alliance between ICAO and the aeronautical authorities of many states. It would therefore not be surprising to find that the aeronautical authorities of states whose domestic air navigation practices are substantially below ICAO standards will invariably lobby for compliance with those standards. The stimulus for such lobbying activities comes not only from the interest which these agencies have in improving air navigation safety, but because they no doubt recognize that the domestic implementation of ICAO Annexes will of necessity increase the size and authority of their own administrative apparatus.

It would thus appear that the real genius of the Organization's regulatory system lies in its non-compulsory character. The complex and sophisticated aviation code, consisting of ICAO SARPS, PANS, SUPPS, and Regional Air Navigation Plans that the Organization has been able to develop over the years with almost no opposition from the Contracting States, would not be in existence today without this built-in flexibility. True, their general level of implementation leaves much to be desired, but the basic cause for this unsatisfactory situation is not the legislative scheme of the Chicago Convention; it is the wide economic and technological gap that separates the developed from the developing nations of the world. Just as domestic laws with all their coercive power cannot force people to do what they cannot do, so no amount of solemn international promise-making will compel states to abide by rules with which they simply cannot comply. This phenomenon also explains why the requirement for the notification of differences prescribed in Article 38 tends to be disregarded by some states, even though it is a binding treaty obligation.

Given the unsatisfactory level of compliance with ICAO regulations, it must be asked whether much has been gained by the promulgation of rules that many states cannot implement? One answer is that those states which can implement them generally do so, and this alone provides a level of standardization which would otherwise not exist. In other words, to the extent that the ICAO regulations, if implemented, perform a useful function, some compliance by all states with a few rules and almost complete compliance by some states with all the rules is better than no compliance with any rules. The second answer is that the international standardization—which ICAO has thus far been able to achieve only in part—cannot but improve as many of the states now incapable of implementing all ICAO regulations gradually acquire this capability. The more ICAO standardization there is at any given moment, the more difficult it becomes for a state to participate in international civil aviation without itself subscribing to these norms. This consideration alone proves the Organization's wisdom in not letting the problem of implementation interfere unduly with its law-making functions.

Part III

ICAO and the Settlement of International Civil Aviation Disputes

INTRODUCTION

The Convention on International Civil Aviation and its two companion agreements—the International Air Services Transit Agreement and the International Air Transport Agreement—establish an elaborate machinery for the settlement of disputes between the Contracting States. In addition, a host of international aeronautical agreements, both multilateral and bilateral, confer arbitral jurisdiction on the ICAO Council or some other body established by the Organization.

This machinery for the settlement of international aviation disputes has been invoked on very few occasions.[1] It may well be that the very existence of this adjudication procedure has been a contributing factor in encouraging the Contracting States to resolve their differences without resorting to it. The availability of international tribunals with jurisdiction to hear a particular dispute no doubt discourages the uncompromising assertion of questionable legal claims. States often have little to gain politically and a great deal to lose economically by engaging in lengthy litigation of international aviation disputes. They are thus probably more willing to resolve these disagreements through the ordinary diplomatic processes. It may also be that many states doubt that a political body such as the ICAO Council would be able to exercise adjudicatory functions with

---

[1] The dispute between the United Kingdom and Spain, which was referred to the ICAO Council for adjudication on 6 September 1967, could not be discussed in this study because the case has not as yet been decided and because most documents relating to it have thus far not been published. It is known, however, that in this dispute the United Kingdom, in reliance on Article 9 of the Convention, has challenged the legality of a prohibited area established by Spain in the vicinity of Gibraltar. See Annual Report of the Council to the Assembly for 1967 (hereinafter cited as [1967] Report of the Council), ICAO Doc. 8724 (A16–P/3), p. 116 (1968).

the requisite judicial impartiality. Not to be overlooked, furthermore, is the fact that the ICAO Council itself has shown very little
enthusiasm for the exercise of the judicial functions that have been
conferred upon it. Finally, the dispute-settling machinery established by the Convention and the Transit and Transport Agreements is by no means a model of legal draftsmanship. It leaves too
many important questions unresolved, and these uncertainties may
well have discouraged some states from resorting to it, lest they find
themselves embroiled in lengthy litigation costlier than the object of
the dispute. The sparse literature on this subject has, furthermore,
done little to dispel these doubts.

Accordingly, it may be of value to analyze the provisions of
various international agreements which vest arbitral powers in
ICAO, and to explore the manner in which the Council has and
might exercise them.

SETTLEMENT OF DISPUTES UNDER THE CHICAGO ACTS

Under the Convention on International Civil Aviation

The Convention on International Civil Aviation confers on the
ICAO Council extensive judicial functions for the settlement of
disputes between the Contracting States.[2] Under Chapter XVIII
(Arts. 84–88) of the Convention, the Council is empowered to
adjudicate any disagreement between two or more Contracting
States relating to the interpretation or application of the Convention
and its Annexes which cannot be settled by negotiation.[3] The Council is vested with jurisdiction to decide such a dispute "on the
application of any State concerned in the disagreement."[4] Its deci-

---

[2] See, on this subject, Erler, RECHTSFRAGEN DER ICAO: DIE INTERNATIONALE
ZIVILLUFTFAHRTORGANISATION UND IHRE MITGLIEDSTAATEN 185–96 (1967);
Cheng, THE LAW OF INTERNATIONAL AIR TRANSPORT 100–05 (1962)
[hereinafter cited as Cheng]; Hingorani, *Dispute Settlement in International
Civil Aviation*, 14 Arb. J. 14 (1959) [hereinafter cited as Hingorani]; Mankiewicz, *Organisation Internationale de l'Aviation Civile*, [1957] Ann. Français
de Droit International 383 [hereinafter cited as Mankiewicz]; Kos-Rabcewicz-
Zubkowski, *Le Règlement des differends internationaux relatifs à la Navigation
aérienne civile*, 2 Rev. Française de Droit Aérien 340 (1948) [hereinafter cited
as Kos-Rabcewicz-Zubkowski]; Domke, *International Civil Aviation Sets New
Pattern*, 1 Int'l Arb. J. 20 (1945) [hereinafter cited as Domke].

[3] Convention, Art. 84.

[4] *Ibid.*

sion may be appealed either to the International Court of Justice or to an *ad hoc* international tribunal,[5] whose judgment "shall be final and binding."[6] The Convention provides two types of sanctions for non-compliance with these decisions. The first applies to cases of non-compliance by airlines. Here, if the Council renders a decision noting such non-compliance, each Contracting State is under an obligation to bar the airline in question from operating through the airspace above its territory.[7] The second type of sanction applies to states. If they are found to be in default of their obligations, the ICAO Assembly must suspend their voting power both in the Assembly and the Council.[8]

JURISDICTION

By adhering to the Convention, each Contracting State has recognized the compulsory jurisdiction of the Council to adjudicate disagreements between it and any other party to the Convention. This jurisdiction is subject to four conditions, however.[9] First, there must be a disagreement between the parties. Second, this disagreement must relate to the interpretation or application of the Convention or its Annexes. Third, only a Contracting State "concerned in the disagreement" can refer the case to the Council for adjudication. Finally, before the Council may assume jurisdiction to decide the case, it must appear that the disagreement "cannot be settled by negotiation." A showing that any one of these requirements is absent would necessarily divest the Council of jurisdiction to hear the case.

The Disagreement

Since Article 84 of the Convention empowers the Council to decide disagreements between the Contracting Parties, its jurisdiction is necessarily limited to contentious as distinguished from advi-

---

[5] Convention, Arts. 84, 85. While the Convention refers to the Permanent Court of International Justice, it is clear that the International Court of Justice is to be regarded as the judicial institution contemplated by the Convention to exercise this function. See ICAO Doc. 4039 (A1–CP/12), p. 22 (1947). See also, I.C.J., Statute, Art. 37.

[6] Convention, Art. 86.

[7] Convention, Art. 87.

[8] Convention, Art. 88.

[9] Convention, Art. 84.

sory proceedings. The term "disagreement," although not defined in the Convention, is no doubt synonymous with what in other international agreements is referred to as a "dispute." According to the International Court of Justice, to make out a case that a justiciable dispute exists, "it must be shown that the claim of one party is positively opposed by the other." In the Court's view ". . . it is not sufficient for one party to a contentious case to assert that a dispute [disagreement] exists with the other party. . . . Nor is it adequate to show that the interests of the two parties to such a case are in conflict."[10] A disagreement within the meaning of the Convention could therefore be characterized as a dispute between two or more Contracting States, in which one state asserts a legal right or claim against another state that contests the validity of the claim.[11]

Jurisdiction over the Subject Matter

The requirement of Article 84 that the disagreement relate to the interpretation or application of the Convention or its Annexes goes to the jurisdiction over the subject matter of the dispute. While this is a basic jurisdictional requirement, a plea based on it will not always be disposable at the procedural stage of the proceedings unless the complaint on its face relates quite clearly to some other subject matter.[12] It may be assumed that complaints *prima facie* devoid of any such jurisdictional basis will rarely be submitted to the Council. The Council may, therefore, in some cases be unable to dispose of an objection based on this ground without examining the

[10] South West Africa Cases (Preliminary Objections), [1962] I.C.J. Rep. 319, 328.

[11] In this connection, see Interpretation of Peace Treaties with Bulgaria, Hungary and Romania, [1950] I.C.J. Rep. 65, 74 (advisory opinion), where the Court reasoned as follows:

> Whether there exists an international dispute is a matter for objective determination. . . . There has . . . arisen a situation in which the two sides hold clearly opposite views concerning the question of the performance or non-performance of certain treaty obligations. Confronted with such a situation, the Court must conclude that international disputes have arisen.

[12] For the form and contents of the application (complaint) to the Council under Chapter XVIII of the Convention, see ICAO Council, *Rules for the Settlement of Differences* [hereinafter cited as 1957 Rules], Art. 2, Doc. 7782 (1959). These Rules were approved by the Council on 9 April 1957.

merits of the case.[13] In doing so, it may find that the dispute or, what is more likely, some of its elements are outside the scope of its jurisdiction.

Here it should be remembered that the jurisdiction of the Council to decide disputes between the Contracting States is not limited to those that arise under the Convention, for various other multilateral and bilateral international agreements relating to international civil aviation also bestow adjudicatory functions on the Council. Since a dispute submitted to it may thus call for the interpretation or application of more than one of these agreements, and since the scope of the Council's judicial powers varies under these agreements, substantial jurisdictional significance attaches to the various elements comprising a given dispute.

Standing

The Council acquires jurisdiction under Article 84 only if the dispute has been submitted to it by a Contracting State "concerned in the disagreement." This requirement resembles the notion of "standing" which has been developed in domestic law to bar suits by persons lacking a recognizable interest in their adjudication. A Contracting State will therefore have to show that the action or inaction on the part of another Contracting State violates or directly and adversely affects its rights under the Convention or one of the Annexes thereto.[14]

[13] 1957 Rules, Art. 5 deals with objections to the jurisdiction of the Council. While Art. 5(3) provides that "upon a preliminary objection being filed, the proceedings on the merits shall be suspended," it is submitted that this provision can have reference only to those instances where a plea to the jurisdiction can in fact be decided at the preliminary stage. That this is not always possible is evidenced by the practice of the Permanent Court of International Justice and the International Court of Justice. These tribunals have on numerous occasions found it necessary to consider the merits of the case before deciding the jurisdictional plea. See Shihata, THE POWER OF THE INTERNATIONAL COURT TO DETERMINE ITS OWN JURISDICTION 113–16 (1965); Rosenne, THE INTERNATIONAL COURT OF JUSTICE 348–59 (1957) [hereinafter cited as Rosenne]; Hudson, THE PERMANENT COURT OF INTERNATIONAL JUSTICE 1920–1940, at 418 (1943) [hereinafter cited as Hudson]. In fact, Article 62(5) of the Rules of the International Court of Justice codifies this practice. See, e.g., Case Concerning the Administration of the Prince von Pless (Preliminary Objection), P.C.I.J., Ser. A/B, No. 52, p. 15 (1933). See also, Shihata, op. cit. supra, at 114; Rosenne 350.

[14] See South West Africa Cases (Judgment), [1966] I.C.J. Rep. 6.

Moreover, the applicant state will have to show that it is a *party* to the dispute. This requirement is implicit in the notion of standing as articulated in the Convention, even though Article 84 speaks of a Contracting State "concerned in the disagreement" rather than of one that is a "party" to it. A state can be "concerned in" a "disagreement" with another state only if there is a disagreement within the meaning of the Convention which "cannot be settled by negotiation." This in turn presupposes that the applicant state has previously addressed to the respondent, through diplomatic channels, a legal claim that the latter has refused to honor.[15] In other words, some sort of diplomatic confrontation—some sort of negotiations— must have taken place between the applicant and the respondent before the former may submit the matter to the Council. If that has not been done, the applicant cannot be said to be "concerned in the disagreement," for it has no justiciable disagreement with the respondent state.[16] One may accordingly conclude that a state has no standing to submit to the Council a disagreement between two other states, unless it too was a party to the negotiations between them.

It might be argued, of course, that this proposition overlooks the fact that one state may be profoundly affected by a dispute between two other states and that its interests may, for all practical purposes, be identical with those of one of the disputing parties. To require this state to join the negotiations merely to enable it to submit the case to the Council might appear to be unduly formalistic. The answer to this argument is that there is considerable wisdom in letting the parties decide when to submit their dispute to adjudication, because their negotiations—even if otherwise unsuccessful—may enable them to narrow or define the issues of their dispute. It must also be recognized that a state may, for political reasons, be unwilling to accede to the demands of one state, although it might be prepared to comply with these same demands if made by another state.

Admittedly, there may be cases where it would make little sense to require a state to go through the motions of negotiations merely to establish itself as a party concerned in the disagreement. This would be true of a dispute which had been the subject of protracted

[15] See Case of the Electricity Company of Sofia and Bulgaria (Preliminary Objection), P.C.I.J., Ser. A/B, No. 77, p. 83 (1939).

[16] See ICAO Doc. GE/RSD/WD#3, p. 14 (1955).

and unsuccessful negotiations or discussions within the ICAO Assembly, for example. In cases of this type, there no longer exist any compelling reasons for denying any interested Contracting State the right to submit the dispute to the Council, particularly when such parliamentary diplomacy has crystallized the issues of the dispute and demonstrated the futility of further direct negotiations by individual states.[17] "Diplomacy by conference or parliamentary diplomacy," the International Court of Justice emphasized in 1962, "has come to be recognized in the past four or five decades as one of the established modes of international negotiation."[18]

That a Contracting State seeking to refer a dispute to the ICAO Council under Article 84 of the Convention must itself have been a party to the negotiations finds support in the Council's disposition of Afghanistan's complaint against Pakistan. This complaint was directly related to the India-Pakistan dispute of 1952, which will be discussed below. Here it is only relevant to note that after India formally invoked Article 84,[19] Afghanistan addressed a communication to the ICAO Council[20] in which it charged that Pakistan was illegally interfering with flights between India and Afghanistan. Although this complaint contained allegations identical in substance to those made by India, the Council concluded that it could not be regarded as an application for the settlement of a disagreement within the meaning of Article 84. If Afghanistan wished to file such an application, the Council stated in a note addressed to that country, Afghanistan would have to furnish the Council, *inter alia* "with a more detailed and explicit statement . . . of the extent to which efforts have been made to settle *its* disagreement with the Government of Pakistan." (Emphasis added.)[21] Since the Indian application, which was found to be *prima facie* in order, spoke of unsuccessful negotiations between that country and Pakistan, it is apparent that the Council believed that Afghanistan lacked the

---

[17] See South West Africa Cases (Preliminary Objections), [1962] I.C.J. Rep. 319, 346.

[18] *Ibid.* On this subject generally, see Sohn, *The Function of International Arbitration Today*, 108 Recueil des Cours 9, 12–14 (1963); Jessup, *Parliamentary Diplomacy: An Examination of the Legal Quality of the Rules of Procedure of Organs of the United Nations*, 89 Recueil des Cours 185 (1956).

[19] The Indian Application can be found in ICAO Doc. C–WP/1169 (1952).

[20] ICAO Doc. C–WP/1222 (1952).

[21] ICAO Council, 16th Sess., Doc. 7291 (C/845), p. 195 (1952).

requisite standing to file its application against Pakistan because Afghanistan had not made a preliminary showing that it was a party to those negotiations.[22]

Prior Negotiations

Before the Council can assume jurisdiction to decide a dispute, it must appear that it "cannot be settled by negotiation."[23] This requirement corresponds in some measure to the principle found in domestic administrative law that a controversy must be ripe for adjudication, which usually means that all available administrative remedies must have been exhausted before the courts will assume jurisdiction. On the international plane, the requirement of prior negotiations, if made a jurisdictional prerequisite,[24] is designed to prevent unnecessary litigation between states and to narrow the issues of their dispute.

Under Article 84 of the Convention, a preliminary showing that prior negotiations to settle the dispute have failed has a dual jurisdictional significance. The first relates to the issue of standing. It has already been discussed in connection with the question whether a state which has a vital interest in a dispute between two other Contracting States can submit the case to the Council without having itself become a party to their negotiations. The other jurisdictional significance of the requirement of prior negotiations has to do with the content or nature of these negotiations.

In principle, the ICAO Council lacks jurisdiction to decide a case submitted to it by a state that has made no effort, beyond going through certain diplomatic formalities, to enter into *bona fide* negotiations with the respondent state. As a practical matter, however, a plea based on this ground will rarely—if ever—succeed, because such an allegation is extremely difficult to prove. Moreover, the Council cannot and probably should not substitute its judgment for that of the applicant state in deciding whether the dispute could

---

[22] In this connection, see 1957 Rules, Art. 2, which also proceeds on the assumption that only a party to the dispute may submit the case to the Council under Article 84 of the Convention.

[23] Convention, Art. 84.

[24] It is generally assumed that no rule of customary international law compels negotiations as a condition precedent to the submission of a dispute to an international tribunal. See Simpson & Fox, INTERNATIONAL ARBITRATION 126 (1959) [hereinafter cited as Simpson & Fox]; Hudson 413. Various international agreements do impose this requirement, however.

have been settled by negotiations, for in the final analysis that decision is political in nature. This was recognized by the Permanent Court of International Justice which, in rejecting a similar plea to its jurisdiction, emphasized that ". . . in applying this rule, the Court cannot disregard, amongst other considerations, the views of the States concerned, who are in the best position to judge as to political reasons which may prevent the settlement of a given dispute by diplomatic negotiation." [25]

In determining, for strictly jurisdictional purposes, when a dispute is one that cannot be settled by negotiations, it is reasonable to assume that the respondent cannot defeat the Council's jurisdiction by simply asserting, at some stage of the proceedings, that it is prepared to reach a friendly settlement. This decision must be made by reference to the situation as it existed at the time the case was submitted to the Council for adjudication.[26] If at that stage the negotiations were deadlocked, the Council's jurisdiction will have vested.

The requirement of prior negotiations does not necessarily demand that the parties engage in direct negotiations. It could undoubtedly also be satisfied by negotiations carried on in a parliamentary or conference forum, provided both parties to the dispute participated therein on opposite sides.[27] The dispute between the United States and Czechoslovakia over the launching of balloons demonstrates how, within the ICAO framework, parliamentary diplomacy can take the place of direct negotiations.

In January of 1956 the Government of Czechoslovakia informed ICAO that leaflet-carrying balloons released in other countries were observed in its airspace. It charged that these balloons were a hazard to air navigation, that this action violated Articles 1 [28] and 8 [29] of the Convention, and requested the Council to take all neces-

[25] Case of the Mavrommatis Palestine Concessions, P.C.I.J., Ser. A, No. 2, p. 15 (1924).
[26] See South West Africa Cases (Preliminary Objections), [1962] I.C.J. Rep. 319, 344.
[27] *Id.* at 346.
[28] Convention, Art. 1 provides that "the contracting States recognize that every State has complete and exclusive sovereignty over the airspace above its territory."
[29] The relevant part of Article 8 of the Convention reads as follows: "No aircraft capable of being flown without a pilot shall be flown without a pilot over the territory of a contracting State without special authorization by that State and in accordance with the terms of such authorization."

sary measures to have it stopped.[30] A few months later the United States, in response to an ICAO inquiry, informed the President of the Council that the U.S. Air Force had discontinued the launching of large weather balloons from the Federal Republic of Germany and that the U.S. ". . . understood that the Free Europe Committee, a privately sponsored enterprise, was limiting itself to the use of balloons of characteristics approximating those of the standard radiosonde balloons, which had never been considered to constitute a hazard to aircraft, even in dense traffic areas." [31] Czechoslovakia promptly reiterated its charges, alleging further violations of its airspace, and again urged the Organization to "take effective steps, vis-à-vis the Governments concerned" to end this practice.[32]

When the ICAO Assembly convened a month later the Czech Delegation, after noting that the Council had made no reference to the balloon controversy in its report to the Assembly, introduced a draft resolution with an explanatory memorandum restating its previous charges, and alleging that a Czech aircraft had crashed after colliding with one of the balloons in question.[33] The preamble to the Czech draft resolution defined a balloon as a pilotless aircraft which, under the Convention, may not be flown over the territory of a Contracting State without its authorization. The operative clause of the resolution "invited" all Contracting States ". . . to refrain from sending uncontrolled balloons over the territory of other States who gave no authorization thereto, and to prevent such activity on the part of persons, organizations or other subjects over which they exercise their sovereignty." [34]

This document died in the Executive Committee of the Assembly, where the United States Delegation took issue with the legal assumptions of the draft resolution and the factual allegations set forth in the Czech explanatory memorandum. And, while expressly refusing to move for an adjournment of the debate, the Delegate of the U.S. indicated that he would welcome such a motion because, apart from the safety aspect of this question which was already before the Council, ICAO was not the proper forum for dealing with

---

[30] [1956] Report of the Council, ICAO Doc. 7788 (A11/P/1), p. 49 (1958).
[31] As reported in ICAO Doc. C–WP/2371, p. 2 (1957).
[32] *Ibid.*
[33] ICAO Doc. A10–WP/87 (EX/24) (1956).
[34] *Id.* at 6.

the other aspects it raised.[35] A motion to adjourn the debate was promptly introduced by the Philippines. It was adopted by 13 votes to 8, with 24 abstentions.[36]

Czechoslovakia thereupon brought the matter formally to the attention of the ICAO Council.[37] In the Council, Czechoslovakia argued among other things that the balloons which were being released by the Free Europe Committee were larger than meteorological balloons and that, even if they were not, they were in a different category and that their release consequently violated the Convention. Invoking Articles 54(j) [38] and 55(e) [39] of the Convention, Czechoslovakia requested the Council to take effective steps against the release of these balloons.[40] In reply, the U.S. Representative denied the Czech assertion that the U.S. Air Force had launched espionage balloons over Czechoslovakia and that the Free Europe Committee was a U.S. Government agency.[41] Following a lengthy debate, the Council took no action on the Czech complaint beyond instructing the ICAO Secretary General to prepare a study "to establish the actual facts on aspects of the situation falling within the scope of the Convention. . . ."[42]

While this study was still in progress, the U.S. Representative notified the President of the ICAO Council that the Free Europe Committee had discontinued its balloon-launching program.[43] At the subsequent Council meeting the U.S. Representative furthermore stated that to his Government's knowledge no other leaflet balloons were being launched by any U.S. citizens or Government agencies.[44] But when the Czech Representative asked whether the U.S. Repre-

---

[35] ICAO Assembly, Executive Committee, 10th Sess., Doc. A10–WP/150 (MIN. EX/1–17), pp. 138–39 (1956).

[36] *Id.* at 142.

[37] See ICAO Docs. C–WP/2248 (1956) and C–WP/2251 (1956).

[38] Convention, Art. 54(j), requires the Council to "report to contracting States any infraction of this Convention."

[39] Under Convention, Art. 55(e), the Council may "investigate, at the request of any contracting State, any situation which may appear to present avoidable obstacles to the development of international air navigation; and, after such investigation, issue such reports as may appear to it desirable."

[40] ICAO Council, 29th Sess., Doc. 7739 (C/894), pp. 36–38 (1956).

[41] *Id.* at 39.

[42] *Id.* at 33–34.

[43] ICAO Doc. C–WP/2350 (1957).

[44] ICAO Council, 30th Sess., Doc. 7766 (C/897), p. 36 (1957).

sentative was "prepared to give the Council a firm assurance that the release of free balloons would not be renewed in [the] future," the latter replied that ". . . he would be happy to supply the Representative of Czechoslovakia with a copy of the statement he had read, which contained all the information his office had on this problem. Beyond that he had nothing further to say at this time." [45] Since the Secretary General's study was not as yet before it, the Council decided to take no action until his report had been received.

A few weeks later this study was presented to the Council.[46] In it the Secretary General concluded, *inter alia*, that "the launching of the balloons in question contravenes the provisions of the Convention as mentioned above [Articles 1, 3(c) and 8]. . . ." He reserved judgment, however, on "the question of specific responsibility in respect thereof." [47] For its part, the U.S. submitted a memorandum to which was attached a lengthy brief prepared by counsel for the Free Europe Committee. The brief described the activities of that organization, its balloon-launching program, and its views on the legal and technical aspects of the controversy.[48] The U.S. memorandum, after calling attention to the fact that Czechoslovakia had filed a diplomatic claim against the U.S. seeking damages for the loss of its aircraft, submitted that in view of these developments it would be improper for the Council to consider the questions raised by the report of the Secretary General.[49] The Representative of Czechoslovakia urged, on the other hand, that the Council was duty-bound to adopt a resolution similar to the one his Government had previously introduced in the Assembly.[50] This the Council was not prepared to do. Having been assured by the U.S. that the Free Europe Committee had discontinued its balloon-launching program, the Council decided merely to consider this matter again during its next session.[51]

Thereafter, in November of 1957, the Representative of Czechoslovakia informed the Council that no balloons had been observed in Czechoslovak airspace since March, 1957. This notwithstanding,

---

[45] *Id.* at 37–38.
[46] ICAO Doc. C–WP/2371 (1957).
[47] *Id.* at 8.
[48] See ICAO Doc. C–WP/2402, Appendix A (1957).
[49] ICAO Doc. C–WP/2402, pp. 1–2 (1957).
[50] ICAO Council, 30th Sess., Doc. 7766 (C/897), p. 116 (1957).
[51] *Id.* at 121–23.

however, he urged the Council to adopt a general resolution to ensure against future balloon launchings.[52] While the Council agreed that ICAO should explore the legal and technical problems bearing on the release of balloons across international boundaries, it concluded that such a study should not be linked to the specific case under consideration.[53] This case having become moot, the Council decided "to take no further action on the particular request made by the Government of Czechoslovakia." [54]

In 1960, Czechoslovakia again informed the Council that balloons launched from the territory of the Federal Republic of Germany had penetrated Czechoslovak airspace.[55] Taking note of these charges and the assurances received from the Federal Republic that it was making every effort to prevent this practice, the Council finally adopted a resolution in this matter. In its operative part, the Council

> DECLARES that the flight of uncontrolled balloons not released under appropriate safeguards and conditions may constitute a definite hazard to the safety of air navigation;

> DRAWS THE ATTENTION of Contracting States to Article 8 of the Chicago Convention; and

> URGES Contracting States to take whatever action they may deem appropriate or necessary to ensure the safety of flight.[56]

Although the ICAO Council did not regard the Czech complaint against the U.S. as an application for adjudication under Article 84 of the Convention because Czechoslovakia had not invoked that provision, this case demonstrates, albeit only partially, that parliamentary diplomacy within the ICAO framework could readily satisfy the requirement of Article 84 for prior negotiations. Here, of course, one could argue that the two Governments were still engaged in bilateral diplomatic negotiations,[57] and that the Council lacked

---

[52] ICAO Council, 31st Sess., Doc. 7815 (C/900), p. 111 (1957).
[53] *Id.* at 111–19.
[54] *Id.* at 108.
[55] ICAO Council, 40th Sess., Doc. 8078 (C/924), p. 61 (1960).
[56] *Id.* at 59–60. This resolution was unanimously adopted.
[57] See *U.S. Replies to Czechoslovak Charges Concerning Free Europe Committee Balloons,* 38 Dep't State Bull. 1010 (1958).

jurisdiction to hear the case under Article 84 until these negotiations had been unsuccessfully concluded.

At various stages of the discussion the issues separating the parties were, however, rather clearly drawn. The U.S. denied the Czech charges that the balloons were a hazard to air navigation, that their launching violated the Convention, and that the U.S. was responsible for the activities of the Free Europe Committee. The Government of Czechoslovakia demanded assurances that no further balloons would be released into its airspace; the U.S. refused to give them. Hence, if both sides had remained adamant in their respective positions, and if Czechoslovakia had thereupon referred the dispute to the ICAO Council under Article 84 of the Convention, it could properly have pointed to the proceedings in the Council and Assembly to sustain the jurisdictional requirement that the dispute "cannot be settled by negotiation."

The Role of the ICAO Council

In examining the manner in which the Council discharges its functions under Article 84 of the Convention, it should be remembered that the Council is not a court of law in the strict sense of the word. It is therefore free to adopt very flexible procedures for dealing with disputes that are referred to it. Illustrative of the conception which the Council has of the role it performs is Article 14(1) of its 1957 Rules for the Settlement of Differences. It provides that "the Council may, at any time during the proceedings and prior to the meeting at which the decision is rendered . . . invite the parties to the dispute to engage in direct negotiations, if the Council deems that the possibilities of settling the dispute or narrowing the issues through negotiations have not been exhausted." [58] This provision indicates that the Council considers that its main task under Article 84 of the Convention is to assist in *settling* rather than in *adjudicating* disputes. Up to the moment of final decision, the Council in fact acts more like a mediator than a court. This conclusion is supported by Article 14(3) of the Rules which empowers the Coun-

---

[58] See 1957 Rules, Art. 6(1) which provides that "upon filing of the counter-memorial by the respondent, the Council shall decide whether at this stage the parties should be invited to enter into direct negotiations as provided in Article 14."

cil to "render any assistance likely to further the negotiations, including the designation of an individual or a group of individuals to act as conciliator during the negotiations." Although Article 14 envisages a procedure that is not strictly in keeping with judicial proceedings, it does not violate the Convention because the Council may only "invite" but not "compel" the parties to enter into further negotiations. Any party to the dispute thus retains the right to force the Council to adjudicate the dispute by declining to accept the Council's "invitation" to negotiate.[59] The experience which the Council gained in dealing with the dispute between India and Pakistan—it prompted Article 14 of the Rules [60] —indicates, moreover, that this flexible procedure is best calculated to result in the settlement of disputes arising under Article 84 of the Convention.[61]

The complaint by India against Pakistan [62] was formally submitted to the Council by India in April of 1952.[63] The complaint charged Pakistan with acts violating Articles 5, 6, and 9 of the Convention, and with violations of the International Air Services Transit Agreement. India alleged, in particular, that Pakistan refused to permit Indian aircraft engaged in commercial air service between India and Afghanistan to fly over West Pakistan.[64]

When the Indian complaint was submitted to the Council, no rules of procedure had as yet been enacted for the settlement of

---

[59] The fear expressed by Cheng 103, that "such a liberal interpretation may well . . . lead one of the parties to employ obstructionist tactics in order to frustrate the jurisdiction of the ICAO Council," overlooks two considerations. The first is that the Council's jurisdiction cannot be frustrated, for it already has jurisdiction when it invites further negotiations. The second consideration which Cheng overlooks is that Article 14(2) of the 1957 Rules stipulates that "the Council may set a time-limit for the completion of such negotiations." This rule provides an adequate safeguard against obstructionist tactics.

[60] See Oral Report to the Council by the Chairman of the Working Group on the Rules Governing the Settlement of Disagreements, ICAO Council, 19th Sess., Doc. 7390 (C/861), p. 5 (1953).

[61] See Hingorani 16 n.15.

[62] For a summary of the India-Pakistan case, see [1952] Report of the Council, ICAO Doc. 7367 (A7-P/1), pp. 74–76 (1953).

[63] The Indian Application is reprinted in ICAO Doc. C-WP/1169 (1952).

[64] For a discussion relating to the legal issues involved in this dispute, see Bhatti, Drion & Heller, *Prohibited Areas in International Civil Aviation—the Indian-Pakistani Dispute*, [1953] U.S. & Can. Av. 109. See also, Schenkman, THE INTERNATIONAL CIVIL AVIATION ORGANIZATION 376–80 (1955).

disputes under Article 84 of the Convention.[65] Recognizing that it would initially have to decide what rules of procedure were to be applied,[66] the Council invited India and Pakistan "to designate representatives to consult with the Council on the future course of action to be followed." [67] This invitation was designed to produce an acceptable procedure for the disposition of this case.[68] The Council recognized that more time would be needed before any generally applicable rules could be drafted.

In the meantime, the Council granted Pakistan's request for a 30-day period within which to file an answer to the Indian complaint.[69] When Pakistan's reply had been received,[70] the Council appointed a Working Group of three Council Representatives to consider and recommend to the Council "what steps could properly be taken by the Council during the remainder of the . . . session." [71]

After consulting with the parties, the Working Group presented a report containing two basic recommendations.[72] The first suggested

[65] The Interim Council of the Provisional International Civil Aviation Organization (PICAO) had in 1946 promulgated the "Rules Governing the Settlement of Differences between Contracting States." These Rules were issued as PICAO Doc. 2121 (C/228). They were approved by the Interim Council on 10 September 1946. These Rules were promulgated mainly to enable the Interim Council to discharge the arbitral functions assigned to it under the Interim Agreement on International Civil Aviation, Art. III, Sec. 6, para. 8. The PICAO Rules did not apply to disputes submitted to the Council under the Convention, however. See Rules Governing the Settlement of Differences between Contracting States [hereinafter cited as 1946 Rules], Art. 1, PICAO Doc. 2121 (C/228) (1946). Besides, they had not been reissued by the ICAO Council and were thus no longer in force. ICAO Doc. C–WP/1171, p. 1 (1952); ICAO Council, 16th Sess., Doc. 7291 (C/845), p. 11 (1952).

[66] Interestingly enough, both India and Pakistan were mistakenly proceeding under the 1946 Rules. See ICAO Council, 16th Sess., Doc. 7291 (C/845), p. 11 (1952).

[67] *Id.* at 48.

[68] This invitation for consultation was based on a proposal submitted to the Council by Canada which suggested that the two Governments should be invited "to designate representatives to consult with the Council on the question of the *method of procedure to be adopted."* (Emphasis added.) ICAO Doc. C–WP/1192 (1952). This language was revised because a number of Council Representatives voiced the sentiment that it was undignified to say to the parties, to use the words of the French Representative, "you have something for us to arbitrate. . . . We have no rules ready. How do you think we should proceed?" See ICAO Council, 16th Sess., Doc. 7291 (C/845), pp. 49–55 (1952).

[69] ICAO Council, 16th Sess., Doc. 7291 (C/845), p. 48 (1952).

[70] See ICAO Doc. C–WP/1205 (1952); Doc. C–WP/1299 (1952).

[71] ICAO Council, 16th Sess., Doc. 7291 (C/845), p. 96 (1952).

[72] ICAO Doc. C–WP/1214 Rev. (1952).

that the parties provide the Council with certain additional information relating to the dispute. The second proposed that the parties be urged "to enter into further direct negotiations as soon as possible with a view to limiting to the greatest possible extent the outstanding issues." [73] This proposal was prompted by the consideration that the Working Group had concluded, after consulting with the parties, that Pakistan and India were receptive to the possibility of reaching a negotiated settlement. [74] The Council accepted these recommendations,[75] and shortly thereafter appointed another Working Group to study the case with a view to ascertaining what further action should be taken.[76]

The new Working Group informed the Council that Pakistan was prepared to discuss with India the possibility of opening two air routes over West Pakistan in exchange for certain concessions by India,[77] and suggested that "no possibility of settlement by direct negotiations should be missed." The Council accepted this suggestion and set a time limit within which the parties were requested to submit a progress report on their negotiations.[78] Before this deadline had expired, the parties informed the Council that they had reached an amicable settlement of their dispute.[79]

It is noteworthy that these consultations between the parties and the Council's Working Groups, which never formally touched upon the merits of the dispute, produced a mutually satisfactory settlement of the dispute. This settlement was worked out in less than nine months. It was achieved mainly because the Council, having brought the parties together, eschewed adjudication in favor of mediation. Had the Council constituted itself immediately into an arbitral tribunal, a few years might have elapsed before the case

[73] In his oral report to the Council in explaining these recommendations, the Chairman of the Working Group noted that his committee "felt that there might not have been negotiations to the extent contemplated by Article 84 of the Convention. . . ." ICAO Council, 16th Sess., Doc. 7291 (C/845), p. 163 (1952). Technically, the correctness of this explanation may be doubted, for the Council had already accepted jurisdiction over the dispute.

[74] *Id.* at 164–65.

[75] *Id.* at 162.

[76] ICAO Council, 17th Sess., Doc. 7328 (C/853), p. 129 (1952).

[77] ICAO Doc. C–WP/1341 (1952).

[78] ICAO Council, 17th Sess., Doc. 7328 (C/853), p. 203 (1953).

[79] See ICAO Council, 18th Sess., Doc. 7361 (C/858), pp. 15–26 (1953); [1952] Report of the Council, ICAO Doc. 7367 (A7–P/1), pp. 74–76 (1953). The exchange of notes constituting the agreement that was reached by India and Pakistan can be found in 164 U.N.T.S. 3 (1953).

could finally have been decided, given the right of the parties to appeal the Council's judgment either to the International Court of Justice or to an *ad hoc* international tribunal.[80] The manner in which the dispute between India and Pakistan was resolved confirms the wisdom of the policy embodied in Article 14 of the Council's Rules for the Settlement of Disagreements. This policy seeks to avoid the full exercise, except as a last resort, of the Council's adjudicatory powers under the Convention. Of course, it also prevents the aggravation of disputes through protracted litigation, which cannot but adversely affect the best interests of international civil aviation generally.

THE DECISION

A dispute submitted to the Council under Article 84 of the Convention is decided by a majority vote of all Council Members not parties to the dispute.[81] Unless reversed or modified on appeal, the decision of the Council must be deemed to be final and binding on the parties, as well as on any other state that has intervened in the proceedings.[82] This conclusion follows, despite the fact that the Convention is silent on the question of the binding effect of such decisions and merely provides that "the decisions of the Permanent Court of International Justice and of an arbitral tribunal shall be final and binding." [83] It must be assumed, however, that if the parties fail to avail themselves of their right of appeal, the decision of the Council takes the place of the final and binding judgment that would otherwise be rendered on appeal.

The contrary conclusion would make little sense, for it would admit that a losing party could, by failing to appeal a Council decision, avoid a final and binding adjudication of the dispute. That the draftsmen of the Convention did not intend to establish such ineffective adjudicatory machinery is apparent from the language of Article 86 of the Convention. It provides in part that "unless the Council decides otherwise, any decision by the Council on whether an international airline is operating in conformity with the provisions of this Convention shall remain in effect unless reversed on

---

[80] Convention, Arts. 84, 85.
[81] Convention, Arts. 84, 52, 53; 1957 Rules, Art. 15.
[82] 1957 Rules, Art. 19.
[83] Convention, Art. 86.

appeal. On any other matter, the decisions of the Council shall, if appealed from, be suspended until the appeal is decided." Implicit in this provision is the assumption that Council decisions are final and binding unless they have been modified or reversed on appeal. This view is shared by the Council, for it has stipulated in its Rules for the Settlement of Differences that a state wishing to intervene in a dispute submitted to the Council "shall undertake that the decision of the Council will be *equally* binding upon it." (Emphasis added.) [84]

All Council decisions, except those relating to the question "whether an international airline is operating in conformity with the provisions" of the Convention, are automatically suspended pending final disposition on appeal. Decisions dealing with the operation of airlines remain in force unless the Council agrees to suspend them.[85] This difference in treatment was prompted by the consideration that the automatic suspension of decisions falling into the latter category might endanger the safety of international air transport.[86] Where such danger does not exist, the Council would probably suspend its decision in order to avoid the serious economic hardship that the requirement of immediate compliance by the airline might entail.

THE APPEAL

A decision rendered by the Council in a dispute submitted to it under Article 84 of the Convention is appealable by the parties either to an *ad hoc* arbitral tribunal or to the International Court of Justice.

Notice of Appeal and Time Limits

The Convention does not contain an express provision establishing a time limit within which an appeal must be lodged. All it provides is that "any such appeal shall be notified to the Council within sixty days of receipt of notification of the decision of the Council." [87] This language indicates that a party, to reserve its right

[84] 1957 Rules, Art. 19(1).
[85] Convention, Art. 86.
[86] See 1 PROCEEDINGS OF THE INTERNATIONAL CIVIL AVIATION CONFERENCE, (CHICAGO, ILLINOIS, NOVEMBER 1–DECEMBER 7, 1944) [hereinafter cited as PROCEEDINGS] 480–81 (1948).
[87] Convention, Art. 84.

of appeal, must notify the Council within this period of its intention to file an appeal. It can also be said to imply, and the International Court of Justice might so find, that an appeal to the Court must be lodged within the same period.[88] This interpretation would not necessarily apply to a party wishing to appeal to an *ad hoc* tribunal, however, for the tribunal will probably first have to be constituted.

It must therefore be asked whether there is any time limit within which an appeal to such a tribunal must be lodged. In theory, the answer would seem to be in the negative. There are certain practical considerations, however, which overcome this drafting omission. In addressing ourselves to them, reference should be made to a statement of the Group of Experts appointed by the ICAO Council to finalize the Council's Rules for the Settlement of Differences. In its report to the Council, this committee took the position that Article 84 of the Convention implies "that an appeal to the International Court of Justice has to be filed within the same period of 60 days. . . ." And, after noting that this interpretation was far from being "self-evident," the Group of Experts expressed the opinion that ". . . in the case of an appeal to an *ad hoc* arbitral tribunal no time limit is fixed within which the tribunal shall be set up or have started its work, and consequently the case may remain pending *ad infinitum*." [89]

Of course, if the parties desire to have the case remain pending before the arbitral tribunal indefinitely, their wishes will probably prevail.[90] That is stating the obvious because, if one of the litigants wants the tribunal to be constituted promptly, it need only invoke Article 85 of the Convention which stipulates that, whenever one of the parties fails to name an arbitrator "within a period of three months from the date of appeal," the President of the Council shall exercise that power on its behalf. Article 85 also provides that if the arbitrators cannot agree within another 30-day period on the choice of an umpire, he will be designated by the President of the Council.

[88] See I.C.J., Rules of Court, Art. 67(2); ICAO Doc. C–WP/2271, p. 7 (1956).

[89] ICAO Doc. C–WP/2271, p. 7 (1956).

[90] Even here it might be possible for the Council to step in. It could do so under Article 85 of the Convention, which authorizes the Council "to determine procedural questions in the event of any delay which in the opinion of the Council is excessive." The Council could invoke this power to prevent an indefinite suspension of its decision.

It must accordingly be concluded that, assuming the President of the Council acts promptly, it will take a maximum of four to five months, following the notice of appeal under Article 84, for the tribunal to be constituted. The absence of an express time limit within which an appeal must be filed cannot therefore have the effect of indefinitely delaying the establishment of the arbitral tribunal or the conduct of the proceedings.

Choice of Appellate Tribunal

The Convention is not entirely clear whether the parties to a dispute have a choice in submitting their appeal to the International Court of Justice [91] or to an *ad hoc* arbitral tribunal.[92] Article 84 provides in part that "any contracting State may, subject to Article 85, appeal from the decision of the Council to an *ad hoc* arbitral tribunal agreed upon with the other parties to the dispute or to the Permanent Court of International Justice." Article 85 states that "if any contracting State party to a dispute . . . has not accepted the Statute of the Permanent Court of International Justice and the contracting States parties to the dispute cannot agree on the choice of the arbitral tribunal, each . . . shall name a single arbitrator who shall name an umpire." Obviously, the appeal cannot be submitted to the Court if one of the parties to the dispute has not accepted the Statute and is unwilling to consent to its jurisdiction to decide this particular case.[93] Articles 84 and 85 also compel the conclusion that the parties, even if they adhere to the Statute, may by mutual agreement bypass the Court,[94] for these provisions speak of the Court and the *ad hoc* tribunal as alternative appellate fora without expressing a preference for one or the other.

It is less clear whether, in the absence of an agreement to submit the case to an arbitral tribunal, each state is free to take the appeal to the International Court of Justice whenever all parties to the dispute adhere to the Statute of the Court. In other words, it must be asked whether the Contracting States which have accepted the

[91] Due to the provisions of Article 37 of the Statute of the International Court of Justice, the reference in Articles 84 and 85 of the Convention to the Permanent Court of International Justice must be understood to apply to the I.C.J. See note 5 *supra*.

[92] See Kos-Rabcewicz-Zubkowski 347.

[93] See I.C.J., Statute, Arts. 35 and 36.

[94] Kos-Rabcewicz-Zubkowski 347; Domke 21 n.6. *But see* Cheng 104.

Statute have, in Articles 84 and 85, consented to the compulsory jurisdiction of the Court to hear such appeals. While the Convention does not expressly so provide, its language compels an affirmative reply.[95]

The procedure envisaged by Article 85 for the establishment of an *ad hoc* tribunal is applicable only if two conditions are met. It must appear that the parties have not accepted the Statute of the Court and that they cannot agree on the composition of the tribunal, but no provisions are made for its establishment if the parties adhere to the Statute but cannot agree on the *ad hoc* tribunal. This would be a serious and inexplicable oversight, unless it was understood that in these circumstances each party to the dispute would have the right to take the case to the Court. The distinction made in Article 85 between states that have and those that have not accepted the Statute would be meaningless, moreover, unless it was intended to have the jurisdictional significance contemplated by Article 36(1) of the Statute,[96] for even a state not a party to the Statute can submit to the Court's jurisdiction in a particular case.[97]

Finally, since Article 36(1) of the Statute provides an independent jurisdictional basis,[98] it can hardly be contended that the appeal under Article 84 of the Convention is subject to a Contracting State's acceptance of the Court's jurisdiction under Article 36(2) of the Statute. It must accordingly be concluded that, if all parties to the dispute have accepted the Statute, each of them has the right to appeal the Council's decision to the International Court of Justice.

Composition of ad hoc Tribunal

Article 85 of the Convention provides that, when the parties have not accepted the Statute of the International Court of Justice and cannot themselves agree on the choice of an *ad hoc* tribunal, each of

---

[95] See Cheng 104.

[96] I.C.J., Statute, Art. 36(1) provides in part that "the jurisdiction of the Court comprises . . . all matters specially provided for . . . in treaties and conventions in force." See Institut für ausländisches öffentliches Recht und Völkerrecht, STATUT ET RÈGLEMENT DE LA COUR PERMANENTE DE JUSTICE INTERNATIONALE: ELÉMENTS D'INTERPRÉTATION 256–66 (1934).

[97] See I.C.J., Statute, Art. 35(2); Rosenne 238–39.

[98] Guggenheim, *L'élaboration d'une clause modèle de compétence obligatoire de la Cour internationale de Justice,* 44/1 Annuaire de l'Institut de Droit International 458, 466 (1952).

them has the right to name an arbitrator. The arbitrators, in turn, designate an umpire. The President of the Council has the power to exercise a party's right to name an arbitrator, if the arbitrator has not been appointed within a period of three months from the date of the appeal. The President must, however, make his selection "from a list of qualified and available persons maintained by the Council." [99]

The list in question, consisting of names submitted to the Council by Member States, was formally established by the Council in 1963.[100] This list has been left open to enable the President to add any new names that the Contracting States might wish to submit.[101] The Council apparently proceeds on the assumption, although Article 85 does not compel it, that this list should consist of names submitted by the Member States. The Council has at the same time recognized that, if it should prove necessary to designate a particular individual whose name is not on the list, the President of the Council may invite his formal designation.[102] Finally, whenever the arbitrators cannot agree on the choice of an umpire within 30 days, that individual will also be designated by the President of the ICAO Council from the list previously referred to.

Scope of Appeal

The Convention does not specify what questions the appellate tribunal may review.[103] All we are told is that "any arbitral tribunal established under this or the preceding Article [84] shall settle its own procedure and give its decisions by majority vote. . . ." [104] Since the Convention does not, however, limit the powers of the appelate tribunal, it can be concluded that the tribunal may review any findings of law and/or fact made by the ICAO Council. Whether new issues—that is, questions of law or fact not argued before the ICAO Council—may be considered by the appellate tribunal is more doubtful. Unless all the parties involved consent

---

[99] Convention, Art. 85.

[100] See [1963] Report of the Council, ICAO Doc. 8402 (A15–P/2), p. 92 (1964).

[101] ICAO Council, 15th Sess., Doc. 8373 (C/948), p. 142 (1964).

[102] *Id.* at 146–48.

[103] The appellate jurisdiction of international tribunals varies considerably depending upon the treaty that establishes them. See generally on this subject, Simpson & Fox 247–50; Hudson 430–33.

[104] Convention, Art. 85.

thereto, these issues would seem to be *ultra vires* the jurisdiction of the appellate tribunal. This is so not because of any formalistic notions of estoppel, but because the consent to the jurisdiction of the appellate tribunal is limited to the review of those issues that were submitted to the ICAO Council for adjudication. However, except for this limitation, the appellate tribunal may hear the case *de novo,* unless the parties agree to limit the scope of review.

While the Convention authorizes the appellate tribunal to fix its own rules of procedure,[105] it reserves to the Council the power to "determine procedural questions in the event of any delay which in the opinion of the Council is excessive." [106] Questions regarding the scope of the appellate tribunal's jurisdiction, while technically procedural in nature, are probably not encompassed by this provision, which in all likelihood applies only to the difficulties that the *ad hoc* tribunal might encounter in the actual conduct of its proceedings.[107]

ENFORCEMENT OF DECISIONS

Articles 87 and 88 of the Convention establish certain enforcement measures to bring about compliance with the decisions rendered under Article 84. Two distinct types of sanctions are provided for.[108]

Penalty for Non-Compliance by Airlines

The first, set out in Article 87, stipulates that "each contracting State undertakes not to allow the operation of an airline of a contracting State through the airspace above its territory if the

[105] For the procedure that will be followed by the International Court of Justice, see its Rules of Court, Art. 67.

[106] Convention, Art. 85.

[107] In this connection, it is interesting to note that Art. 30 of the 1946 Rules provided:

(1) In the event of any delay which in the opinion of the Council is excessive, the Council shall determine the rules of procedure of the arbitral tribunal.

(2) These rules shall include the provisions of the Articles 5, 6, 7, 9, 10, 11, 13 and 14 of the present rules.

(3) The Council shall also fix the seat of the arbitral tribunal.

The rules to which Article 30(2) referred deal with questions relating to the actual conduct of the proceedings. See Domke 28–29.

[108] See Mateesco Matte, TRAITÉ DE DROIT AÉRIEN-AÉRONAUTIQUE 222–23 (2d ed. 1964).

Council has decided that the airline concerned is not conforming to a final decision rendered in accordance with the previous Article." [109] The sanction envisaged by this provision cannot be imposed until the Council "has decided that the airline concerned is not conforming to a final decision rendered in accordance with the previous Article." The "previous Article" is Article 86 of the Convention, which provides that the decisions of the International Court of Justice or the *ad hoc* arbitral tribunal are final and binding. It also stipulates that a Council decision relating to the question whether an international airline is operating in conformity with the provisions of the Convention "shall remain in effect unless reversed on appeal," provided that the Council has not authorized its suspension. Reading these two provisions together, a number of conclusions and problems emerge.

Initially, it will be noted that it is not for the Contracting States themselves to determine whether the airline in question has failed to comply with a final judgment. A Council decision to that effect is a condition precedent to the application of this penalty, but any Contracting State, even if not a party to the dispute, may request the Council to take this action because Article 54(n) of the Convention empowers the Council to "consider any matter relating to the Convention which any contracting State refers to it."

The determination that an airline is in default of its obligations under a final decision is bound to have serious economic consequences for the airline. The Council should therefore not act without giving the airline or the state of its nationality an opportunity to be heard. In some cases, such a hearing might reveal difficult questions of law or fact bearing directly on the issue of compliance. There may be defenses justifying non-compliance,[110] or differences of opinion relating to the interpretation of the judgment. Neither

---

[109] Since only Contracting States can be applicants and respondents in an action under Article 84, the original decision will have been rendered in a proceeding to which the airline was not a formal party.

[110] As one commentator rightly notes, "rarely, if ever, is the failure to comply unsupported by a legal claim; the decision it will be argued, cannot be binding if it is invalid under law or unenforceable in practice." Schachter, *Enforcement of International Judicial and Arbitral Decisions*, 54 Am. J. Int'l L. 1, 3 (1960). See, in this connection, International Law Commission, Model Rules on Arbitral Procedure, Art. 35, [1958] YEARBOOK OF THE INTERNATIONAL LAW COMMISSION, Vol. 2, p. 83, which recognizes four grounds upon which the validity of a decision of an arbitral tribunal may be challenged.

the Convention nor the present Rules for the Settlement of Differences contain any provisions relating to the procedure to be followed in disposing of these questions.[111] They might, however, be treated in a number of ways. Because Article 87 of the Convention empowers the Council to decide upon the existence of a default, it is arguable that the Council alone is competent to pass on these issues. In doing so, the Council could seek an advisory opinion from the International Court of Justice pursuant to Article X of the Agreement between the United Nations and ICAO.[112] Where the existence of a default depends upon the interpretation of the underlying judgment, or when it is sought to be justified on the ground of newly discovered evidence, the state of the airline's nationality should be given an opportunity to obtain an interpretation or revision of the judgment from the appellate tribunal that rendered it. This could easily be done if the case was appealed to the International Court of Justice.[113]

On the other hand, if the appeal was taken to an *ad hoc* tribunal, an interpretation or revision of the judgment will not always be obtainable, because it may be impossible to reconstitute the tribunal. Besides, even if this hurdle can be surmounted, it must be remembered that "the general rule is that an international tribunal has no power to interpret its award, unless it is expressly authorised

---

[111] Articles 19 and 20 of the Rules for the Settlement of Differences Between Contracting States, ICAO Doc. 7392 (C/862), provisionally promulgated by the Council in 1953, provided for the revision and interpretation of Council decisions. These provisions were not incorporated in the 1957 Rules because the Group of Experts concluded that "the Council would have no authority to revise or interpret a decision given by it." ICAO Doc. C–WP/2271, p. 6 (1956). This conclusion can be traced to the opinion expressed by the ICAO Legal Bureau, which asserted that these provisions were "outside the competence of the Council to promulgate." In its view, "powers of 'revision' or of 'interpretation of decisions' do not exist unless they are provided for in the Statute constituting the tribunal (in the present case Chapter XVIII of the Chicago Convention) or are included in the *compromis* from which an arbitral tribunal derives its powers." ICAO Doc. C–WP/1685 (1954). This conclusion is no doubt true as far as it goes, but its proponents seem to have overlooked the fact that, unlike other international arbitral tribunals, the ICAO Council also has the express power to determine the existence of a default and to impose sanctions for non-compliance with its decisions. It would therefore seem that this power presupposes the authority to interpret the decision which is to be applied and, in proper cases, to sustain defenses justifying non-compliance.

[112] 8 U.N.T.S. 316 (1947).

[113] See I.C.J. Statute, Arts. 60–61; and Rules of Court, Arts. 78–81.

to do so by its constitutive instruments, or unless the parties reach a fresh agreement inviting it to do so." [114]

Assuming, however, that such an interpretation or revision can be obtained from the International Court of Justice or the *ad hoc* tribunal, it would still have to be ascertained whether the Council must follow it in passing on the question of non-compliance. The Council, not being a party to the proceedings, is not bound by the decision of the appellate tribunal in the sense that a party would be. It should not be forgotten, however, that the Council's decision imposing a penalty for non-compliance with a final judgment must be based on a finding that the judgment is not being complied with. So long as the competent appellate tribunal interprets or revises that judgment,[115] the Council will have to take that interpretation into account before deciding whether a default does in fact exist. These problems will not arise in cases where the parties to the dispute failed to appeal the original decision of the Council. Since decisions rendered by the Council under Article 84 become final when no appeal has been taken, it would follow that in this context the power to decide all issues of law and fact relating to non-compliance rests exclusively with the Council.

It remains to be noted that no appeal can be taken against a determination by the ICAO Council that an airline is in default of the obligations incumbent upon it under a final decision. Once this ruling has been made, all Contracting States are bound to bar the airline from operating through the airspace above their territory.

Penalty for Non-Compliance by States

Article 88 of the Convention provides that "the Assembly shall suspend the voting power in the Assembly and in the Council of any contracting State that is found in default under the provisions of this Chapter." The language of Article 88 indicates that this provi-

---

[114] Simpson & Fox 245. The same view was expressed by the Permanent Court of International Justice. See Advisory Opinion regarding the delimitation of the Polish-Czechoslovak Frontier (Question of Jaworzina), P.C.I.J., Ser. B, No. 8, p. 38 (1923).

[115] See Interpretation of Judgments Nos. 7 and 8 (The Chorzów Factory), P.C.I.J., Ser. A, No. 13, p. 21 (1927), where the Court stated that an interpretation of a judgment "adds nothing to the decision, which has acquired the force of *res judicata*, and can only have binding force within the limits of what was decided in the judgment construed."

sion can be invoked against a state party to a dispute which has failed to comply with a final judgment, as well as against any other Contracting State which continues to allow a defaulting airline, contrary to a decision of the Council under Article 87, to operate through the airspace above its territory.[116] It is thus readily apparent that Article 88 gives the Organization considerable leverage for the enforcement of decisions rendered under Chapter XVIII of the Convention.

Unlike Article 87, Article 88 does not specifically identify the ICAO organ that is empowered to determine the existence of the default to which Article 88 applies. All it provides is that "the Assembly shall suspend" the voting powers of the state found to be in default of its obligations under Chapter XVIII. A number of considerations do support the conclusion, however, that this power is vested in the ICAO Assembly.

The only other body which could have been empowered to make this decision is the Council. Since Article 87 gives the Council similar powers expressly, it is only reasonable to assume that if Article 88 had contemplated like functions for the Council it would have contained a clause to that effect. The question to be decided by the Council under Article 87 is in all respects a legal question. Since the Council has been given judicial powers, it is only proper that it should also be competent to decide the legal questions which might arise under Article 87. Article 88, on the other hand, presents issues which are not strictly legal in nature. True, the question whether a state is in default of its obligations under Chapter XVIII is legal in character, but the resultant obligation placed upon the Assembly to suspend a state's voting power in the Organization cannot be divorced from the political and economic implications inherent in such action.[117]

Accordingly, since the Assembly *must* impose this penalty once the state has been found to be in default,[118] it may be assumed that

[116] Hingorani 23.

[117] Analogous considerations will have to be taken into account by the Security Council in applying Article 94 of the U.N. Charter. See Schachter, *supra* note 110, at 20–21.

[118] *Compare* Convention, Art. 88 *with* Art. 62. Under Article 62 the Assembly "may" suspend the voting powers of a state that has defaulted in its financial obligations to the Organization. Article 88, on the other hand, makes such action mandatory, since it provides that the Assembly "shall" do so.

the Assembly was also assigned the function of ascertaining the existence of the default. This would enable it to appreciate the various non-legal considerations involved in depriving a state of its vote without appearing to condone lawlessness by refusing, for example, to implement a Council recommendation that sanctions should be imposed. In other words, if it should deem the imposition of the sanction politically unwise, the Assembly could simply find that the alleged default has not been proved or that the state should be given more time to discharge its obligations.

Since the draftsmen of the Convention were undoubtedly aware of these considerations, it is only reasonable to assume that they took them into account in formulating Article 88. This conclusion is not weakened by the fact that Article 54(k) requires the Council to report to the Assembly "any infraction of this Convention," for the Council's report to the Assembly concerning an infraction of the Convention does not *ipso facto* deprive the Assembly of the power to verify the Council's findings.[119]

Before suspending a state's voting powers in accordance with Article 88, the Assembly will no doubt adopt a policy of restraint similar to that it has followed in applying Article 62 of the Convention, which calls for the suspension of the voting powers of states found to be in default of their financial obligations.[120] While it is true that under Article 62 the Assembly "may" impose this sanction, whereas Article 88 provides that it "shall" do so, it has already been shown that as a practical matter Article 88 gives the Assembly considerable discretion in applying these enforcement measures. The difference between Articles 62 and 88 may therefore be more apparent than real. It is accordingly unlikely that a state will be deprived of its vote under Article 88 unless it has made no effort to persuade the Assembly of its attempts in good faith to remedy the default.[121] Such considerations as *bona fide* delays resulting from the lack of implementing legislation, serious economic dislocations that might result from too rapid a compliance with the decision in

---

[119] The argument made by Hingorani 23, who asserts that the Assembly should exercise its powers under Article 88 in accordance with the Council recommendation, would deprive the Assembly of the flexibility it needs to appreciate the political considerations implicit in the exercise of this power.

[120] See discussion in Part I, pp. 47–51 *supra.*

[121] See Assembly Res. A9–6, ICAO Doc. 7595 (A9–P/12) (1955).

question, lack of requisite technical skills or equipment, and so on, will undoubtedly be factors which the Assembly would take into account before ruling on the existence of a default.

If the Assembly does find, however, that a state has not discharged the obligations incumbent upon it under Article 88, it will have to suspend that state's voting powers in the Council and in the Assembly. Should that state remain recalcitrant, the Assembly will no doubt proceed in a manner analogous to the practice it has developed under Article 62. That is to say, its next step might be to extend the suspension to all or only some of the subsidiary bodies of the Council and the Assembly.[122] This action might in due time be supplemented by a resolution authorizing the Council to withhold the general services furnished by the Organization to that state.[123] Ultimately, the Assembly might even recommend that the delinquent state be barred from participation in some or all meetings or conferences convened by the Organization.[124]

One final point bearing on the application of Article 88 has to do with a problem that could arise if a case submitted to the Council under Article 84 was appealed to the International Court of Justice, and the successful party sought to seize the U.N. Security Council under Article 94 of the Charter with a request for assistance in implementing the judgment of the Court. Article 94 of the Charter of the United Nations provides that

> 1. Each Member of the United Nations undertakes to comply with the decision of the International Court of Justice in any case to which it is a party.
>
> 2. If any party to a case fails to perform the obligations incumbent upon it under a judgment rendered by the Court, the other party may have recourse to the Security Council, which may, if it deems necessary, make recommendations or decide upon measures to be taken to give effect to the judgment.[125]

---

[122] Compare Assembly Res. A2–1, ICAO Doc. 5692 (A2–P/37) (1948), with Assembly Res. A3–6, ICAO Doc. 6459 (A3–P/28) (1949).

[123] See Assembly Res. A5–2, ICAO Doc. 7173 (A5–P/3) (1951).

[124] See ICAO Assembly, Commission No. I, ICAO Doc. 4013 (A1–CP/1), p. 5, para. 10(b) (1947).

[125] Under Article 93(2) of the U.N. Charter, states which are not Members of the United Nations may become parties to the Statute of the International Court of Justice "on conditions to be determined in each case by the General Assembly upon the recommendation of the Security Council." See also, I.C.J.

While much has been written about the role of the Security Council under Article 94 of the Charter,[126] the question here under consideration does not seem to have been explored.

In answering this question, it would appear that an appeal taken to the International Court of Justice from a Council decision rendered under Article 84 of the Convention, while subject to the Court's Statute and its Rules of Court [127]—and therefore implicitly also to Article 94 of the Charter—should not be divorced from the general scheme of the Convention. A party to such a dispute should therefore have to resort initially to the enforcement measures which the Convention provides. Only if they have failed to produce compliance with the Court's judgment would it be proper for the successful party to seek the assistance of the Security Council. In short, since the Convention establishes enforcement measures applicable to disputes under Article 84, they should first be exhausted.

While the possibility of a Security Council intervention under Article 94 of the Charter might prompt certain states to bypass the Court by submitting their appeal to an *ad hoc* tribunal, this step will not necessarily enable them to escape U.N. involvement. True, Article 94 of the Charter, unlike Article 13(4) of the Covenant of the League of Nations, does not apply to arbitral awards.[128] This does not mean, however, that the Security Council, the General Assembly, or some other international institution is without power, in a proper

---

Statute of the Court, Art. 35(2). On 15 October 1946, the U.N. Security Council resolved that the adherence of such non-Member States to the Statute of the Court should be conditioned, *inter alia*, on their undertaking "to accept all obligations of a Member State of the United Nations under Article 94 of the Charter." U.N. Security Council, Off. Rec., 1st year, 2d Ser., No. 19, pp. 467–68 (1946). The General Assembly has imposed this condition. See, *e.g.*, U.N. Gen. Ass. Res. 91 (I), of 11 December 1946, U.N. Gen. Ass. Off. Rec., 1st Sess., 2d pt., RESOLUTIONS 182–83 (A/64 Add. 1) (1947), relating to the adherence of Switzerland to the Statute of the Court. Accordingly, even states that are not Members of the United Nations might be subject to the provisions of Article 94 of the U.N. Charter.

[126] See, *e.g.*, Schachter, *supra* note 110, at 17–24; Tuncel, L'EXÉCUTION DES DÉCISIONS DE LA COUR INTERNATIONALE DE JUSTICE SELON LA CHARTE DES NATIONS UNIES (1960); Rosenne 102–15; Vulcan, *L'Exécution des Decisions de la Cour Internationale de Justice d'Après la Charte des Nations Unies*, 51 Revue Générale de Droit International Public 187 (1947).

[127] See I.C.J., Rules of Court, Art. 67.

[128] For an analysis of Article 13(4) of the Covenant, see Hambro, L'EXÉCUTION DES SENTENCES INTERNATIONALES 68–95 (1936).

case, to take appropriate action designed to obtain compliance with a judgment rendered by an arbitral tribunal.[129] On this score, there is therefore little to be gained from preferring an arbitral tribunal to the Court.

Under the International Air Services Transit and Air Transport Agreements

The International Air Services Transit Agreement[130] and the International Air Transport Agreement[131] are companion agreements to the Convention on International Civil Aviation. Approximately seventy states are parties to the Transit Agreement, while the Transport Agreement is in force only with regard to a dozen countries. This is not at all surprising, because the former is much less burdensome than the latter. The Transit Agreement provides for the reciprocal exchange of transit rights—the so-called Two Freedoms.[132] That is to say, it stipulates in part that

> Each contracting State grants to the other contracting States the following freedoms of the air in respect of scheduled international air services:
> (1) The privilege to fly across its territory without landing;
> (2) The privilege to land for non-traffic purposes.[133]

The Transport Agreement, on the other hand, contemplates the reciprocal exchange of the Five Freedoms of the Air. It accords the transit rights set forth in the Transit Agreement and, in addition, recognizes three more. These are:

> The privilege to put down passengers, mail and cargo taken on in the territory of the State whose nationality the aircraft possesses;
> The privilege to take on passengers, mail and cargo destined for the territory of the State whose nationality the aircraft possesses;
> The privilege to take on passengers, mail and cargo destined for the

---

[129] See Sohn, *The Role of International Institutions as Conflict—Adjusting Agencies*, 28 U. Chi. L. Rev. 205, 225–27 (1961); Simpson & Fox 268; Rosenne 108–09.

[130] The International Air Services Transit Agreement, 59 Stat. 1693, E.A.S. No. 487, 84 U.N.T.S. 389 (1951), entered into force on 30 January 1945.

[131] The International Air Transport Agreement, 59 Stat. 1701, E.A.S. No. 488, 171 U.N.T.S. 387 (1953), entered into force on 8 February 1945.

[132] For an analysis of the Freedoms of the Air, see Cheng 8–17.

[133] Transit Agreement, Art. I, Sec. 1.

territory of any other contracting State and the privilege to put down passengers, mail and cargo coming from any such territory.[134]

The Transit and Transport Agreements contain identical provisions for the settlement of differences between the Contracting States. These provisions establish one procedure for the adjudication of disputes, and another for the disposition of complaints.

DISPUTES

Disputes between the Contracting Parties to the Transit and Transport Agreements are subject to the same procedure that applies to differences arising under the Convention on International Civil Aviation. Thus both Agreements provide:

> If any disagreement between two or more contracting States relating to the interpretation or application of this Agreement cannot be settled by negotiation, the provisions of Chapter XVIII of the . . . Convention shall be applicable in the same manner as provided therein with reference to any disagreement relating to the interpretation or application of the . . . Convention.[135]

Although we already considered Chapter XVIII (Articles 84–88) of the Convention and thus do not have to restate the procedure it establishes, it should be noted that the adjudicatory machinery provided for under the Transit and Transport Agreements presents certain special problems which need to be discussed.

The most serious problem results from the language of Article 66 of the Convention. It reads as follows:

> (a) The Organization shall also carry out the functions placed upon it by the International Air Services Transit Agreement and by the International Air Transport Agreement . . . in accordance with the terms and conditions therein set forth.
>
> (b) Members of the Assembly and the Council who have not accepted the International Air Services Transit Agreement or the International Air Transport Agreement . . . shall not have the right to vote on any questions referred to the Assembly or Council under the provisions of the relevant Agreement.

---

[134] Transport Agreement, Art. I, Sec. 1. A state not wishing to accord the Fifth Freedom may indicate its intention by a reservation or subsequent notice. Transport Agreement, Art. IV(1).

[135] Transit Agreement, Art. II, Sec. 2; Transport Agreement, Art. IV, Sec. 3.

On its face, Article 66(b) of the Convention applies also to the judicial functions which the Transit and Transport Agreements assign to the ICAO Council. If that conclusion is valid, a number of Council Members would be disqualified from rendering a decision under the Transit Agreement. Moreover, there would not even be a quorum in the Council to discharge its functions under the Transport Agreement.[136] This result can be avoided only if it can be shown that Article 66(b) does not apply to the judicial functions assigned to the Council by these two Agreements. Since the Transit and Transport Agreements stipulate that ". . . the provisions of Chapter XVIII of the . . . Convention shall be applicable *in the same manner as provided therein* . . ." (emphasis added),[137] it can be contended that the phrase "in the same manner" equates disputes under these Agreements to those arising under the Convention, thus excluding the application of Article 66(b).[138] This is a permissible interpretation because Article 66(a) of the Convention requires ICAO to carry out the functions assigned to it under the Transit and Transport Agreements "in accordance with the terms and conditions therein set forth."

The ICAO Council has apparently adopted this interpretation, since its Rules for the Settlement of Differences do not disfranchise those Members of the Council which are not parties to these Agreements.[139] Furthermore, in many cases it would be extremely difficult to do so. As the dispute between India and Pakistan indicates, one case may call for the application of the Convention as well as one or both of the Agreements. The elements of the dispute may accordingly be so interrelated that it would make little sense, if it were possible at all, to establish different voting patterns for their adjudication.

If disputes under the Transit and Transport Agreements are to be handled in exactly the same manner as those arising under the Convention, can the sanctions provided for in Articles 87 and 88 of

---

[136] ICAO Council, Rules of Procedure, Rule 34, Doc. 7559/3, Rev. 3 (1959), provides that "a majority of the Members of the Council shall constitute a quorum for the conduct of the business of the Council."

[137] Transit Agreement, Art. II, Sec. 2; Transport Agreement, Art. IV, Sec. 3.

[138] Cheng 455.

[139] 1957 Rules, Art. 15(5) provides merely that "no Member of the Council shall vote in the consideration by the Council of any dispute to which it is a party."

the Convention also be imposed for non-compliance with decisions relating to the Transit and Transport Agreements? Article 87 of the Convention, it will be recalled, deals with the measure that may be taken against an airline which has failed to comply with a final decision. Once the ICAO Council has ruled that such a default exists, "each contracting State" is under an obligation to bar the airline from operating through the airspace above its territory. But if the dispute is one relating to the Transit or Transport Agreements, to whom does the phrase "each contracting State" apply? Since Chapter XVIII of the Convention applies to disputes arising under these Agreements "in the same manner" as it does to disputes under the Convention, the phrase "each contracting State" can be said to refer to the parties to the Convention. This interpretation would create the somewhat anomalous, albeit not entirely novel, situation whereby states not parties to a treaty would be required to assist in its implementation. On the other hand, it is by no means impermissible to assume that in this context the phrase "each contracting State" refers only to the State Parties to the Transit and Transport Agreements. Valid arguments can thus be adduced in favor of either result although, if a dispute relates both to the Convention and one of these Agreements, it would not be unreasonable for the Council to require all parties to the Convention to impose the prohibition envisaged by Article 87.

Similar difficulties might arise in the application of the sanctions provided for in Article 88 of the Convention. It authorizes the suspension of a state's voting power in the Assembly and the Council for non-compliance with a decision rendered under Chapter XVIII. In applying this provision to disputes arising under the Transit or Transport Agreements we face two problems. The first is attributable to the language of Article 66(b) of the Convention and presents the question, discussed earlier, whether only parties to these Agreements may vote on the imposition of this penalty.

The second problem concerns the scope of the voting suspension. If the dispute arises under one of the Agreements, may the non-complying state be deprived of its vote in these bodies on all matters or only on those that relate to these Agreements? While the Assembly might in such a case initially impose the more limited suspension, it would seem to be authorized to disfranchise the state altogether. Since both the Transit and Transport Agreements refer to

Chapter XVIII as a whole, they can be said to incorporate by reference the entire enforcement machinery envisaged in Articles 87 and 88. Even if it be accepted that these provisions are modified by Article 66(b) and that certain countervailing considerations may be applicable to Article 87, this in no way affects the enforcement measures of Article 88. Had the draftsmen of the Agreements intended to limit the application of Article 88, they could easily have done so. That this was not an oversight on their part is apparent from the enforcement machinery they established for complaints, where they expressly stipulated that, if a state fails to take the corrective action recommended by the Council, it may be "suspended from its rights and privileges *under this Agreement. . . ."* (Emphasis added.) [140]

COMPLAINTS

The Transit and Transport Agreements establish the following identical procedure for dealing with complaints: [141]

A contracting State which deems that action by another contracting State under this Agreement is causing injustice or hardship to it, may request the Council to examine the situation. The Council shall thereupon inquire into the matter, and shall call the States concerned into consultation. Should such consultation fail to resolve the difficulty, the Council may make appropriate findings and recommendations to the contracting States concerned. If thereafter a contracting State concerned shall in the opinion of the Council unreasonably fail to take suitable corrective action, the Council may recommend to the [ICAO] Assembly . . . that such contracting State be suspended from its rights and privileges under this Agreement until such action has been taken. The Assembly by a two-thirds vote may so suspend such contracting State for such period of time as it may deem proper or until the Council shall find that corrective action has been taken by such State.[142]

---

[140] Transit Agreement, Art. II, Sec. 1; Transport Agreement, Art. IV, Sec. 2.

[141] The term "complaint" is here used to designate this action because it is so described in the Council's Rules for the Settlement of Differences. See 1957 Rules, Art. 1(2).

[142] Transit Agreement, Art. II, Sec. 1; Transport Agreement, Art. IV, Sec. 2. For an extensive analysis of these provisions, see Cheng 479–81; Kos-Rabcewicz-Zubkowski 352–56.

The Nature of the Proceedings

The language of the Transit and Transport Agreements is sufficiently unambiguous to indicate that Article 66(b) of the Convention applies to the complaint procedure that these Agreements establish.[143] Accordingly, only parties to these Agreements will have a vote in the ICAO Council and Assembly on matters relating to the functions which the Agreements assign to these ICAO organs.

Notwithstanding the silence of the Agreements on this question, Council Members which are parties to a complaint proceeding may not vote on Council decisions relating thereto.[144] Dr. Cheng, in reliance on the maxim *nemo debet esse judex in propria sua causa*, argues that this disqualification also extends to the functions assigned to the Assembly.[145] The validity of this contention is open to doubt. There is first the consideration that Article 53 of the Convention expressly disqualifies Council Members from voting in any dispute to which they are parties. No corresponding provision applies to the Assembly. Second, the functions which the Transit and Transport Agreements assign to the Assembly are not, strictly speaking, judicial in character. They merely empower, but do not require, the Assembly to impose sanctions for non-compliance. Here, as a result, the Assembly exercises the same political judgment that characterizes its work generally. Furthermore, the merits of the case will already have been decided by the Council. It is therefore rather doubtful whether the Assembly is exercising adjudicatory functions within the meaning of the principle that no one shall be a judge in his own case.

A state which "deems that action by another contracting State under this [Transit or Transport] Agreement is causing injustice or hardship to it, may request the Council to examine the situation." That is to say, it may file a complaint. The facts justifying the submission of a complaint could include questions relating to the interpretation or application of the Agreements. The states involved thus have a choice between filing a complaint or instituting a formal action under Chapter XVIII of the Convention.[146] In other words,

[143] See Cheng 455.
[144] Convention, Art. 53 provides that "no Member of the Council shall vote in the consideration by the Council of a dispute to which it is a party."
[145] Cheng 481.
[146] Kos-Rabcewicz-Zubkowski 355.

an "injustice or hardship" may be caused by action on the part of a Contracting State which is in violation of the Agreements, but it is not limited thereto. An "injustice or hardship" may encompass measures which, while otherwise permissible, are in a particular case improper or inequitable because of the effect they have or because of the manner in which they are applied.

Under Article I, Section 3, of the Transit Agreement, for example, airlines enjoying the privilege of stopping for non-traffic purposes in the territory of a Contracting State, may be required by the granting state "to offer reasonable commercial service at the points at which such stops are made." The exercise of this right is subject, *inter alia*, to the requirement that it not "involve any discrimination between airlines operating on the same route." The determination of the question whether or not a state is exercising this right in a discriminatory manner calls for the interpretation of the Agreement. It could accordingly form the basis for a formal application under Chapter XVIII of the Convention. If the measure were discriminatory, it would *ipso facto* be an injustice justifying the filing of a complaint.

These alternative remedies will not always be available. Under the Transit Agreement, for example, each Contracting State "reserves the right to . . . revoke a certificate or permit to an air transport enterprise of another State . . . where it is not satisfied that substantial ownership and effective control are vested in nationals of a contracting State. . . ." [147] If such effective control is in fact not vested in nationals of a Contracting State, a state would be free to revoke the permit it had granted to the airline in question. If the case were submitted for adjudication to the ICAO Council, the legal right to take this action would have to be sustained. This would be true, notwithstanding a showing that the permits of other airlines equally situated were not withdrawn, and that this particular airline was singled out because certain political disagreements had developed between the state of its nationality and the granting state. This situation is one in which an action lawful in itself might be characterized as being unjust by virtue of the motives that prompted it. [148]

---

[147] Transit Agreement, Art. I, Sec. 5.

[148] In some legal systems, notably the French and that governing the European Communities, it could be set aside as an abuse of power (*détournement de pouvoir*). See Buergenthal, *Appeals for Annulment by Enterprises in the Euro-*

If the permit were to be withdrawn on very short notice, it might cause the airline severe economic hardship. Here, no other remedy but that provided by the complaint procedure could be invoked.

This example indicates that the complaint procedure is designed primarily to provide a machinery for the adjustment of frictions of an economic or political type that might otherwise disrupt the orderly operation of the system established by the Transit and Transport Agreements. The role which the ICAO Assembly and Council here perform, and the nature of the complaint procedure, were well described by Dr. Cheng in the following passage:

> The jurisdiction which these two multilateral agreements confer on the Assembly and the Council of the ICAO is not strictly arbitral. The recommendations of the Council and the decisions of the Assembly are to be based not exclusively on the legal rights and duties of the parties. They may take into account considerations of equity and convenience, and their function, from this point of view, is not unlike that which the International Court of Justice is entitled to discharge . . . under Article 38(2) of its Statute, that is to say, settlement of a dispute *ex aequo et bono*.[149]

It should be noted, however, that the Council has rather limited powers when it deals with complaints. After it has received a complaint, the Council must inquire into the matter by consulting with the states concerned. If these consultations fail to resolve the controversy and the Council concludes that a given measure is causing injustice or hardship, it "may make appropriate findings and recommendations to the contracting States concerned."[150] The state to which a recommendation for corrective action is addressed has no clear obligation to comply with it, because the Transit and Transport Agreements provide that the Council may recommend enforcement measures only if "a contracting State concerned shall in the opinion of the Council unreasonably fail to take suitable corrective

pean Coal and Steel Community, 10 Am. J. Comp. L. 227, 239–42 (1961). Under French law an administrative act will be set aside as an abuse of power if it was prompted by illegal motives, even though the act is within the administrator's granted powers and all objective legal requirements have been complied with in promulgating it. Rohkam & Pratt, STUDIES IN FRENCH ADMINISTRATIVE LAW 37 (1947); Odent, CONTENTIEUX ADMINISTRATIF 615–16 (1953–54).

[149] Cheng 481–82.
[150] Transit Agreement, Art. II, Sec. 1; Transport Agreement, Art. IV, Sec. 2.

action." [151] At most, therefore, a state has undertaken not to be unreasonable in its refusal to comply with the recommendation of the Council. It is thus probably under no legal obligation to take the specific action recommended by the Council or, for that matter, to take any action, provided it can adduce valid reasons in support of its position. In deciding whether to seek enforcement measures, the Council will therefore have to balance the equities. Since the reasons justifying non-compliance apparently need not be related to international civil aviation,[152] enforcement measures will rarely be forthcoming. As a practical matter, they will probably be granted only if a state makes no effort to cooperate or to participate in the consultations that the Agreements envisage.

The primary role which the Council thus performs in dealing with complaints is to provide a forum where difficulties between Contracting States can be ironed out in an institutional setting that is particularly well suited for compromise solutions. This is illustrated by a dispute which arose between Jordan and the United Arab Republic in 1958. It was brought to the attention of ICAO by Jordan, which requested the Council to "review the charges imposed by Syria for use of aeronautical services and facilities and report and make the necessary recommendations to Syria, in accordance with Article 15 of the Convention." [153] In its communication to the Council, Jordan also charged that it was subjected to great inconvenience and hardship because Syria was illegally requiring Jordanian air carriers in transit over Syria to land in that territory.[154] Shortly thereafter, the newly established United Arab Republic prohibited Jordanian planes to fly over or land in the U.A.R.[155] This action was ostensibly based on the charge that substantial ownership and effective control of the Jordanian airlines in question was not vested in Jordanian nationals as required by a bilateral agree-

---

[151] Transit Agreement, Art. II, Sec. 1; Transport Agreement, Art. IV, Sec. 2.

[152] This follows from the fact that the Council may recommend enforcement measures only if the state concerned "shall in the opinion of the Council *unreasonably* fail to take suitable corrective action. . . ." (Emphasis added.) Transit Agreement, Art. II, Sec. 1; Transport Agreement, Art. IV, Sec. 2.

[153] ICAO Doc. C–WP/2661, p. 5 (1958).

[154] It was never clear whether Jordan was submitting this matter to the Council as a complaint or dispute under the Transit Agreement, to which it and Syria, but not Egypt, were parties.

[155] Cable No. 1, ICAO Doc. C–WP/2743, p. 5 (1958).

ment between the two countries.[156] Jordan immediately retaliated by issuing a decree excluding U.A.R. carriers from its territory [157] and, shortly thereafter, requested the ICAO Council to intervene.[158] The U.A.R. followed suit. In a communication addressed to the Council, which charged Jordan with a violation of the Convention and the bilateral agreement, the U.A.R. asked the Council to "take the necessary measures to obtain a quick cancellation of the decision taken by Jordan against U.A.R. Carriers." [159]

The ICAO Council considered this matter on a number of occasions.[160] The orderly review of the charges and countercharges was hampered by the manner in which they had been submitted to the Council because, while the parties either expressly or implicitly relied on the Convention, the Transit Agreement, and their bilateral air agreement, they never formally invoked the jurisdiction of the Council under Chapter XVIII of the Convention or filed the requisite complaint under the Transit Agreement. Not wishing to transform this case—which was closely related to the then-prevailing explosive political situation in the Middle East [161]—into a formal dispute unless forced to do so, the Council simply asked the parties for more information on their respective positions.[162] The U.A.R. responded with the previously mentioned communication in which it charged Jordan with a violation of the Convention and the bilateral agreement.[163]

After discussing the matter again at some length,[164] the Council concluded that it was still not clear what specific action it was being requested to take, and instructed the Secretary General to ascertain

[156] Cable No. 3, ICAO Doc. C–WP/2743, p. 5 (1958).

[157] Cable No. 2, ICAO Doc. C–WP/2743, p. 5 (1958).

[158] Letter by Jordan to ICAO Secretary General, ICAO Doc. C–WP/2743, pp. 7–9 (1958).

[159] Letter from the U.A.R. Representative to the President of the ICAO Council, ICAO Doc. C–WP/2743, pp. 3–4 (1958).

[160] See ICAO Council, 33rd Sess., Doc. 7878 (C/905), pp. 243–46 (1958); ICAO Council, 34th Sess., Doc. 7902 (C/910), pp. 38–41, 60–67 (1958); ICAO Council, 35th Sess., Doc. 7934 (C/912), pp. 11–19 (1958).

[161] See ICAO Council, 35th Sess., Doc. 7934 (C/912), pp. 17–18 (1958).

[162] See Action of the Council, 33rd Sess., ICAO Doc. 7895 (C/908), p. 18 (1958); Action of the Council, 34th Sess., ICAO Doc. 7903 (C/911), p. 24 (1958).

[163] Letter from the U.A.R. Representative to President of the ICAO Council, ICAO Doc. C–WP/2743, pp. 3–4 (1958).

[164] ICAO Council, 35th Sess., Doc. 7934 (C/912), pp. 12–19 (1958).

whether the parties wished the Council to decide the dispute under Chapter XVIII of the Convention or under the arbitral clause of their bilateral agreement. At the same time, the Council invited Jordan and the U.A.R. "to permit air service between their countries to be resumed" and authorized its President "to offer his own good offices or those of the Secretary General towards finding a settlement of the difference."[165] The President of the Council entered into consultations with the two parties, and shortly thereafter informed the Council that both had agreed to permit the temporary resumption of air services between their respective countries.[166] Once air services were reestablished, the parties did not pursue the matter further.

While this case was not, of course, submitted to the Council as a formal complaint within the meaning of the Transit or Transport Agreements, it does indicate how difficulties arising under these Agreements might for the most part be resolved. Since the Council will usually succeed in getting the parties to reestablish the *status quo ante,* it will thereby be able to create an atmosphere conducive to compromise. The Council will therefore rarely have to rely on sanctions to obtain compliance with any recommendations that it might address to the parties. It is accordingly not surprising that the Council's Rules for the Settlement of Differences do not, in dealing with complaints,[167] contain any provisions relating to sanctions. But since the availability of sanctions may well make a state more receptive to compromise solutions, this topic merits consideration.

The Sanctions

The Transit and Transport Agreements both provide that, after the Council has made appropriate findings and recommendations, "if thereafter a contracting State concerned shall in the opinion of the Council unreasonably fail to take suitable corrective action, the Council may recommend to the Assembly . . . that such contracting State be suspended from its rights and privileges under this Agreement until such action has been taken."[168] The wording of this

---

[165] Action of the Council, 35th Sess., ICAO Doc. 7958 (C/914), p. 20 (1958).
[166] ICAO Doc. C–WP/2788, p. 5 (1958); [1958] Report of the Council, ICAO Doc. 7960 (A12–P/1), p. 60 (1959).
[167] 1957 Rules, Arts. 21–26.
[168] Transit Agreement, Art. II, Sec. 1; Transport Agreement, Art. IV, Sec. 2.

provision indicates that the Council may not seek these enforcement measures simply because the state concerned has not complied with the Council recommendation as such. Enforcement measures may be imposed only if the Council concludes that the state has "unreasonably" failed to take "suitable corrective action." A state thus runs no risk when it disregards the Council's recommendation, provided the steps it takes are intended to ameliorate the injustice or hardship complained of.[169] Accordingly, before the Council may recommend to the ICAO Assembly that the state be suspended from its rights and privileges under the applicable Agreement, three elements must be present. It will have to appear that the injustice or hardship persists, that the state has made no effort to mitigate it, and that it has advanced no valid reasons for its inaction. The Council is under no obligation, however, to request these sanctions, because both Agreements provide merely that the Council "may" do so.[170]

The power to impose enforcement measures is reserved to the ICAO Assembly. To demonstrate how difficult it will be in practice to obtain the sanctions provided for by the Transit and Transport Agreements, it should be noted initially that the Assembly may impose them only if they have been recommended by the Council. Second, even if the Council makes this recommendation, the Assembly is free to disregard it for it has the power, but not the obligation, to give effect to it. The victim of an injustice or hardship thus has no standing to compel the appropriate relief.[171] Finally, a majority of two-thirds is required in the Assembly to implement the Council's recommendation. For political reasons this may be extremely difficult to achieve, even assuming that the requisite quorum could be obtained.

However, the sanctions that may be imposed are quite severe, for the delinquent state can be suspended from its rights and privileges under the applicable Agreement. Thus, if the Transit Agreement is involved, its scheduled airlines will for the duration of the suspension no longer enjoy the right to fly over or to land for non-traffic

[169] If the measure which led to the submission of the complaint is lawful in itself, the state in question has the obligation only to mitigate its effect, but if it violates the Transport or Transit Agreement it will have to be rescinded.

[170] Transit Agreement, Art. II, Sec. 1; Transport Agreement, Art. IV, Sec. 2. See Kos-Rabcewicz-Zubkowski 355.

[171] See Kos-Rabcewicz-Zubkowski 355.

purposes in the territory of another Contracting State. A suspension under the Transport Agreement would have the effect of depriving those airlines of the Five Freedoms it guarantees. In theory, the delinquent state would at the same time have to accord these very rights to all Contracting States, because the suspension does not relieve it of its duties under the applicable Agreement.[172] It would be unrealistic, however, to believe that a state which has shown such a degree of recalcitrance as to warrant the imposition of sanctions would discharge this obligation. Instead, it would probably withdraw from the Agreement and decline to comply with any provision of the Agreement even before the effective date of its denunciation.[173]

In the final analysis, the effectiveness of the complaint procedure established by the Transit and Transport Agreements depends in large measure upon the willingness of the Contracting States to compromise for the sake of enjoying the benefits these Agreements confer. Because of its expertise in matters relating to international civil aviation, the ICAO Council can quite often provide the assistance necessary to achieve these compromise solutions. If the complaint machinery is viewed in this light, it hardly matters that the enforcement measures are for all practical purposes little more than an illusory remedy.

JUDICIAL FUNCTIONS ASSIGNED TO ICAO BY OTHER INTERNATIONAL AGREEMENTS

In addition to the Convention and the Transit and Transport Agreements, some multilateral and a large number of bilateral agreements confer judicial functions on the ICAO Council.

Under Multilateral Agreements

In three multilateral agreements, concluded under the auspices of and administered by ICAO, some ICAO Member States have undertaken to share in the financial support of air navigation facilities and services deemed vital to the safety of international air services

---

[172] *Id.* at 354.

[173] Both Agreements may be denounced on one year's notice to be given to the United States as depositary Government. Transit Agreement, Art. III; Transport Agreement, Art. V.

flying the busy North Atlantic air routes.[174] Two of these agreements provide for the joint financial support of certain ground stations operated by Iceland [175] and Denmark.[176] The third, entitled "Agreement on North Atlantic Ocean Stations," [177] deals with the financing, operation, and maintenance of ocean-station vessels providing navigational assistance to international air services.

Each of these agreements provides, in a substantially identical provision, that "any dispute relating to the interpretation or application of this Agreement . . . which is not settled by negotiation shall, upon the request of any Contracting Government party to the dispute, be referred to the Council for its recommendation." [178] The stipulation that the dispute may be "referred to the Council for its recommendation," indicates that the decision of the Council is not intended to be binding on the parties to the dispute.[179] Under these

---

[174] The Convention on International Civil Aviation contemplates the effectuation under ICAO auspices of such arrangements for the joint support of air navigation services. See Convention, Ch. XV. For a description of these services, see ICAO Secretariat, MEMORANDUM ON ICAO 31–37 (5th ed. 1966); Cheng 76–98.

[175] Agreement on the Joint Financing of Certain Air Navigation Services in Iceland [hereinafter cited as Joint Financing–Iceland], ICAO Doc. 7727 (JS/564) (1957), 334 U.N.T.S. 13 (1959). It was concluded at Geneva on 25 September 1956, and entered into force on 6 June 1958.

[176] Agreement on the Joint Financing of Certain Air Navigation Services in Greenland and the Faroe Islands [hereinafter cited as Joint Financing–Denmark], ICAO Doc. 7726 (JS/563) (1957), 334 U.N.T.S. 89 (1959). This agreement was concluded at Geneva on 25 September 1956, and entered into force on 6 June 1958.

[177] The Agreement on North Atlantic Ocean Stations, ICAO Doc. 7510 (JS/559), Appendix 8 (1954), 215 U.N.T.S. 268 (1955), was concluded at Paris on 25 February 1954, and entered into force on 1 February 1955.

[178] Agreement on North Atlantic Ocean Stations, Art. XV; Joint Financing–Denmark, Art. XVIII; Joint Financing–Iceland, Art. XVIII. The Agreement on North Atlantic Ocean Stations speaks of "any dispute relating to . . . this Agreement or [its] Annex II. . . ." The Joint Financing Agreements with Denmark and Iceland both refer to "any dispute relating to . . . this Agreement or the Annexes thereto."

[179] Article 15 of the Convention, which deals with airport and other charges, confers a similar advisory function on the Council. It provides in part that "upon representation by an interested Contracting State, the charges imposed for the use of airports and other facilities shall be subjected to review by the Council, which shall report and make *recommendations* thereon for the consideration of the State or States concerned." (Emphasis added.) See Cooper, *The Chicago Convention—After Twenty Years*, 14 Zeitschrift für Luftrecht und Weltraum—Rechtsfragen 273, 286–88 (1965).

agreements the ICAO Council thus has the power to render only advisory opinions.[180]

Much more extensive judicial powers are vested in the ICAO Council by the (Paris) Multilateral Agreement on Commercial Rights of Non-Scheduled Air Services in Europe.[181] The Paris Agreement, concluded under the auspices of the European Civil Aviation Conference,[182] regulates the reciprocal grant of commercial rights for the non-scheduled air services of the Member States of the ECAC. Article 4 of the Paris Agreement establishes an elaborate machinery for the settlement of disputes. It provides:

(1) If any dispute arises between Contracting States relating to the interpretation or application of the present Agreement, they shall in the first place endeavour to settle it by negotiation between themselves.

(2) (a) If they fail to reach a settlement they may agree to refer the dispute for decision to an arbitral tribunal or arbitrator.

(b) If they do not agree on a settlement by arbitration within one month after one State has informed the other State of its intention to appeal to such an arbitral authority, or if they cannot within an additional three months after having agreed to refer the dispute to arbitration reach agreement as to the composition of the arbitral tribunal or the person of the arbitrator, any Contracting State concerned may refer the dispute to the Council of the International Civil Aviation Organization for decision. No member of the Council shall vote in the consideration by the Council of any dispute to which it is a party. If said Council declares itself unwilling to entertain the dispute, any Contracting State concerned may refer it to the International Court of Justice.

---

[180] See ICAO Doc. C–WP/1457, p. 1 (1953).

[181] The Multilateral Agreement on Commercial Rights of Non-Scheduled Air Services in Europe [hereinafter cited as Paris Agreement], ICAO Doc. 7695 (1956), 310 U.N.T.S. 229 (1958), was concluded at Paris on 30 April 1956, and entered into force on 21 August 1957.

[182] The European Civil Aviation Conference, a regional affiliate of ICAO, was brought into being by ICAO and the Council of Europe. See Conference on Coordination of Air Transport in Europe, ICAO Doc. 7575 (CATE/1) (1954); European Civil Aviation Conference, Report of the First Session (Strasbourg, 29 November–16 December 1955), Res. No. 1, ICAO Doc. 7676 (ECAC/1), p. 5 (1956). On the organizational structure and functions of the ECAC, see Wheatcroft, THE ECONOMICS OF EUROPEAN AIR TRANSPORT 311–20 (1956); Cheng 56–62.

(3) The Contracting States undertake to comply with any decision given under paragraph (2) of this Article.[183]

Article 4 indicates that the jurisdiction of the Council to decide a dispute referred to it under the Paris Agreement is contingent, apart from the requirement of prior negotiations, on the failure of the parties to agree on the submission of the dispute to arbitration or on the composition of the tribunal. The ICAO Council thus has compulsory jurisdiction under Article 4 only when the parties cannot find a mutually acceptable forum.[184] If this happens, the case may be referred to the Council under Article 4(2)(b) by "any Contracting State concerned." In the context of the Paris Agreement, "any Contracting State concerned" can be read to include states not parties to the dispute.[185] True, we reached the opposite conclusion in interpreting the almost identical language found in Article 84 of the Convention, but that construction was justified by considerations which are inapplicable in the present context.

Article 4(2)(b) of the Paris Agreement specifies a definite time limit within which the parties must proceed to arbitration after one of them has given notice of its intention to do so. When such notice has been given, it is clear that at least one of them has concluded that further *inter partes* talks would serve no useful purpose. Article 84 of the Convention does not fix such a time limit. A state not involved in the negotiations is consequently in no position to judge whether the dispute is ripe for adjudication under Article 84. Here it would be unwise to give a third state standing to submit the dispute to the ICAO Council. No such countervailing considerations arise under Article 4 of the Paris Agreement.

If this interpretation of Article 4 of the Paris Agreement is correct, it must be asked to what states the phrase "any Contracting States concerned" applies. Dr. Cheng takes the position that, since all states adhering to a multilateral treaty are in some way "concerned" in its interpretation or application, each of them has the

---

[183] This Article provides further that "if and so long as any Contracting State fails to comply with a decision given under paragraph (2) of this Article, the other Contracting States may limit, withhold or revoke any rights granted to it by virtue of the present Agreement." Paris Agreement, Art. 4(4).

[184] It can be assumed, of course, that the parties could agree to select the Council, instead of some other body, to settle their dispute.

[185] Cheng 223.

right to submit the dispute to the Council.[186] The language of Article 4(2)(b) may neither compel nor permit this result, however, for under Cheng's construction the word "concerned" after "any Contracting State" becomes superfluous. To avoid this result, one could construe this clause as according standing to the parties to the dispute and to those states directly affected by it.[187] This construction may in some cases—e.g., cost-sharing—include all Contracting States.

The most interesting feature of Article 4 is the provision in paragraph 2(b) which permits the reference of the dispute to the International Court of Justice, if the ICAO Council "declares itself unwilling to entertain the dispute." [188] This clause was prompted by the consideration that, although the ICAO Assembly authorized the Council in 1947 "to act as an arbitral body on any differences arising among Contracting States relating to international civil aviation matters submitted to it, when expressly requested to do so by all parties to such differences," [189] the Council never accepted this broad grant of power.[190] Moreover, the Council's Rules for the Settlement of Differences, provisionally promulgated by it in 1953,[191] like the present 1957 Rules, apply only to disputes arising under the Convention and the Transit and Transport Agreements. And despite the fact that the Council, in adopting these Rules,

---

[186] *Ibid.*

[187] See 1957 Rules, Art. 19(1), where the right to intervene in a dispute submitted to the Council under Article 84 of the Convention is limited to Contracting States "directly affected by the dispute." The Council would probably reach a similar conclusion in applying Article 4 of this Agreement.

[188] The original draft of Article 4 contained the words "unwilling or unable." See European Civil Aviation Conference, Report of the First Session (Strasbourg, 29 November–16 December 1955), ICAO Doc. 7676 (ECAC/1), p. 34 (1956). The words "or unable" were dropped at a subsequent conference, which accepted a German draft of Article 4. See European Civil Aviation Conference, Report of the First Intermediate Meeting (Paris, 26 April 1956), ICAO Doc. 7696 (ECAC/IMI), p. 10 (1956). No reasons are given for this deletion.

[189] Assembly Res. A1–23, ICAO Doc. 4411 (A1–P/45) (1947).

[190] Here it should be noted, however, that the functions conferred on the Council by the Agreement on North Atlantic Ocean Stations was accepted by it on 7 April 1954. Action of the Council, 21st Sess., ICAO Doc. 7484 (C/872), p. 18 (1954). On 28 November 1956, it accepted the same obligations arising under the Agreements on the Joint Financing of Certain Air Navigation Services in Greenland and the Faroe Islands as well as in Iceland. Action of the Council, 29th Sess., ICAO Doc. 7763 (C/896), p. 27 (1957).

[191] ICAO Doc. 7392 (C/862) (1953).

reserved the right to apply them to disputes arising under other agreements,[192] the draftsmen of the Paris Agreement nevertheless had no real guarantee that the Council would accept the judicial functions assigned by Article 4 of the Agreement. It is therefore interesting to note that when the ICAO Council reviewed the Report of the First Session of the European Civil Aviation Conference,[193] which contained the draft of the Paris Agreement,[194] most of the discussion centered on Article 4, even though the Paris Agreement confers a number of other functions on the Organization. In this debate, the Representative of the United States suggested that "the Council should consider very carefully, and should certainly have the advice of the Legal Bureau, before accepting the responsibility, placed upon it by Article 4 . . . to arbitrate disputes over the interpretation or application of the Agreement." He took this position, the U.S. Representative explained, because "he doubted very much whether the Council would be able to consider such disputes, which would be between European States, when European States formed such a high proportion of its [the Council's] membership." [195]

When it was pointed out that the possibility that the Council might lack a quorum to decide a dispute was not a serious problem, since Article 4(2)(b) left the Council free not to adjudicate a particular case, the U.S. Representative replied that "it was not only the ability of the Council to arbitrate disputes under the Agreement about which he was doubtful. He wondered whether the Council had the right to take on any quasi-judicial functions beyond those given to it by the Convention." [196] Although the other Council Representatives apparently did not share these constitutional doubts, they agreed to a suggestion that the Council reserve its position with regard to Article 4 of the Agreement at least until after the Assembly had considered the relationship between ICAO and ECAC. The Council accordingly decided to inform ECAC "that ICAO will assume responsibility for the performance of the functions assigned to the Organization in Articles 5, 6, 7, 8 and 9 of the proposed Agree-

---

[192] Action of the Council, 19th Sess., ICAO Doc. 7408 (C/864), p. 29 (1953).
[193] ICAO Doc. 7676 (ECAC/1) (1956).
[194] Id. at 31.
[195] ICAO Council, 27th Sess., Doc. 7662 (C/890), p. 163 (1956).
[196] Ibid.

ment, but for the time being reserves its position in relation to the functions assigned to it in Articles 4 and 10." [197]

When the ICAO Assembly convened a few months later, it adopted a resolution in which it decided "to assume, on behalf of ICAO, the responsibilities that will devolve upon the Organization as a result of acceding to the request of ECAC. . . ." [198] This resolution prompted the Council to reconsider its earlier position and to accept the functions assigned to it under Article 4 of the Paris Agreement. [199]

Mention should also be made of the role assigned to the ICAO Council by a multilateral agreement on private international air law, namely, the (Rome) Convention on Damages Caused by Foreign Aircraft to Third Parties on the Surface. [200] The Rome Convention establishes uniform rules governing liability for surface damage inflicted by foreign aircraft. Paragraph (7) of Article 15, which deals with the recognition of certificates of financial responsibility issued to aircraft operators, contains the following provision:

(a) Where the State overflown has reasonable grounds for doubting the financial responsibility of the insurer, or of the bank which issues a guarantee under paragraph 4 of this Article, that State may request additional evidence of financial responsibility, and if any question arises as to the adequacy of that evidence the dispute affecting the States concerned shall, at the request of one of those States, be submitted to an arbitral tribunal which shall be either the

[197] *Id.* at 162. Article 10 of the Agreement deals with the role of ICAO in convening a conference to consider amendments to the Agreement. No reasons are given in the Council debates for the reservation relating to Article 10.

[198] Assembly Res. A10–5, ICAO Doc. 7707 (A10–P/16) (1956).

[199] See Action of the Council, 29th Sess. [1956], ICAO Doc. 7763 (C/896), p. 25 (1957).

For the view that the ICAO Council is not properly equipped to perform the judicial functions under the Paris Agreement, see Riese, *Das mehrseitige Abkommen über gewerbliche Rechte im nichtplanmässigen Luftverkehr in Europa,* 8 Zeitschrift für Luftrecht 127, 136 (1959).

[200] The Convention on Damages Caused by Foreign Aircraft to Third Parties on the Surface [hereinafter cited as Rome Convention], 310 U.N.T.S. 181 (1958), was signed in Rome, on 7 October 1952, and entered into force on 4 February 1958. See generally Rinck, *Damage Caused by Foreign Aircraft to Third Parties,* 28 J. Air L. & Com. 405 (1961–62); Kistler, DAS RÖMER HAFTUNGSABKOMMEN VON 1952 (1959).

Council of the International Civil Aviation Organization or a person or body mutually agreed by the parties.[201]

Article 15(7)(a) indicates that if the parties to the dispute fail to agree upon its submission to a different tribunal, each of them may seize the ICAO Council with jurisdiction to decide it. This result was clearly intended by those who drafted Article 15. Thus, when the Chairman of the "Committee on Article 15" was asked at the Rome Conference whether "it was the intention of the Conference in the case covered by this provision [Article 15(7)(a)] that, if the parties did not agree on an arbitrator, it would be compulsory for them to accept the arbitration of the ICAO Council if either party so requested," [202] he replied that

> in accordance with the decision of the Conference, the arbitration procedure was compulsory if one of the States concerned requested it. The other State would have to submit its dispute to arbitration with the State so requesting. The objective of this provision was to have the parties submit to the decision of the ICAO Council or of a court specially appointed by common agreement between the parties.[203]

It is therefore surprising to find a statement in the Report of the U.S. Delegation to the Rome Conference that it is not clear under Article 15(7)(a) "whether, in the event of the failure of the parties to agree upon another person or body, the Council of the ICAO automatically becomes the arbitral tribunal." [204] This statement is valid only if it is interpreted to mean that the Council's jurisdiction seems to be contingent on the case being submitted to it by one of the parties to the dispute. It cannot be doubted, however, that upon the failure of the parties to reach agreement on some other arbitral tribunal, each of them has the right to seize the Council with jurisdiction to decide the dispute.

[201] Pursuant to Article 15(7)(b) of the Rome Convention, the insurance or guarantee is to be considered "provisionally valid by the State overflown" until the tribunal envisaged in paragraph (7)(a) has rendered its decision.

[202] 1 CONFERENCE ON PRIVATE INTERNATIONAL AIR LAW (ROME, SEPTEMBER–OCTOBER 1952), ICAO Doc. 7379 (LC/34), p. 527 (1953).

[203] *Ibid.*

[204] United States Delegation to the International Conference held at Rome, Italy, September 9–October 7, 1952, *Summary Analysis of Convention on Damage Caused by Foreign Aircraft to Third Persons on the Surface—Annex to Delegation Report,* 20 J. Air L. & Com. 92, 99 (1953).

Whether the ICAO Council has the requisite professional qualifications to adjudicate disputes arising under Article 15 may well be doubted. Here it would have to pass upon the "adequacy" of the evidence of financial responsibility of the aircraft operator's insurer or guarantor, as certified by the state of the aircraft's registry or by the state where the insurer or guarantor has its principal place of business.[205] The Council's competence in matters of international air law might well be of little value in deciding questions closely related to the law and economics of the banking and insurance business. It is therefore surprising that the Council accepted the judicial functions assigned to it under the Rome Convention.[206]

Under Bilateral Agreements

In 1952, when the dispute between India and Pakistan was before the Council, the ICAO Secretariat prepared a paper on the rules of procedure applicable to disputes that might be submitted to it.[207] In it the Secretariat examined over 200 bilateral aeronautical agreements registered with ICAO up to the year 1951, and classified them according to the dispute-settling machinery they envisaged.[208] Using the Secretariat's classifications, its findings may roughly be summarized as follows.

Conventions and Agreements recognizing the exclusive competence of Council: Final binding decision, 2; Decision subject to appeal, 1; Advisory report, 12.

Agreements recognizing competence of the Organization for matters covered by provisions of Chapter XVIII [of the Convention] and providing for submission of other matters to arbitration: [Type of decision not specified by Secretariat], 5.

Agreements recognizing competence of Council with possible alternative choice of arbitral tribunal, body, or person: Final binding decision, 60; Decision subject to appeal, 9.

Agreements recognizing competence of Council after failure of an

---

[205] See Rome Convention, Arts. 15(1)–(4). The dispute envisaged by Article 15(7)(a) would be between the Contracting State overflown and the Contracting State or States certifying the insurer's or guarantor's financial responsibility.

[206] The Council accepted this responsibility on February 10, 1953. Action of the Council, 18th Sess., ICAO Doc. 7388 (C/860), p. 16 (1953).

[207] ICAO Doc. C–WP/1171 (1952).

[208] *Id.* at 15–20.

agreement between the parties on choice of an arbitral tribunal, body, or person: Final binding decision, 8; Advisory report, 11.

Agreements recognizing competence of Council after failure of an agreement between the parties on an arbitral tribunal, body, or person, and if there is no special tribunal established in ICAO for the purpose: Final binding decision, 30.

Agreements recognizing competence of a special tribunal established in ICAO for the purpose, after failure of agreement between parties on an arbitral tribunal, body, or person (without reference to the Council): Final binding decision, 7.

Agreements recognizing competence of an arbitral tribunal (without reference to Council nor any body of the Organization, but with the possible participation of the President of the Council in appointing arbitrators): Final binding decision, 5; Advisory opinion, 13.

Agreements recognizing competence of an arbitral tribunal (without reference to the Council, other body of the Organization, or President): Decision, 23; Advisory opinion, 1.

Agreements recognizing competence of the Interim Council [of PICAO] (with no reference to ICAO Council), or of arbitral tribunal, or other body or person: [Type of decision not specified by Secretariat], 10.

Agreements where there is no provision on settlement of disagreements: 18.

Between 1952 and 1965, approximately 2,000 bilateral aeronautical agreements and protocols thereto have been registered with ICAO.[209] Although it would therefore be a monumental task to update the Secretariat's statistical findings,[210] it might nevertheless be instructive to examine aeronautical treaties registered with ICAO in the year 1960, for example, to ascertain to what extent more recent agreements still look to the Council as an arbitral tribunal for the settlement of disputes arising thereunder.[211]

---

[209] See AERONAUTICAL AGREEMENTS AND ARRANGEMENTS REGISTERED WITH THE ORGANIZATION (1 JANUARY 1946–31 DECEMBER 1964), ICAO Doc. 8473 (LGB/215) (1965).

[210] For a more recent, but for our purposes not very helpful, survey of arbitral clauses found in bilateral air transport agreements, see HANDBOOK ON ADMINISTRATIVE CLAUSES IN BILATERAL AIR TRANSPORT AGREEMENTS, ICAO Circular 63–AT/6, pp. 72–83 (1962).

[211] I selected the year 1960 for two reasons. First, it is sufficiently removed in time from the period covered by the Secretariat's study to permit the discern-

About forty bilateral air treaties registered by the Organization in 1960 contain a provision relating to the settlement of disputes. None of these confers exclusive judicial competence on the ICAO Council. By far the largest number of these agreements provide for the settlement of disputes through diplomatic channels,[212] or by an arbitral tribunal. Those contemplating arbitration can be divided into four groups.

The first makes no provisions for the composition of the tribunal, if the parties are unable to agree thereon.[213] The second envisages the appointment of a tribunal of three arbitrators by mutual agreement among the parties. It provides further, however, that, if the parties fail to reach such an agreement, the arbitrators may be designated by the President of the ICAO Council.[214] The third group follows for all practical purposes the pattern just described, except that the functions conferred therein on the President of the ICAO Council are assigned in these agreements to the President of the International Court of Justice.[215] The fourth group calls for arbitration by a tribunal mutually agreed upon by the parties, and provides that the dispute may be referred to the International Court of Justice if no such agreement can be reached.[216]

Among those bilateral agreements—approximately one-third of the total registered in 1960—which call for some sort of arbitration

---

ment of a trend. Second, most of the bilateral agreements registered with ICAO in 1960 have in the meantime also been published in the United Nations Treaty Series and are thus accessible.

[212] These are mainly agreements concluded with Communist Bloc countries. See, *e.g.*, Agreement (with Annexes) between the United Arab Republic and Bulgaria concerning Civil Air Services, Article XVIII. This agreement was signed at Cairo on 9 July 1959, and is reprinted in 411 U.N.T.S. 185 (1961).

[213] See, *e.g.*, Air Transport Agreement (with schedule of routes) between Thailand and France, Article 7. This Agreement was signed at Bangkok on 26 February 1960, and may be found in 392 U.N.T.S. 279 (1961).

[214] See, *e.g.*, Agreement (with schedule) between the United Kingdom and Czechoslovakia for air services between and beyond their respective territories, Article 12, 374 U.N.T.S. 207 (1960). This agreement was signed at Prague on 15 January 1960.

[215] See, *e.g.*, Agreement (with schedule and exchange of notes) between Sweden and Sudan on air services between and beyond their respective territories, Article IX. This agreement was signed at Khartoum on 17 February 1958, and may be found in 393 U.N.T.S. 161 (1961).

[216] See, *e.g.*, Air Transport Agreement (with annex) between the Netherlands and Guinea, Article 9. This Agreement was signed at Conakry on 9 March 1960. It is reproduced in 392 U.N.T.S. 242 (1961).

under the auspices of ICAO, a mere handful vests judicial function in the Council. Illustrative of provisions which do is Article 15 of the Air Services Agreement between Denmark and Ceylon.[217] It reads as follows:

> If the Contracting Parties fail to reach agreement on any question relating to the interpretation or application of this Agreement or of the Annex thereto, the dispute shall be referred for decision to the Council of the International Civil Aviation Organization, unless the Contracting Parties agree to settle the dispute by reference to an Arbitral Tribunal appointed by agreement between the Contracting Parties, or to some other person or body. The Contracting Parties undertake to comply with the decision rendered.

Interestingly enough, the remaining agreements falling in this category provide for the settlement of disputes by an arbitral tribunal or, in the alternative, a competent tribunal established by ICAO. They usually stipulate further that, if such a tribunal has not been established by the Organization, the case may be referred to the Council. Thus the Air Services Agreement between Ghana and the Netherlands,[218] after providing in Article 10(1) for the settlement of the dispute through direct negotiation, stipulates further that

> (2) If the Contracting Parties fail to reach a settlement by negotiation,
> (a) they may agree to refer the dispute for decision to an arbitral tribunal appointed by agreement between them or to some other person or body; or
> (b) if they do not so agree or if, having agreed to refer the dispute to an arbitral tribunal, they cannot reach agreement as to its composition, either Contracting Party may submit the dispute for decision to any tribunal competent to decide it which may hereafter be established within the International Civil Aviation Organisation or, if there is no such tribunal, to the Council of the said Organisation.
> (3) The Contracting Parties undertake to comply with any decision given under paragraph (2) of this Article.

[217] Agreement (with annex, Protocol, and exchange of letters) between Denmark and Ceylon relating to air services, signed at Colombo on 29 May and 8 September 1959, 348 U.N.T.S. 225 (1960).

[218] Agreement (with annex) between Ghana and the Netherlands for air services between and beyond their respective territories, signed at The Hague on 30 July 1960, 412 U.N.T.S. 51 (1961).

Even some of these agreements bypass the Council. They provide that, if the parties are unable to agree on an arbitral tribunal and if none has been established by ICAO, the dispute may be submitted to the International Court of Justice. The language employed in the Air Services Agreement between Sweden and Pakistan [219] is characteristic of this approach. Article XI of this agreement provides:

> (B) If the Contracting Parties fail to reach a settlement by negotiation,
> (i) they may agree to refer the dispute for decision to an arbitral tribunal or some other person or body appointed by agreement between them; or
> (ii) if they do not so agree or if, having agreed to refer the dispute to an arbitral tribunal they cannot reach agreement as to its composition, either Contracting Party may submit the dispute for decision to any tribunal competent to decide it established within the International Civil Aviation Organization, or, if there be no such tribunal, to the International Court of Justice.

On the assumption that the year 1960 is fairly characteristic of recent state practice, the proportion of bilateral air agreements vesting adjudicatory functions in the ICAO Council has been declining. A superficial perusal of similar agreements registered with the Organization in the years 1961–64, reveals that this trend may well have gained even greater momentum since 1960.[220] One reason for this trend may be that some states have concluded that the ICAO Council would be unwilling to act as an arbitral tribunal. Another reason might be that these states do not believe that a political body like the ICAO Council is a proper forum for the adjudication of legal disputes.[221]

It is therefore interesting to note that some of the bilateral agreements anticipate the possibility that ICAO might establish a

---

[219] Agreement (with annex and exchange of notes) between Sweden and Pakistan relating to air services, signed at Stockholm on 6 March 1958, 393 U.N.T.S. 181 (1961).

[220] This trend may either be the cause or the result of the fact that Article 13 of the Standard Clauses for Bilateral Agreements, adopted by the European Civil Aviation Conference, envisages no arbitral functions for the ICAO Council. See ECAC, Report of the 3rd Session, Records of the Session, Vol. I, ICAO Doc. 7977 (ECAC/3–1), p. 61 (1959).

[221] See Goedhuis, *Problems of Public International Air Law*, 81 Recueil des Cours 205, 223–25 (1952).

special arbitral tribunal to decide disputes relating to the interpretation or application of these agreements. The Organization does not
seem to have considered this step. Suggestions to that effect, however, have come from various commentators.[222] A permanent ICAO
arbitral tribunal would avoid the difficulties that are usually encountered in establishing *ad hoc* tribunals. It might furthermore develop
a substantial body of law and thus clarify many of the current
uncertainties relating to the application of international aviation
agreements. The varied and complicated technical issues that are
raised by disputes relating to multilateral and bilateral air agreements may, on the other hand, demand considerable flexibility in the
selection of arbitrators especially qualified to adjudicate a particular
case. This consideration may outweigh the benefits to be derived
from a permanent tribunal. Here the list of available arbitrators
maintained by the ICAO Council since 1963 [223] performs a useful
service. It may, of course, also be that these bilateral agreements
can be read as authorizing the ICAO Council or the Organization to
establish an *ad hoc* tribunal to decide such disputes.[224] ICAO should
therefore promulgate appropriate rules for the establishment of
such tribunals.

THE ICAO RULES FOR THE SETTLEMENT OF DISPUTES

Evolution and Scope of the Rules

The Interim Council of the Provisional International Civil Aviation Organization promulgated on September 24, 1946, the "Rules
Governing the Settlement of Differences between States." [225] They
were expressly made applicable [226] to disputes and complaints arising under the Transit and Transport Agreements; to the review of

---

[222] See, *e.g.*, *id.* at 300–01.

[223] See [1963] Report of the Council, ICAO Doc. 8402 (A15–P/2), p. 92 (1964).

[224] Article 17 of the Draft Multilateral Agreement on Commercial Rights in International Civil Air Transport, prepared by the PICAO Air Transport Committee, PICAO Doc. 2866 (AT/169) (1947), reissued as ICAO Doc. 4014 (A1–EC/1) (1947), contemplated the establishment of such an *ad hoc* tribunal to be designated by the President of the ICAO Council. For an analysis of Article 17, see Cooper, *New Problems in International Civil Aviation Arbitration Procedure*, 2 Arb. J. 119 (1947).

[225] Rules Governing the Settlement of Differences between States [hereinafter cited as 1946 Rules], PICAO Doc. 2121 (C/228) (1946).

[226] 1946 Rules, Art. 1.

charges imposed for the use of airports and other facilities as contemplated in the Interim Agreement on International Civil Aviation; [227] to the settlement of disputes relating to international air matters as envisaged in Article III, Section 6(8) of the Interim Agreement; [228] and to "any differences referred to the Interim Council under provisions of other agreements relating to international civil aviation matters concluded by the States concerned." [229]

These Rules did not apply to disputes under Article 84 of the Convention because it had not as yet entered into force. And, since no cases were submitted to the Interim Council for adjudication, they were never applied. They were, furthermore, not reissued when ICAO was established.[230] On May 21, 1952, the ICAO Council established a Working Group to review the set of draft rules which the ICAO Secretariat had prepared for the Council's consideration in connection with the India-Pakistan case.[231] This Working Group submitted a revised set of draft rules to the Council on March 31, 1953.[232] These rules were extensively debated in the Council and then remanded to the Working Group for reexamination in the light of the comments made in the Council.[233] A few weeks later, after receiving the Working Group's second report containing the necessary revisions,[234] the Council provisionally adopted these rules [235] and ordered them to be circulated to the Member States for their comments.[236]

The 1953 Rules which, with some changes,[237] formed the basis for

---

[227] See Interim Agreement, Art. VIII, Sec. 9.

[228] Interim Agreement, Art. III, Sec. 6(8) read in part that "when expressly requested by all parties concerned, [the Council shall] act as an arbitral body on any differences arising among member States relating to international civil aviation matters which may be submitted to it."

[229] 1946 Rules, Art. 1(g).

[230] For an analysis of the 1946 Rules, see Kos-Rabcewicz-Zubkowski 356–65.

[231] Action of the Council, 16th Sess., ICAO Doc. 7314 (C/849), p. 26 (1952). The Rules prepared by the Secretariat can be found in ICAO Doc. C–WP/1171 Appendix A (1952).

[232] ICAO Doc. C–WP/1457 (1953).

[233] ICAO Council, 19th Sess., Doc. 7390 (C/861), pp. 5–13 (1953).

[234] ICAO Doc. C–WP/1503 and Corr. (1953).

[235] Rules for the Settlement of Differences between Contracting States [hereinafter cited as 1953 Rules], ICAO Doc. 7392 (C/862) (1953).

[236] ICAO Council, 19th Sess., Doc. 7390 (C/861), p. 103 (1953).

[237] The specific amendments to the 1953 Rules which were taken over by the 1957 Rules can be found in ICAO Doc. C–WP/2271 (Annex B) (1956).

the present Rules, were made applicable to disputes under the Convention and its Annexes, and to disagreements and complaints under the Transit and Transport Agreements.[238] In its first report, the Working Group on the Rules for the Settlement of Disputes between Contracting Parties gave the following reasons for limiting the Rules to these disputes:

> The Working Group explored the possibilities of preparing rules which may apply to any case which may be submitted to the Organization. In addition to the provisions of the Chicago Acts, there are also in a number of bilateral and multilateral aeronautical agreements provisions relating to the settlement of disputes by the Organization or its Council. But the responsibility placed upon the Organization or the Council by these agreements has not yet been accepted except in the case of the Ocean Weather Stations Agreement and the Rome Convention [on Damage Caused by Foreign Aircraft to Third Parties on the Surface]; in the first case, Council is to give only an advisory opinion, and in the second the differences which may be referred to the Council are of a special nature which would not readily fit into general rules. In respect of other bilateral and multilateral agreements, it is believed that if and when cases arise, it will be more appropriate to decide then what rules of procedure should apply.[239]

When this report was submitted to the Council, a number of Representatives expressed the view that the Rules should be made applicable to all disputes that might be submitted to the Council.[240] The Director of the ICAO Legal Bureau counseled against this course, however, on the ground that the arbitral proceedings envisaged for the settlement of disputes arising under bilateral agreements ". . . were of a different character than judicial proceedings (the kind involved in the settlement of disputes under the Chicago Acts). For example, in the former there would be an agreed presentation of the facts and the issues by the two parties concerned; in the latter there would not."[241]

Of course, neither the reasons nor the example given by the Director of the Legal Bureau compel the conclusion that the Rules should not be applicable to disputes arising under bilateral agree-

---

[238] 1953 Rules, Art. 1.
[239] ICAO Doc. C–WP/1457, p. 1 (1953).
[240] See ICAO Council, 19th Sess., Doc. 7390 (C/861), pp. 5–8 (1953).
[241] *Id.* at 7.

ments. The addition of one or two provisions to the Rules could readily have overcome the problems he anticipated, even assuming that they are more than distinctions without a difference. Be that as it may, his arguments did not persuade those Council Representatives who favored making the Rules applicable to all disputes. To prevent further delays, however, they agreed to a compromise under which the Council, in its resolution promulgating the 1953 Rules, decided that "as far as practicable and appropriate, these Rules would be applied to any disputes other than those specifically provided for therein, submitted to the Council." [242]

The Council's 1957 resolution adopting the present Rules makes no reference to the possible applicability of these Rules to disputes other than those arising under the Chicago Acts.[243] The 1957 Rules are expressly limited to disputes arising under the Convention and its Annexes, and to disagreements and complaints under the Transit and Transport Agreements.[244] During the four-year period that elapsed between the provisional adoption of the 1953 Rules and the promulgation of the present Rules, the Council never considered the question of their applicability to disputes arising under other agreements. It is therefore not clear whether the 1953 resolution was superseded by the resolution adopting the present Rules. It matters little what conclusion is accepted, for if the Council decided to act as an arbitral tribunal under some other agreement it would in all likelihood apply these Rules, provided such a course proved to be "practicable and appropriate."

Before analyzing the provisions of the present Rules, it should be asked why their final adoption was delayed for almost four years. Contrary to what one might assume, this delay cannot be attributed to any controversies in the Council relating to the substance of the Rules. Rather, apart from the time that was consumed in obtaining and analyzing the comments of the Contracting States,[245] the delay was caused by the insistence of some Council Representatives that the Rules not be adopted until they had been carefully studied by a committee of qualified legal experts. After debating the composition

---

[242] Action of the Council, 19th Sess., ICAO Doc. 7408 (C/864), p. 29 (1953).

[243] See Action of the Council, 30th Sess., ICAO Doc. 7818 (C/901), p. 33 (1957).

[244] 1957 Rules, Art. 1.

[245] An analysis of these comments, prepared by the ICAO Secretariat, can be found in ICAO Doc. C–WP/1685 (1954).

of this committee at two sessions,[246] the Council decided to entrust the "finalization" of the Rules to a group of legal experts nominated by the Chairman of the ICAO Legal Committee in consultation with the President of the Council.[247] The Group of Experts presented its report and revisions of the 1953 Rules to the Council in 1956.[248] These Rules, as revised by the Group of Experts, were then promulgated by the Council without any amendments at its next session on April 9, 1957.[249]

Contents of the Rules

The 1957 Rules[250] consist of one set of rules that applies to disputes and another which governs complaints. They also contain some general provisions applicable to both types of proceedings.[251]

RULES APPLICABLE TO DISPUTES

The Pleadings

The Rules envisage the usual exchange of pleadings, commencing with an application and memorial,[252] followed by a counter-memorial,[253] a reply by the applicant state, and the respondent's rejoinder.[254] If the respondent state questions the Council's jurisdiction, it must file the appropriate objections in a "special pleading" before the time limit set for the submission of the counter-memorial has expired. This step will have the effect of suspending the proceedings on the merits until the Council, after hearing the parties, has passed on the question of jurisdiction.[255]

As far as the pleadings are concerned, three points should be noted. First, after the application has been filed with the Secretary

---

[246] See ICAO Council, 21st Sess., Doc. 7464 (C/871), pp. 4–6 (1954); ICAO Council, 23rd Sess., Doc. 7525 (C/875), p. 204 (1955).

[247] Action of the Council, 23rd Sess., ICAO Doc. 7556 (C/877), p. 36 (1955).

[248] ICAO Doc. C–WP/2271 (1956).

[249] Action of the Council, 30th Sess., ICAO Doc. 7818 (C/901), p. 33 (1957). They were subsequently issued as ICAO Doc. 7782 (1959).

[250] For an analysis of the 1957 Rules, see Hingorani 15–21; Mankiewicz 388–94.

[251] See 1957 Rules, Art. 1.

[252] 1957 Rules, Art. 2.

[253] 1957 Rules, Art. 4.

[254] 1957 Rules, Art. 7.

[255] 1957 Rules, Art. 5.

General of ICAO, who under the Rules performs the functions of a court registrar, he must inform all parties to the particular agreement that the action has been instituted.[256] This provision is undoubtedly designed, among other things, to give these states an opportunity to consider the advisability of intervening in the proceedings. Second, the Rules do not contain any time limits for the pleadings. This matter is left to the Council, or to its President if the Council is not in session, subject to the stipulation that "any time-limit fixed pursuant to these Rules shall be so fixed as to avoid any possible delays and to ensure fair treatment of the party or parties concerned." [257] Third, under Article 4(2) of the Rules, the respondent state may in its counter-memorial assert "a counter-claim directly connected with the subject matter of the application provided it comes within the jurisdiction of the Council." If such a counter-claim is presented, the Council must accord the parties a hearing before passing on its admissibility.

Article 4(2) was recommended in 1956 by the Group of Experts who patterned it on Rule 63 of the I.C.J. Rules of Court.[258] Although the Group's report does not explain the intended scope of this provision, Article 4(2) would seem to be broad enough to encompass counter-claims based on agreements other than the three Chicago Acts. This would mean that if a dispute arising under the Convention, for example, is directly related to a claim based on a bilateral air transport agreement, the Council will have to decide the counter-claim, provided that the bilateral agreement confers the requisite jurisdiction on the Council or that the parties consent thereto.[259]

The Proceedings

The Council's policy of encouraging the Contracting States to settle their disputes by direct negotiations finds expression in two separate provisions of the Rules. Under Article 6(1) of the Rules the Council, after receipt of the counter-memorial, may decide "whether at this stage the parties should be invited to enter into

---

[256] 1957 Rules, Art. 3.
[257] 1957 Rules, Art. 28(1).
[258] ICAO Doc. C–WP/2271, p. 4 (1956).
[259] See Asylum Case, [1950] I.C.J. Rep. 266, 280–81.

direct negotiations as provided in Article 14." Under Article 14(1) this invitation may be extended to the parties at any time during the proceedings before the decision is rendered, "if the Council deems that the possibilities of settling the dispute or narrowing the issues through negotiations have not been exhausted." As soon as the parties accept this invitation the proceedings are suspended. The Council may, however, fix a time limit within which the negotiations are to be completed.[260] With the consent of the parties, moreover, "the Council may render any assistance likely to further the negotiations, including the designation of an individual or a group of individuals to act as conciliator during the negotiations." [261] A settlement of the dispute by the original parties prior to the Council's decision terminates the proceedings.[262] This result obtains even if other states have intervened, although the dismissal of the dispute under these circumstances is without prejudice to the intervenor's right to lodge its own application.[263] The terms of a settlement are recorded and communicated to all states that are parties to the instrument under which the dispute arose.[264]

If the Council does not invite the parties to enter into further negotiations after receipt of the counter-memorial, or if these negotiations were unsuccessful, the Council will either consider the case itself or delegate this task to a "Committee . . . of five individuals who shall be Representatives on the Council of Member States not concerned in the disagreement." [265] Since it is highly unlikely that the Council as a whole will conduct the proceedings itself, the Committee will no doubt perform this role in most, if not all, cases. The functions assigned to the Committee are set forth in Article 13 of the Rules, which provides that the Committee

> shall, on behalf of the Council, receive and examine all documents submitted in accordance with these Rules and, in its discretion, hear evidence or oral arguments, and generally deal with the case with a view to action being taken by the Council under Article 15. The

---

[260] 1957 Rules, Art. 14(2).
[261] 1957 Rules, Art. 14(3).
[262] 1957 Rules, Arts. 14(4) and 20(1)(a).
[263] 1957 Rules, Art. 20(1)(b).
[264] 1957 Rules, Art. 20(2).
[265] 1957 Rules, Art. 6(2).

procedures governing the examination of the case by the Committee shall be those prescribed for the Council when it examines the matter itself.[266]

The "action" envisaged under Article 15 refers to the decision in the case which only the Council may render. When considering the Committee's report, the Council does have the power, however, to "make such further enquiries as it may think fit or obtain additional evidence." [267] This provision was inserted in the 1957 Rules by the Group of Experts to emphasize that, while the Committee could deal with the case up to the final decision, "the Council should, in all stages, be in final control of the proceedings, and that the right to give a decision must be reserved to the Council." [268]

The Committee's report, which must contain a summary of the evidence, findings of fact, and the Committee's recommendations, becomes a part of the record of the proceedings.[269] After receipt of a copy of the report, the parties may submit to the Council their written comments and, if the Council consents, they may also be given an oral hearing.[270]

The Committee, as we have seen, is to consist of "five individuals who shall be Representatives on the Council of Member States not concerned in the disagreement." [271] The same language was employed in the 1953 Rules.[272] This provision was adopted by the Council after an extensive debate that was sparked by the Representative of the United Kingdom, who wondered whether the Convention and the Transit and Transport Agreements precluded the appointment of a Committee consisting of individuals other than Council Representatives.[273] The 1946 Rules spoke of a Committee consisting either of Interim Council Representatives or of "qualified persons" chosen from a list that was to be maintained for that purpose by the Interim Council.[274] The U.K. Representative and

---

[266] 1957 Rules, Art. 14(1) further provides that "while the Committee has charge of the proceedings, the functions of the President of the Council under these Rules shall be exercised by the Chairman of the Committee."

[267] 1957 Rules, Art. 13(4).

[268] ICAO Doc. C–WP/2271, p. 4 (1956).

[269] 1957 Rules, Art. 13(2).

[270] 1957 Rules, Art. 13(3).

[271] 1957 Rules, Art. 6(2).

[272] 1953 Rules, Art. 6(2).

[273] ICAO Council, 19th Sess., Doc. 7390 (C/861), p. 8 (1953).

[274] 1946 Rules, Art. 8(2).

some of his colleagues favored a similar approach,[275] but this view did not prevail because the Director of the Legal Bureau asserted that the Council could lawfully delegate a part of its judicial functions only to a body composed of its own members.[276]

The fact that the Committee must be composed of Council Representatives does not preclude the Council or the Committee from seeking outside expert advice. Article 8(1) therefore provides that "the Council may at any time, but after hearing the parties, entrust any individual, body, bureau, commission, or other organization that it may select, with the task of carrying out an enquiry or giving an expert opinion." This provision to some extent overcomes the disadvantages which inhere in the requirement that the Committee must be composed of Council Representatives, for it permits the Council to seek the assistance of any specially qualified person who might otherwise have been asked to serve on the Committee. Article 8(1) is broad enough, furthermore, to permit the Council to request an advisory opinion from the International Court of Justice on difficult questions of international law.

The right of intervention, while recognized by the Rules, is strictly delimited.[277] To qualify as an intervenor, a state must be a party to the agreement under which the dispute arose and be "directly affected by the dispute." The intervenor must also "undertake that the decision of the Council will be equally binding upon it." [278] The parties have a right to object to the admissibility of the intervention, in which case the matter is decided by the Council.[279]

Strangely enough, Article 19(4) of the Rules provides that

> if no objection has been notified . . . or if the Council decides in favour of the admissibility of an intervention, as the case may be, the Secretary General shall take the necessary steps to make the documents of the case available to the intervening party.

This provision could be taken to mean that if no objections to the intervention have been received, the intervention is automatically admissible. It can be argued, however, that this may well be a drafting oversight, for it would seem that the Council must in any

---

[275] ICAO Council, 19th Sess., Doc. 7390 (C/861), p. 9 (1953).
[276] *Id.* at 8.
[277] See Hingorani 18–20.
[278] 1957 Rules, Art. 19(1).
[279] 1957 Rules, Art. 19(2).

event inquire whether the intervenor is a party to the particular instrument and directly affected by the dispute.[280] This conclusion finds support in the legislative history of Article 19, which indicates that this provision was designed to discourage interventions as much as possible. Under an earlier draft of Article 19, any state was permitted to intervene in the proceedings provided it was a party to the agreement giving rise to the dispute.[281] When that provision was considered by the Council, three different views relating to intervention were advanced. The U.S. Representative proposed that only states "directly affected by the dispute" should be permitted to intervene.[282] India urged that no provision should be made for interventions, because it was "not conducive to expeditious action." [283] The Representatives of Canada [284] and France [285] felt that every State Party to an instrument had a right to intervene in the dispute because it had an interest in its interpretation and application.

Eventually the view of the United States prevailed, mainly, it seems, because it was a compromise between the two extreme positions that had been advanced and because it permits the Council to limit interventions to a minimum.[286] This decision may also have been prompted by the consideration that the intervention of too many states might deprive the Council of the requisite quorum to decide the dispute.[287] It cannot therefore be doubted that the Council has an obligation to limit interventions *sua sponte* in accordance with the standards set forth in the Rules.[288]

To be admissible, the intervention must come from a state which is "directly affected by the dispute." That state must, of course, also be a party to the instrument to which the dispute relates, but while the latter requirement is self-explanatory, the former is not. What standard will the Council employ in deciding whether a state is "directly affected by the dispute"? The discussions in the Council do

[280] See Statement by Mr. Söderberg, Chairman of the 1953 Working Group on the Rules for the Settlement of Differences, ICAO Council, 19th Sess., Doc. 7390 (C/861), pp. 11 and 113 (1953).

[281] See Article 16(1) of the Draft Rules prepared by the Working Group on Rules for the Settlement of Differences, ICAO Doc. C–WP/1457, p. 9 (1953).

[282] ICAO Council, 19th Sess., Doc. 7390 (C/861), p. 11 (1953).

[283] *Ibid.*

[284] *Ibid.*

[285] *Id.* at 113.

[286] *Id.* at 111–13.

[287] See ICAO Doc. GE/RSD/WD#3, pp. 14–15 (1955).

[288] See Mankiewicz 393.

not throw much light on this question, although they indicate that the intervenor's interest in the Council's decision must be more immediate or greater than the general interest which all other parties to the instrument have.

This consideration, taken together with the fact that the Council was motivated by a desire to limit interventions as much as possible, permits the conclusion that a state will be deemed to be "directly affected by the dispute," if it can show (1) that its interest in the dispute is distinguishable from the general interest which all parties to the particular agreement have, and (2) that this special interest might be jeopardized by disallowing the intervention. A state, for example, which is a supplier of certain aircraft or navigational instruments might qualify as intervenor in a dispute relating to their airworthiness. This would equally be true of a state such as Afghanistan, whose air link to India was at stake in the India-Pakistan dispute. Needless to say, one can imagine cases that could not be as easily decided. Considering the Council's professed policy against interventions, any doubts will probably be resolved against the intervenor.

An interesting feature of the Rules is their emphasis on written proceedings.[289] The parties do not have a right to an oral hearing, although the Council may in its discretion accord it. Even the final arguments of the parties must be presented in writing, "but oral arguments may be admitted at the discretion of the Council." [290] This policy against oral proceedings is probably designed to reduce the time that the Council would have to devote to a given case.[291]

The 1957 Rules, unlike those provisionally enacted in 1953,[292] do not provide for the interpretation or revision of a Council decision.[293] They do, however, contain a provision not found in the 1953 Rules, which empowers the Council to render a default judgment if one of the parties does not appear or fails to defend the case.[294] Before taking this action, the Council must "satisfy itself not only that it has jurisdiction in the matter but also that the claim is well founded in fact and law." [295]

---

[289] See 1957 Rules, Arts. 9, 12(2), and 13(3).
[290] 1957 Rules, Art. 12(2).
[291] See ICAO Doc. C–WP/2271, p. 4 (1956).
[292] See 1953 Rules, Arts. 19 and 20.
[293] The reasons for this change are discussed in note 111 *supra*.
[294] 1957 Rules, Art. 16(1).
[295] 1957 Rules, Art. 16(2).

The power to render a decision in a dispute submitted to the Council cannot be delegated by it.[296] The decision must be in writing and must be motivated.[297] Dissenting opinions are permissible.[298] And, as previously noted, "no Member of the Council shall vote in the consideration by the Council of any dispute to which it is a party." [299] This provision is identical to the language found in Articles 84 and 53 of the Convention. Its meaning is by no means clear, however. Obviously, a state represented on the Council may not vote in a case in which it is the applicant, respondent, or intervenor. But a state could well be "a party to the dispute" in all but name whenever its interests are identical or closely related to those of one of the litigants. This would have been true of Afghanistan, for example, had it served on the Council at the time of the India-Pakistan dispute.[300]

On the other hand, all states adhering to the particular instrument to which the dispute relates have some, albeit not always the same, interest in the outcome of the controversy. In order to assure elementary fairness without paralyzing the Council's power to render a decision, the applicable test should be the same that the Rules employ to limit interventions. Thus, a state which could have intervened in the proceedings because it was "directly affected by the dispute," should not have a vote in the case. This test will not always be easy to apply, and it may be open to the charge that it substitutes one vague standard for another. But the fact of the matter is that it does articulate with somewhat greater precision the policy inherent in Article 84 of the Convention, while recognizing that the principle of strict judicial impartiality cannot be fully applied to a political body like the Council.

When submitting their report to the Council, the Group of Experts called attention to a subject that is closely related to the issue which has just been discussed. They explained this problem in the following terms:

> According to Article 52 of the Convention: "Decisions by the Council shall require approval by a majority of its members." In the opinion of the Group, this provision requires 11 votes for a decision. However, since, according to Articles 53 and 84, no member of the

[296] Compare 1957 Rules, Art. 13(1), with Art. 15(4).
[297] 1957 Rules, Art. 15(2).
[298] 1957 Rules, Art. 15(3).
[299] 1957 Rules, Art. 15(5).
[300] See Hingorani 21.

Council may vote in the consideration by the Council of a dispute to which it is a party, it may well happen that the Council finds itself unable to give a decision. The possibility of a tie vote has also to be taken into account in this connection.[301]

While the Council has in the meantime been enlarged from a membership of 21 to 27,[302] these problems could still arise although the odds are somewhat reduced. How might these problems be resolved? The Group of Experts did not offer any solutions, and when its chairman, Mr. Loaeza of Mexico, was asked in the Council whether it would be desirable to amend the Convention to anticipate these problems, he replied that "the difficulties inherent in them could be resolved quite easily in practice, and in the opinion of the Group certainly would not justify going through the complicated and protracted process of amendment."[303] The practical solution Mr. Loaeza apparently had in mind would consist of a ruling that the parties to the dispute, if they are Council Members, will not be counted in ascertaining the votes required for a Council decision on the ground that for this purpose they are not deemed to be "Members of the Council."[304] This seems to be but another way of saying that a dispute would be decided by a simple majority of those Council Members who are qualified to vote in deciding the particular case. Since the draftsmen of the Convention would probably have adopted this solution had the problem occurred to them, the Council may be expected to resort to it should the occasion arise.[305]

The problem that might arise in case of a tie vote is dealt with by the Council's Rules of Procedure.[306] Rule 53 of these Rules provides:

> In the event of a tie vote, a second vote on the motion concerned shall be taken at the next meeting of the Council, unless a majority of

[301] ICAO Doc. C–WP/2271, p. 6 (1956).

[302] This amendment to Article 50(a) of the Convention was adopted by the ICAO Assembly on 17 July 1961. See Assembly Res. A13–1, ICAO Doc. 8167 (A13–P/2) (1961). It came into force on 17 July 1962.

[303] ICAO Council, 30th Sess., Doc. 7766 (C/897), p. 107 (1957).

[304] See Hingorani 21, who attributes this suggestion to Mr. Loaeza.

[305] Support for the legality of this interpretation can be found in the jurisprudence of the Permanent Court of International Justice. See Advisory Opinion Concerning the Interpretation of Article 3, paragraph 2, of the Treaty of Lausanne (Frontier between Turkey and Iraq), P.C.I.J., Ser. B, No. 12, p. 32 (1925). See also, Hexner, *Interpretation by Public International Organizations of their Basic Instruments,* 53 Am. J. Int'l L. 341, 367–70 (1959).

[306] ICAO Doc. 7559/3, Rev. 3 (1953).

its Members represented at the meeting decides that such second vote be taken during the meeting at which the tie vote took place. Unless there is a majority in favour of the motion on this second vote, it shall be considered lost.

Under Rule 53, the decision would turn on the form in which the motion is presented. It may therefore be assumed that, to prevent such an unsatisfactory result, one or two Council Members might change their vote and support the recommendations that the Committee of Five made in the case. This solution would not be unreasonable under the circumstances, especially since the parties have an opportunity to appeal the Council's decision.

The Rules make no provisions relating to the enforcement measures that may be imposed to implement Council decisions rendered in disputes arising under the Convention, its Annexes, and the Transit or Transport Agreements. With regard to the appeal that is open to the parties under Article 84 of the Convention, the Rules merely stipulate that notice of such appeal shall be given within sixty days after the Council's decision has been communicated to the parties.[307]

COMPLAINTS

The Rules prescribe the same process of pleadings for complaints that applies to disputes, except that in the case of complaints the formal pleading stage ends with the submission of the counter-memorial.[308] When the counter-memorial has been received, a meeting of the Council must be convened for the purpose of formally deciding "whether the matter falls under the category of complaints" within the meaning of the Transit or Transport Agreement.[309] If the decision is in the affirmative,[310] the Council must appoint the previously described Committee of Five and refer the case to it.[311] Thus, whereas the reference of a dispute to the Committee rests in the Council's discretion, it is mandatory in the case of a complaint.

In dealing with a complaint, the Committee acts very much like

---

[307] 1957 Rules, Art. 18(2).

[308] 1957 Rules, Arts. 21 and 22.

[309] 1957 Rules, Art. 23(1).

[310] A negative decision results of necessity in a dismissal of the case, although the Rules are silent on this question.

[311] 1957 Rules, Art. 23.

a fact-finding and conciliation commission. The Rules require the Committee to begin its consideration of the case by calling the states concerned into consultation.[312] The Committee must "arrange the procedures for the consultation as far as possible in agreement with the parties, and on an informal basis in accordance with the circumstances of each case." [313] It may ask the parties for additional information,[314] and will no doubt explore with them the possibility of reaching a mutually satisfactory solution of their differences. Thereafter the Committee must report to the Council "as expeditiously as possible" on the outcome of the consultations.[315] If the consultations proved unsuccessful, the Committee "may" also include in its report "proposed findings and recommendations to the States concerned." [316] If the Committee obtained a settlement, its terms are recorded and communicated to the parties.[317] If the difficulties have not been resolved, "the Council may make appropriate findings and recommendations to the States concerned." [318] The use of the permissive "may" is intentional because neither the Transit nor the Transport Agreement requires the Council to exercise this power.[319]

The provisions of Article 15, which relate to the procedure that the Council must follow when rendering a decision in a dispute submitted to it, also apply to complaints.[320] This means that the recommendation which the Council may address to the parties must be motivated, that dissenting opinions will be permissible, and that parties to the complaint will not be able to vote in the Council on questions relating to their case.

GENERAL PROVISIONS

Part III of the Rules contains certain general provisions applicable to disputes as well as to complaints. They regulate the appointment of agents and provide, among other things, that Council Rep-

---

[312] 1957 Rules, Art. 24(1).
[313] 1957 Rules, Art. 24(2).
[314] *Ibid.*
[315] 1957 Rules, Art. 25(1).
[316] 1957 Rules, Art. 25(2).
[317] 1957 Rules, Art. 26(2).
[318] 1957 Rules, Art. 26(3).
[319] See Transit Agreement, Art. II, Sec. 1; Transport Agreement, Art. IV, Sec. 2.
[320] 1957 Rules, Art. 26(3).

resentatives may not serve in this capacity.[321] They stipulate that the proceedings may be conducted in any of the three official languages of the Organization (English, French, and Spanish),[322] and that the record of the proceedings shall be open to the public unless the Council decides otherwise.[323] Further provisions stipulate that each party is to bear its own costs, although the Council's right to provide otherwise is reserved,[324] and that the costs of the proceedings may be assessed to the parties in a manner to be fixed by the Council.[325]

Of these general provisions, the most interesting one is Article 32. It provides that "subject to agreement of the parties, any of these Rules may be varied or their application suspended when, in the opinion of the Council, such action would lead to a more expeditious or effective disposition of the case." It is not inconceivable that the parties to a dispute might, in reliance on this provision, seek to waive their right to a Council decision and agree instead to accept as binding upon them a decision rendered by the Committee of Five. There is no reason to assume that the Council would reject such a motion so long as it is acceptable to the parties. This approach would be entirely consistent with the Council's policy, which favors settlement of disputes by negotiation. Moreover, the granting of such a motion would not be contrary to Article 84 of the Convention, for if the parties are free by mutual agreement to terminate the litigation at any stage of the proceedings,[326] they would seem to be equally free to do so with a view towards a final disposition of the case by the Committee.[327] Article 32 of the Rules might thus be utilized to avoid some of the shortcomings inherent in the ICAO

---

[321] 1957 Rules, Art. 27(1).

[322] 1957 Rules, Art. 29(1).

[323] 1957 Rules, Art. 30.

[324] 1957 Rules, Art. 31(1).

[325] 1957 Rules, Art. 31(2).

[326] See 1957 Rules, Art. 20(1).

[327] To reserve their right to invoke the enforcement measures provided for in the Convention, the parties would be wise to include a stipulation to this effect in their motion under Article 32 of the Rules. But if the Group of Experts is correct in its conclusion that the Council may not under the Convention delegate its power of decision, see ICAO Doc. C–WP/2271, p. 4 (1956), then it is doubtful whether the enforcement measures envisaged under Articles 87 and 88 of the Convention could validly be imposed for non-compliance with a Committee decision stipulated under Article 32 of the Rules.

dispute-settling machinery. It could streamline the proceedings and substantially de-politicize the adjudicatory process.

CONCLUSION

In dealing with disputes arising under the Chicago Acts, the ICAO Council has been guided by a policy that favors settlements by political and diplomatic rather than judicial means. This policy has thus far proved to be effective and will probably remain so in the future. Its effectiveness may be attributed, in part at least, to the fact that the Council does possess rather extensive adjudicatory powers, which place the Council in a much stronger position to compel negotiated settlements than a body lacking this authority. Thus, when the Council "invites" the parties to enter into further negotiations, for example, it is rather difficult for them to decline such an invitation, for there is always the possibility—real or imagined—that this uncompromising stance might affect the Council's decision in the case.

Disputes arising under the Convention and the Transit or Transport Agreements are often the by-product of temporary political frictions between the parties. Here the chances for an amicable adjustment improve in proportion to the Council's ability to delay the institution of formal arbitral proceedings. As we have seen, the Council has used this method most effectively. It is thus readily apparent that the Council disposes of strong institutional pressures that can be employed to discourage litigation and to encourage settlement.

Furthermore, most Council Representatives are better qualified to assist the parties in adjusting their dispute than they are in adjudicating it. They are appointed to the Council by their governments because of their technical, administrative, and diplomatic experience in civil aviation matters. It is often only a coincidence that some of them happen to have legal training as well. And, since the Council has very extensive legislative and administrative functions to perform, it is not surprising that those serving on it, because of their training, temperament, and the pressure of their work, are more interested in having differences resolved than in adjudicating them.

All of these factors tend to produce a result probably not anticipated when the Chicago Acts were drafted. The Council's *modus operandi* in dealing with disputes has, for all practical purposes, done away with the legal distinction between disputes and complaints. Since the conciliator's role which it performs when dealing with complaints is in greater harmony with its institutional character, the Council prefers to use the same approach when a dispute is submitted to it, although in this context it was intended to act as an arbitral tribunal. By remaining adamant the parties can, of course, force the Council to adjudicate their dispute. But the institutional pressures to which the litigants are subjected, together with the ambiguities surrounding the appellate remedies and enforcement measures provided for in Chapter XVIII of the Convention, all tend to make it very difficult for the parties to "buck" the system.

It may seriously be doubted, however, whether this system, which is so well calculated to preserve harmony within the Organization, should also be employed in dealing with disputes arising under other international agreements conferring arbitral jurisdiction on the Council. The balloon controversy between the United States and Czechoslovakia indicates that the legal issues presented in disputes relating to the Convention and the Transit or Transport Agreements can probably be resolved more effectively by the Organization without litigation. This can be accomplished because ICAO has at its disposal other methods—such as ICAO studies, reports, debates, and eventually resolutions—which tend to clarify doubtful legal issues and provide some impartial fact-finding machinery.

These alternative methods are for the most part not available for the interpretation or application of other international aeronautical agreements. The bilateral air transport agreements, for example, usually contain rather complicated and ambiguous standard capacity [328] and route clauses.[329] They are widely used, although there is little agreement on their meaning. It would therefore undoubtedly be in the interest of international civil aviation to have a body of case law upon which states could draw in drafting or adopting such clauses. Since adjudication would here seem to be more important in the long run than negotiated settlements, the

---

[328] See HANDBOOK ON CAPACITY CLAUSES IN BILATERAL AIR TRANSPORT AGREEMENTS, ICAO Circular 72–AT/9 (1965).

[329] See Decision of the Arbitration Tribunal Established Pursuant to the Arbitration Agreement signed at Paris on 22 January 1963, between the United States of America and France, decided at Geneva on 22 December 1963, 3 Int'l L. M. 668 (1964).

Council's predilection for the latter should give way when it is seized with disputes arising under agreements other than the Chicago Acts.

These same considerations also justify the conclusion that the best interests of international civil aviation are not served by the Council's generally negative attitude toward the arbitral functions assigned to ICAO by various multilateral and bilateral agreements. It may be that the Council lacks the requisite competence and time to discharge this role properly. If so, it should nevertheless respond to the need for appropriate arbitral tribunals—the arbitral provisions found in many of these agreements envisage such tribunals— by promulgating rules for the establishment of such institutions under ICAO auspices. The Council's Rules for the Settlement of Differences could be applied to these proceedings with minor adjustments. It would therefore be relatively easy for ICAO to establish such an arbitral system to enable states to obtain judicial determinations on disputed questions of law or fact. The present practice, which puts a premium on negotiated settlements that often leave the underlying legal issues unresolved, is certainly far from satisfactory.

Part IV

ICAO and the Law Governing Amendments to the Convention on International Civil Aviation

INTRODUCTION

The constitutive instruments of some international organizations perform a dual function. In addition to establishing these organizations and serving as their charters, they very often also create rights and duties for the Contracting States that apply outside the institutional framework of the particular organization. This is true of the Chicago Convention. It is ICAO's fundamental law as well as a multilateral air navigation treaty that regulates the relations of the Contracting States *inter se*.

Because of the dual function which such constitutive instruments perform, it is extremely difficult to devise an acceptable method for their amendment.[1] Today most states are no longer opposed in principle to a procedure under which organizational amendments, *i.e.*, amendments relating to the internal operation of an international organization, enter into force with *erga omnes* effect once they have been ratified by a specified majority of the Contracting States. Many of these same states, however, are strongly committed to the unanimity requirement for non-organizational amendments because important treaty rights and obligations may be affected by such

---

[1] On the practice and law governing the amendment and revision of international conventions, see generally, Winterhager, DIE REVISION VON GRÜNDUNGSVERTRÄGEN INTERNATIONALER UND SUPRANATIONALER ORGANISATIONEN (Diss., Frankfurt/Main, 1963); Stabreit, DIE REVISION MULTILATERALER VÖLKERRECHTLICHER VERTRÄGE DURCH EINE BEGRENZTE ANZAHL DER VERTRAGS-PARTEIEN (Diss., Heidelberg, 1964); Leca, LES TECHNIQUES DE REVISION DES CONVENTIONS INTERNATIONALES (1961); Girand, MODIFICATIONS ET TERMINAISON DES TRAITÉS COLLECTIFS (Institut de Droit Internationale, 1960); Hoyt, THE UNANIMITY RULE IN THE REVISION OF TREATIES: A RE-EXAMINATION (1959); Schwelb, *The Amending Procedure of Constitutions of International Organizations*, 31 Brit. Yb. Int'l L. 49 (1954); Aufricht, *Supersession of Treaties in International Law*, 37 Cornell L.Q. 655 (1951–52); Jenks, *Some Constitutional Problems of International Organizations*, 22 Brit. Yb. Int'l L. 11, 65–68 (1945).

amendments. A compromise solution based on a formula that abandons the unanimity requirement for organizational amendments while retaining it for other amendments will not always be acceptable. It entails the risk—real or imagined—that by characterizing certain non-organizational amendments as organizational in nature, a majority might be able to vary or alter the substantive rights of the non-consenting states.

The constitutive instruments of some international organizations avoid this latter problem by providing that amendments shall enter into force only *inter se* the states that have accepted or ratified them.[2] This modified unanimity formula leaves the rights and obligations of the non-consenting states unaffected by the amendment, and has the advantage of depriving one or a small group of states of the power to block amendments that a majority wishes to adopt. It does have a very undesirable side effect, however, in that the entry into force of an amendment which has not been ratified by all Contracting States splits the particular constitutive instrument into two parts: one applicable to the states that have accepted the amendment, the other governing the relations between the consenting and the non-consenting states.

In a multilateral convention that is not also the constitutive instrument of an international organization the resulting multiplicity of obligations poses no greater problems than those that a state encounters when it adheres to a large number of bilateral treaties governing the same subject matter. The modified unanimity system does create havoc, however, when it is embodied in a multilateral convention that is also the charter of an international organization. Here, unless the entry into force of organizational amendments is governed by a different procedure, the internal operations of the particular organization may be governed by two constitutive instruments. Since no entity can function effectively when it is subject to equally binding yet conflicting sets of fundamental laws, international organizations that have to operate under the modified unanimity system often deal with the problems it poses by resorting to a variety of methods whose efficacy depends in large measure on the acquiescence of the Member States.

[2] For a collection of the various amendment clauses found in international conventions, see U.N. Secretariat, HANDBOOK OF FINAL CLAUSES, U.N. Doc. ST/LEG/6, pp. 130–49 (1957).

A study of the amendment practice of these international organizations is rewarded by the insights it provides about a particular organization's institutional maturity, viewed in terms of its capacity to develop techniques for coping with seemingly insurmountable legal obstacles. ICAO's amendment process is unusually well suited for such a study.

Article 94 of the Chicago Convention—the provision governing amendments—not only adopts the previously discussed modified unanimity formula; it is also a clause that is extremely poorly drafted. This latter factor undoubtedly accounts for the fact that it has been the subject of more attempted amendments than any other provision of the Convention.[3] Article 94 reads as follows:

> (a) Any proposed amendment to this Convention must be approved by a two-thirds vote of the Assembly and shall then come into force in respect of States which have ratified such amendment when ratified by the number of contracting States specified by the Assembly. The number so specified shall not be less than two-thirds of the total number of contracting States.
>
> (b) If in its opinion the amendment is of such a nature as to justify this course, the Assembly in its resolution recommending adoption may provide that any State which has not ratified within a specified period after the amendment has come into force shall thereupon cease to be a member of the Organization and a party to the Convention.

To date the Chicago Convention has been amended on five separate occasions.[4] Article 94 has thus been extensively interpreted by the Organization. The study that follows analyzes the manner in which ICAO has applied Article 94 and seeks to ascertain what, if

[3] For an analysis of the various attempts to amend Article 94, see ICAO Doc. C–WP/3456, Annex I, pp. 8–10 (1961).

[4] See Assembly Res. A1–3, ICAO Doc. 4411 (A1–P/45) (1947), adding Article 93 *bis* to the Convention; Assembly Res. A8–1, ICAO Doc. 7499 (A8–P/9) (1954), amending Articles 48(a), 49(e), and 61 (Frequency of Assembly Sessions); Assembly Res. A8–4, ICAO Doc. 7499 (A8–P/9) (1954), amending Article 45 (Permanent Seat of the Organization); Assembly Res. A13–1, ICAO Doc. 8167 (A13–P/2) (1961), amending Article 50(a) (Increasing Membership of the Council); Assembly Res. A14–5, ICAO Doc. 8268 (A14–P/20) (1962), amending Article 48(a) (Calling of Extraordinary Meetings of Assembly). Of these amendments only the last one has not as yet entered into force.

any, transformation this provision has undergone in the two decades following the establishment of ICAO.

APPLICATION OF ARTICLE 94(a)

The Two-Thirds Vote of the Assemby

Article 94(a) provides that "any proposed amendment to this Convention must be approved by a two-thirds vote of the Assembly. . . ." This clause can be interpreted in a number of different ways. The requirement of a "two-thirds vote of the Assembly" could mean: (1) a two-thirds vote of the states entitled to be represented in the Assembly, *i.e.*, two-thirds of all Contracting States; (2) a two-thirds vote of the states represented at the particular Assembly session; (3) a two-thirds vote of the states represented at the Assembly meeting on the day of the vote; or (4) two-thirds of the votes cast in a meeting of the Assembly after the existence of a quorum has been ascertained.[5] The Legal Commission of the ICAO Assembly considered these four possible interpretations in 1947 and concluded that ". . . the correct interpretation of Article 94(a) . . . is that any proposed amendment to the Convention must be approved by a vote of two-thirds of the Contracting States represented by accredited delegations at any Assembly (in this case at the First Assembly) of the Organization." [6]

Even though the Legal Commission's ruling on Article 94(a) had been expressly requested by the Assembly to clarify the procedure that was to be followed in amending the Convention by the addition of an Article 93 *bis*,[7] it is doubtful that this ruling was actually adhered to when the Assembly adopted Article 93 *bis*. The Assembly's minutes reveal only that this amendment was passed following a roll call to determine the existence of a quorum for the meeting.[8] No attempt seems to have been made to ascertain whether any Contracting States represented at the Assembly by accredited delegations were absent from the meeting. This omission is probably attributable to the fact that the ICAO Secretariat had found that

---

[5] See ICAO Doc. 4292 (A1–LE/47), p. 2 (1947).

[6] ICAO Doc. 4409 (A1–LE/69), p. 1 (1947).

[7] For an analysis of Article 93 *bis* and the reasons prompting this amendment to the Convention, see Part I, pp. 39–46 *supra*.

[8] See ICAO Assembly, 1st Sess., Doc. 4184 (A1–P/24), pp. 3–5 (1947).

the list of accredited delegations could not be relied upon, since "it appeared that the number of States shown as represented by the official registry of the Assembly could not be considered an accurate record of the number of delegations actually represented in Montreal, as delegations would sometimes leave the Assembly without notifying the registry of their departure." [9]

These difficulties prompted the Convention Committee to suggest that Article 94(a) be amended so as to provide that the adoption of an amendment required "a two-thirds vote of all Contracting States represented at the Assembly *at the time the vote is taken.*" (Emphasis added.) [10] The phrase "all Contracting States represented at the Assembly," the Convention Committee explained, should as far as possible be understood to refer to "the number of States actually represented . . . and that the official records kept during the Assembly should not, in principle, be considered as the determining factor." [11] Although Article 94(a) was never formally amended, the result which the Convention Committee sought to accomplish has been achieved through the promulgation of Rule 54 of the Assembly's Standing Rules of Procedure. [12]

Rule 54 provides that the two-thirds vote of the Assembly required under Article 94(a) ". . . shall be construed as meaning . . . two-thirds of the total number of Contracting States represented at the Assembly and qualified to vote at the time the vote is taken." It stipulates further that in computing the total number of "Contracting States represented at the Assembly," three categories of states shall not be counted. These are:

> (a) Contracting States whose Delegations had given notice in writing or otherwise of their withdrawal or departure from the Assembly prior to the time when the vote is taken;
>
> (b) Contracting States whose Delegations' credentials or instructions, filed with the Secretary General, expressly deprive them of the right to vote on the question with respect to which the required majority is being determined; and
>
> (c) Contracting States whose voting power is under suspension at the time the vote is taken.

[9] Committee on the Convention on International Civil Aviation [hereinafter cited as Convention Committee], ICAO Doc. 4802 (IC/504), p. 9 (1947).

[10] *Id.* at 7.

[11] *Id.* at 9.

[12] ICAO Doc. 7600/2 (1963).

Under Rule 54, read in conjunction with Article 48(c) of the Convention which specifies that a majority of the Contracting States constitutes a quorum, it is theoretically possible for the Assembly to adopt an amendment to the Convention even though less than one-half of all Contracting States have voted for it. Thus, if only 51 per cent of all Contracting States were to be represented at a particular Assembly, a two-thirds vote of these states would suffice to carry the amendment.[13]

The constitutionality of Rule 54 was challenged at the 1954 session of the ICAO Assembly by the Portuguese Delegate who contended that Rule 54 was in conflict with Articles 94(a) and 48(c) of the Convention, as well as with Rule 46 of the Assembly's Standing Rules of Procedure.[14] He argued that Article 48(c), which stipulates in part that "unless otherwise provided in this Convention, decisions of the Assembly shall be taken by a majority of the votes cast," indicated that states represented at the Assembly but not voting and states abstaining should not be counted in ascertaining the two-thirds vote required under Article 94(a) for the adoption of an amendment, because these states could not be deemed to have "cast" a vote. The Portuguese Delegate supported his contention by pointing to Rule 46 of the Assembly's Standing Rules of Procedure, which provides that "an abstention shall not be considered as a vote."

The Portuguese Delegate had challenged the constitutionality of Rule 54 shortly before the Assembly was to vote on two proposed amendments to the Convention. He therefore urged that Rule 54 be suspended for the duration of the session lest these amendments be dealt with under an illegal procedure.[15] When it appeared that those opposing the amendments viewed this motion as a maneuver to facilitate the adoption of these amendments, the Portuguese Delegate withdrew it and moved in its stead that the Assembly request the Council to study the constitutionality of Rule 54.[16] The Assem-

[13] That such a situation could very well arise is apparent from the fact that in the 1952 Session of the Assembly, for example, 36 states out of a total of 57 were represented. See Reply by the Secretary General, ICAO Assembly, Executive Committee, 8th Sess., Doc. 7501 (A8–EX/MIN. 1–13), p. 72 (1954).

[14] ICAO   Assembly,   Executive   Committee,   8th   Sess.,   Doc.   7501 (A8–EX/MIN. 1–13), p. 63 and pp. 96–97 (1954).

[15] *Id.* at 63.

[16] *Id.* at 97.

bly passed a resolution to this effect,[17] but applied the provisions of Rule 54 in voting on the two amendments.[18]

In compliance with the wishes of the Assembly, the Council requested the ICAO Legal Committee to examine the constitutionality of Rule 54.[19] After a thorough study,[20] the Legal Committee advised the Council that Rule 54 was not in conflict with Articles 94(a) and 48(c) of the Convention.[21] The Legal Committee's conclusion was based primarily on the ground that the phrase "unless otherwise provided in this Convention" found in Article 48(c), expressly exempted the voting requirements laid down in Article 94(a) from the application of Article 48(c).[22] The Legal Committee also pointed out that the practice of other international organizations on this question was not sufficiently uniform to compel a different interpretation of Article 94(a).[23]

This report was transmitted by the Council to the Contracting States for their comments. Since it received no negative comments on the conclusions of the Legal Committee, the Council advised the Assembly that in its view Rule 54 did not have to be revised.[24] The Assembly's Executive Committee accepted the Council's communication without discussion and reported it to the plenary meeting,[25] where the matter was not further considered. The constitutionality of Rule 54 has not been challenged again. It can, therefore, be

[17] Assembly Res. A8–6, ICAO Doc. 7499 (A8–P/9) (1954).

[18] See ICAO Assembly, 8th Sess., Doc. 7505 (A8–P/10), pp. 52–63 (1954). Interestingly enough, one draft resolution containing a proposed amendment to Article 45 of the Convention, which failed to pass in the form submitted, would have been adopted had the Portuguese interpretation of Article 94(a) prevailed. The vote on that draft resolution was 29 in favor, 6 against, with 9 states abstaining. *Id.* at 57. Since there were 44 states represented at the Assembly and qualified to vote, 30 affirmative votes were needed for adoption under Rule 54. Under the Portuguese interpretation of Article 94(a) the resolution would have passed, since abstaining states would not have been counted in establishing the required two-thirds vote of the Assembly.

[19] ICAO Council, 22nd Sess., Doc. 7490 (C/873), p. 104 (1954).

[20] This study is reproduced in ICAO Legal Committee, 10th Sess. [1954], Doc. 7601 (LC/138), Vol. II, pp. 61–70 (1955).

[21] Final Report of the Sub-Committee on Rule 54, ICAO Legal Committee, 10th Sess. [1954], Doc. 7601 (LC/138), Vol. I, p. liii, at lvi (1955).

[22] *Id.* at liv.

[23] *Id.* at lv–lvi.

[24] ICAO Council, 24th Sess. [1955], Doc. 7555 (C/876), p. 128 (1958).

[25] ICAO Assembly, Executive Committee, 9th Sess., Doc. 7597 (A9–EX/MIN. 1–12), p. 5 (1955).

regarded as an authoritative interpretation of the voting requirements laid down in Article 94(a) for the adoption of an amendment to the Convention.

Entry into Force of Amendments

EFFECT OF ENTRY INTO FORCE

Article 94(a) of the Convention provides that after an amendment has been adopted by the Assembly, it "shall then come into force in respect of States which have ratified such amendment when ratified by the number of contracting States specified by the Assembly. The number so specified shall not be less than two-thirds of the total number of contracting States." This clause raises a number of questions which will be treated separately.

Inter Se and Organizational Effect

On its face, Article 94(a) does not distinguish between amendments affecting the internal operations of the Organization and those relating to the rights and obligations of the Contracting States *inter se*. While it is not unreasonable to provide that amendments of the latter type should bind only those states that have ratified them, the same cannot be said of organizational amendments which relate to the internal operations of the Organization. It makes little sense to stipulate that an amendment governing the frequency of Assembly sessions, for example, even though it has entered into force, binds only those Contracting States that have ratified it. If this is in effect what Article 94(a) provides, it is clear that unless the Assembly invokes Article 94(b) of the Convention—something it has not done to date—and expels all states which fail to ratify the amendment after it has entered into force, ICAO will have to operate under two constitutive instruments.[26] It is accordingly not surprising

---

[26] The constitutive instruments of a number of international organizations therefore quite wisely distinguish between organizational amendments and amendments imposing so-called "new obligations" on the Contracting States. See Constitution of the Food and Agriculture Organization, Art. 20(2), 60 Stat. 1886, T.I.A.S. No. 1554 (1946); Constitution of the United Nations Educational, Scientific and Cultural Organisation, Art. 13(1), 61 Stat. 2495, T.I.A.S. No. 1580, 4 U.N.T.S. 275 (1947); Convention of the World Meteorological Organization, Art. 28(b) and (c), T.I.A.S. No. 2052, 77 U.N.T.S. 143 (1950–51). See also, U.N. Secretariat, HANDBOOK OF FINAL CLAUSES 130–49, U.N. Doc. ST/LEG/6 (1957).

that ICAO considered various proposals for the amendment of Article 94(a) to cope with this problem.

The Proposals to Amend Article 94(a). The first suggestion for the revision of Article 94(a) came from the Convention Committee.[27] It urged that Article 94 be amended to distinguish between "important amendments," which it described as those creating "new obligations" on the part of the Contracting States, and amendments "procedural or organizational in nature." Since the latter did not involve substantive obligations, the Committee proposed that Article 94 be revised to allow such amendments to enter into force without ratification.[28] The Convention Committee recognized that it would not always be easy to decide whether or not an amendment created "new obligations." It therefore suggested that any disputes relating to the character of an amendment be resolved by a two-thirds vote of all Contracting States.[29]

Substantially similar recommendations were made in other proposals considered by ICAO.[30] The most interesting of these is the "revised New York text" of Article 94.[31] Under the "revised New York text," if the Assembly decided that an amendment neither imposed a "new obligation" on the Contracting States nor deprived them of "any right," the amendment would enter into force without ratification. The Assembly's decision regarding the character of the amendment could, however, be formally challenged by any Contracting State. Once such a challenge was made, the Organization would have to seek an advisory opinion from the International Court of Justice, whose characterization of the amendment would be binding. The "revised New York text" also contained a provision

[27] ICAO Doc. 4039 (A1–CP/12), pp. 8–11 (1947).

[28] *Id.* at 8.

[29] *Id.* at 9. The draft resolution containing the Committee's proposed amendment of Article 94 is reprinted in the same document. *Id.* at 28–30. The Convention Committee took substantially the same position in its second report to the Council. See ICAO Doc. 4802 (IC/504) (1947).

[30] See, *e.g.*, Report of the Sub-Committee on Amendments to Article 94 of the Chicago Convention, ICAO Legal Committee, Doc. 5089 (LC/80) (1948); Committee on the Convention on International Civil Aviation, Fourth Report to the Council, ICAO Doc. 5176 (IC/509) (1948); Report of the Legal Committee on Amendments to Article 94, ICAO Doc. C–WP/130 (1949).

[31] This text is reprinted in ICAO Doc. C–WP/130, pp. 12–13 (1949). It was one of two proposals for the amendment of Article 94 that the Council referred to the ICAO Legal Committee for study and revision.

under which the Assembly, in approving an amendment, could decide that it was "essential for the objectives of the Convention that such amendment shall bind all Contracting States." States failing to ratify such an amendment within a period specified by the Assembly would be deemed to have denounced the Convention.

These proposals encountered considerable opposition. The discussions in the Legal Committee and in the Council revealed that any provision which would permit the Assembly to determine that a proposed amendment shall enter into force without ratification was quite unacceptable to a number of Contracting States.[32] Thus the U.S. Representative on the Council asserted that it was not "necessary or desirable" to amend Article 94. Pointing to the provisions of Article 94(b) as a means for achieving uniformity, he emphasized that the U.S. "did not favor any amendment of Article 94 which would permit amendments not imposing new substantive obligations to come into force without ratification." While he recognized that the charters of some other international organizations contained a similar provision, he felt that "an attempt to introduce it, by means of an amendment, into an existing instrument, particularly one of the character of the Chicago Convention, would appear most unwise."[33]

It is undoubtedly true that a formula that distinguishes between amendments imposing new substantive obligations and those not having this effect might in certain cases have given rise to disagreements, but this would have been a comparatively small price to pay for a system which was designed to assure that in matters relating to the internal organization of ICAO all states were bound by one and the same constitutive instrument. Here uniformity of obligations is an administrative necessity, yet it is most unrealistic to assume that the Assembly, in adopting such "housekeeping" amendments, will invoke the provisions of Article 94(b) to hasten ratification. These types of amendments are simply not important enough, when weighed against the benefits which international civil aviation derives from as universal an ICAO membership as possible, to justify the expulsion of states failing to ratify them.[34] Moreover, Article 94

[32] See ICAO Legal Committee, 3rd Sess., Doc. 6024 (LC/121), p. 75 (1949); ICAO Council, 6th Sess., Doc. 6574 (C/747), pp. 4–8 (1949).

[33] ICAO Council, 6th Sess., Doc. 6574 (C/747), p. 5 (1949).

[34] It could be argued, of course, that such amendments are left unratified not

might have been amended in such a manner as to substantially diminish the risk that the Assembly would characterize an amendment imposing new obligations as a "housekeeping measure." This could have been achieved either by expressly identifying the "housekeeping" provisions of the Convention that the Assembly was authorized to amend without ratification, or by enumerating the provisions of the Convention which, if amended, would bind only ratifying states.[35]

It may well be that Article 94 was never amended because the amendment, until ratified by all Member States, would not have accomplished the end it was designed to serve. This problem was noted by the Argentine Representative during a Council debate on the "revised New York text" and a similar United Kingdom proposal,[36] when he stated that he was sure "that many States would not accept an amendment to Article 94 along the lines of the New York text or the United Kingdom proposal. The result would be that there would be two Articles 94, some States abiding by the present Article, others by the new. This was a curious way to work towards uniformity." [37] At any rate, the attempts to revise ICAO's amendment process ended in 1950, when the ICAO Assembly resolved "that Article 94 of the Convention should be maintained in its present form." [38]

The Practice of the Organization under Article 94(a). The prac-

---

because of any objections to them, but because they are simply neglected by national authorities. A threat of expulsion under the provisions of Article 94(b) would serve to overcome this bureaucratic inertia, for no state would risk expulsion for failure to ratify an amendment to which it was not really opposed. This argument may well be valid, although the Assembly has thus far not been willing to test it.

[35] The International Bank for Reconstruction and Development and the International Monetary Fund operate under a somewhat similar system. Under the Articles of Agreement of these Organizations, amendments thereto, except those relating to three enumerated provisions, enter into force for all Contracting Parties "when three-fifths of the members, having four-fifths of the total voting power" have ratified them. Amendments to the three enumerated provisions have to be accepted by all Member States. See Articles of Agreement of the International Bank of Reconstruction and Development, Art. 8, T.I.A.S. No. 1502, 2 U.N.T.S. 134 (1947); Articles of Agreement of the International Monetary Fund, Art. 17, 60 Stat. 1401, T.I.A.S. No. 1501, 2 U.N.T.S. 39 (1947).

[36] The United Kingdom proposal is contained in ICAO Doc. C–WP/461 (1949).

[37] ICAO Council, 6th Sess., Doc. 6574 (C/747), p. 6 (1949).

[38] Assembly Res. A4–3, ICAO Doc. 7017 (A4–P/3) (1950).

tice of the Organization indicates that over the years ICAO has indirectly accomplished much of what it could not achieve directly by formal amendment of Article 94. Illustrative is the Assembly's handling of a problem that arose in connection with the amendment of Article 50(a) of the Convention, which enlarged the Council from a membership of 21 to 27 Member States.[39] Shortly before this amendment was adopted in 1961, the Assembly's Executive Committee considered the question whether states that did not ratify the amendment were eligible, once the amendment had entered into force, to vote for more than 21 Council Members and to be elected to the Council themselves.[40] Some delegates initially thought that this issue could be resolved by omitting from the Protocol of Amendment the usual clause stating that upon its entry into force the amendment bound only the states that had ratified it. This suggestion was dropped after the Director of the ICAO Legal Bureau stated that this action would be devoid of any legal significance, because under Article 94(a) only states which had ratified the amendment were bound by it. However, when asked "what would be the position of States that had not ratified the amendment in regard to voting or being a candidate for a Council of 27 members," the Director of the Legal Bureau replied that after a careful study by his Bureau "the conclusion had been reached that there was nothing in the Convention making the exercise of voting power by a Contracting State, or eligibility for election to the Council, dependent upon the fulfilment of such a condition as ratification of an amendment." [41] This opinion was subsequently accepted by the Council.[42]

As far as it goes, the opinion of the Legal Bureau is no doubt sound. It should be noted, however, that it is one thing to say that the Convention does not make the exercise of a state's voting power dependent upon its ratification of an amendment, but it is quite another matter to draw therefrom any conclusions regarding the constitutionality of a body composed in accordance with an amendment not ratified by all Contracting States. For if the Legal Bureau's

[39] This amendment, Assembly Res. A13–1, ICAO Doc. 8167 (A13–P/2) (1961), entered into force on 17 June 1962.

[40] ICAO Assembly, Executive Committee, 13th (Extraordinary) Sess., Doc. 8167 (A13–P/2), p. 30, at 55–56 (1961).

[41] *Id.* at 56.

[42] See ICAO Council, 46th Sess., Doc. 8247 (C/939), p. 69 (1962).

interpretation of Article 94(a) is correct, a state that had not ratified the amendment of Article 50(a) could validly assert, whether or not it participated in the vote on the enlarged Council, that a Council of 27 members was not legally constituted. It misses the point to argue, as the Secretariat subsequently did, that no state could challenge the constitutionality of decisions rendered by a 27-Member Council "because such decisions would be taken by a majority out of the 27 members of the Council, *i.e.*, by at least 14 votes, which would cover the requirement, prior to the amendment, of only 11 votes (*i.e.*, majority in a Council of 21 members)." [43]

What this argument overlooks is that in a 27-Member Council, 11 votes no longer suffice to carry a motion. In some cases a state might therefore have a valid ground upon which to challenge the legality of a Council action. Let us assume, for example, that the ICAO Council in dealing with a dispute submitted to it under Article 84, decides by a vote of 11 to 16 that State X has violated the Convention. If State X has not ratified the amendment to Article 50(a) it could validly claim that, in a 21-Member Council, the 11 votes cast against the Council decision would have prevented its adoption, and that for this reason the decision of the 27-Member Council was void as far as State X was concerned.

On July 17, 1962, a year after its adoption by the Assembly, the amendment of Article 50(a) entered into force. Meeting in August of 1962, the Assembly elected 27 Contracting States to serve on the Council. Prior to the balloting the Assembly, apparently without any objections, approved the recommendation of the Executive Committee that any Contracting State, whether or not it had ratified the amendment to Article 50(a), "could be a candidate in the election of the new Council of twenty-seven members and that any Contracting State represented at this session, whether it had ratified that amendment or not, would be entitled to vote in the election." [44]

A similar approach was followed by ICAO with regard to another organizational amendment. At its eighth session in 1954 the Assembly adopted an amendment to Articles 48(a), 49(e), and 61 of the Convention.[45] This amendment permits the Assembly to dispense with annual meetings and provides that the Assembly meet "not less

[43] ICAO Doc. C–WP/3456, Annex I, p. 22 n.3 (1961).
[44] ICAO Assembly, 14th Sess., Doc. 8269 (A14–P/21), p. 59 (1962).
[45] Assembly Res. A8–1, ICAO Doc. 7499 (A8–P/9) (1954).

than once in three years." Although this amendment did not enter into force until 12 December 1956, the ICAO Assembly, having been informed that the required number of ratifications would be forthcoming within the next few months, adopted a resolution on 16 July 1956 requesting the Council "to convene an Assembly session in 1959 and another session either in 1957 or 1958." [46] A similar resolution was adopted in 1959. [47] Finally, in 1962 the Assembly resolved "that the triennial arrangement of Assembly sessions should be regarded as the normal practice of the Organization. . . ." [48] The legality of these resolutions was never challenged, although the amendment in question had not been ratified by all Contracting States either in 1956, 1959, or 1962.

Appraisal of the Organization's Practice: A New Approach to Article 94(a). The practice just described justifies the conclusion that the institutional amendments of the type here under consideration will be applied by the Organization as soon as they have entered into force even though they have not been ratified by all Contracting States. [49] As a practical matter, this is the only rational solution short of the application of the provisions of Article 94(b). Furthermore, this result can be justified on the ground that it does not contravene Article 94(a). While it is conceptually sound to provide that an amendment relating to the rights and obligations of the Contracting States *inter se* "shall . . . come into force in respect of States which have ratified such amendment," the same cannot be said of institutional amendments. Of necessity, they either come into force as far as the Organization is concerned or they do not, for if they only come into force "in respect of States which have ratified such amendment," these states have the legal right to have the Organization conduct its business in accordance with the amendment as soon as the requisite number of ratifications is in. States which have not ratified it would at the same time have the right not to have the amendment applied. A literal application of Article 94(a) would require giving effect to both the rights of the states that have and those that have not ratified the amendment. It is therefore arguable that the language of Article 94(a) pertinent here can be

[46] Assembly Res. A10–13, ICAO Doc. 7707 (A10–P/16) (1956).
[47] Assembly Res. A12–7, ICAO Doc. 7998 (A12–P/3) (1959).
[48] Assembly Res. A14–4, ICAO Doc. 8268 (A14–P/20) (1962).
[49] ICAO Doc. C–WP/3456, Annex I, p. 21 (1961).

read as applying only to amendments affecting the rights and obligations of the Contracting States *inter se,* for it is only in this context that the clause can be effectively and meaningfully applied.

The validity of this argument is not weakened by the fact that the Convention furnishes the Assembly, in Article 94(b), with a method that can avoid the absurd result which a strict reading of Article 94(a) produces. If Article 94(b) applied automatically to the organizational amendments here under consideration or referred to them in any way, one could not reasonably assert that Article 94(a) does not govern the entry into force of such amendments for organizational purposes. But Article 94(b) is completely silent on this point, and Article 94(a) does not deal at all with the entry into force of an amendment for organizational purposes. It is therefore permissible to adopt the view that the Convention permits the Assembly to stipulate when a given amendment shall enter into force for organizational purposes. This action by the Assembly would not affect the rights and obligations of the Contracting States *inter se,* because the provisions of Article 94(a) would still apply to any matters regulated by the amendment which do not relate to the institutional framework of the Organization. A state could then be said to be bound by the provisions of an amendment *qua* member of the Organization if the amendment is in force for the Organization. If that state has not ratified the amendment, however, the amendment will not affect its rights or obligations *qua* Contracting State in its *inter partes* relations with other Contracting States.

The application of this interpretation of Article 94(a) can be illustrated by reference to a 1947 amendment which added an Article 93 *bis* to the Convention.[50] Article 93 *bis* provides that

> A State whose government the General Assembly of the United Nations has recommended be debarred from membership in international agencies established by or brought into relationship with the United Nations shall automatically cease to be a member of the International Civil Aviation Organization.[51]

This amendment, it will be recalled, was prompted by the refusal of the U.N. General Assembly to accord ICAO the status of a U.N. specialized agency unless Franco Spain, which had ratified the Con-

[50] Assembly Res. A1–3, ICAO Doc. 4411 (A1–P/45) (1947).
[51] Convention, Art. 93(a) *bis.*

vention before the first Assembly convened in 1947, was expelled from the Organization.[52] The implementation of this amendment posed two problems resulting from the language of Article 94. The first concerned the manner in which the Organization might comply with the condition imposed by the U.N. Since under Article 94(a) an amendment can come into force only after it has been ratified by at least two-thirds of the Contracting States, the mere adoption of the amendment would not have brought about the expulsion of Spain. A number of proposals addressing themselves to this problem were therefore considered by the Assembly.[53] They were not acted upon, however, since Spain advised the Assembly shortly before the vote that it would not participate in the Organization if the amendment was adopted.[54]

Once Spain had given this notice the Assembly no longer had to resolve the second problem, which bears directly on the subject of our discussion and concerns the legal effect of the amendment once it has entered into force.[55] This question could, of course, have been resolved had the Assembly invoked the provisions of Article 94(b), but this it did not do. Therefore, if the entry into force of the amendment is in all respects governed by the provisions of Article 94(a), one would have to conclude that unless all Contracting States have ratified Article 93 *bis*, an "expelled" state would remain a member of the Organization with regard to some states. Besides, even if all the Contracting States except the "expelled" state did ratify the amendment, the latter's membership in ICAO could not as a matter of law be regarded as terminated, because under Article 94(a) an amendment is only binding *inter se* the parties that have ratified it.[56]

If it is assumed that a state expelled under Article 93 *bis* also ceases to be a party to the Convention, Article 94(a) produces an

---

[52] See Part I, pp. 39–46 *supra*.

[53] See ICAO Assembly, Commission No. 1, Doc. 4013 (A1–CP/1), pp. 4–6, (1947).

[54] Statement by the Spanish Delegation, ICAO Assembly, Proceedings of the First [1947] Sess., Doc. 7325 (C/852), p. 127, at 128 (1952).

[55] This question is by no means academic. Article 93 *bis* did not obtain the necessary number of ratifications until 1961. It then entered into force but has still not been ratified by a substantial number of Contracting States, among them the United States and France.

[56] See ICAO Doc. C–WP/3456, Annex I, p. 21 (1961).

entirely rational and workable result as far as the rights and obligations of the Contracting States *inter se* are concerned. Until it has
ratified the amendment, the "expelled" state remains a party to the
Convention. It is thus entitled to the performance of those obligations which the other Contracting States have assumed toward it
qua Contracting States. Pursuant to Article 5 of the Convention, for
example, such a state could claim landing and transit rights for its
non-scheduled air services in and over the territory of any other
Contracting State.[57] However, the result becomes absurd when the
provisions of Article 94(a) are made to govern the "expelled"
state's membership status in the Organization. Its logical effect is to
convert ICAO into two organizations. The membership of one would
consist of all states that have ratified Article 93 *bis,* the other, of
these states plus the "expelled" state, if the latter has not ratified
the amendment.

Such a result can be avoided, without in any way affecting the
rights and obligations of the Contracting States *inter se,* if one
assumes that the entry into force of an amendment for organizational purposes is not governed by the provisions of Article 94(a).
This interpretation would give the ICAO Assembly the power to
stipulate when an amendment shall enter into force for purely
organizational purposes. The Organization's practice relating to the
amendments of Articles 50(a) and 48(a) indicates, as we have seen,
that the Assembly has in fact exercised this power while giving lip
service to the language of Article 94(a).

This approach makes it unnecessary, furthermore, to decide
whether an amendment creates new obligations or is merely organizational in nature. Some amendments, such as that relating to Article 93 *bis* for example, cannot be classified as falling in one or the
other category. It would therefore sometimes be impossible to characterize an amendment in a manner that is conceptually sound. The
need for such characterization can be avoided, however, by providing in each Protocol of Amendment when an amendment shall enter
into force for organizational purposes, and when it shall be binding
inter se the parties in their relations not as members of the Organization but as Contracting States. The first date would then apply

---

[57] See International Law Commission, Draft Articles on the Law of Treaties,
Arts. 36(4) and 26(4)(b), Gen. Ass. Off. Rec., 21st Sess., Supplement No. 9,
U.N. Doc. A/6309/Rev. 1 (1966).

whenever it is found that the amendment affects the internal operations of the Organization; the second date would govern to the extent that the amendment is capable of affecting any rights or obligations which one state might assert against another in their relations as Contracting Parties to the Convention.

Effect on New Contracting Parties

ICAO practice indicates that a state which becomes a member of the Organization after an amendment to the Convention has entered into force is not deemed to have ratified the amendment by depositing its instrument of ratification or adherence to the Convention.[58] This result is in part attributable to the fact that instruments of ratification and adherence to the Convention must be deposited with the Government of the United States,[59] whereas the Assembly has in each instance designated the Organization as the depositary for instruments ratifying the amendments. A state cannot therefore ratify the Convention together with its amendments in a single instrument of ratification. It must be remembered, moreover, that under Article 94(a) the entry into force of an amendment does not *ipso facto* deprive the original provision of the Convention of its effect *inter se* the Contracting Parties.[60] That is to say, as long as an amendment has not been ratified by all Contracting States, there does not theoretically exist one document that can be said to be *the* Convention although, if the amendment affects the internal operations of the Organization, it may be deemed to have come into force for organizational purposes only. The situation would be different if a new ratification of the Convention were to be deposited after all Contracting States had ratified the amendment. Here, provided the problem of dual depositaries is resolved, the ratification by all States could be said to have resulted in a novation.[61]

The Assembly could, of course, have required every new Contracting State, as a condition precedent to ICAO membership, to ratify all amendments that had previously entered into force. It has not done so, however, even though a suggestion to that effect was made

---

[58] ICAO Doc. C–WP/3456, Annex I, p. 26 (1961); Mankiewicz, *Air Law Conventions and the New States*, 29 J. Air L. & Com. 52, 57 (1963).

[59] Convention, Arts. 91(a) and 92(b).

[60] See ICAO Doc. C–WP/2862, p. 1 (1959).

[61] ICAO Doc. C–WP/3456, Annex I, p. 27 (1961).

as early as 1947.[62] As a result, some new Contracting States may not even know that their ratification does not also apply to the amendments or, for that matter, that the Convention has ever been amended. This confusion is compounded by the fact that no reference to amendments appears in the certified copy of the Convention which the U.S. Government transmits to states upon the deposit of their instruments of ratification or adherence. To cope with these problems, the ICAO Secretariat now informs all new Contracting States that the Convention has been amended and invites them to ratify these amendments.[63]

NUMBER OF RATIFICATIONS REQUIRED FOR ENTRY
INTO FORCE

Article 94(a) provides that an amendment comes into force when it has been "ratified by the number of contracting States specified by the Assembly," which number "shall not be less than two-thirds of the total number of contracting States." The Assembly has to date never required a larger number of ratifications than the two-thirds minimum provided for in Article 94(a). In 1954, when the Assembly discussed a proposal to amend Article 45 of the Convention,[64] the United Kingdom Delegate moved that the entry into force of this amendment be conditioned upon the deposit of a substantially larger number of ratifications than the minimum two-thirds prescribed by Article 94(a). This motion was withdrawn before it could be voted upon.[65]

In theory, the two-thirds requirement is an adequate guarantee against the entry into force of amendments that do not enjoy the support of a substantial number of Contracting States, but this has not been true in the case of ICAO. The most striking illustration of

[62] See ICAO Doc. 4039 (A1–CP/12), p. 10 (1947).
[63] ICAO Doc. C–WP/3456, Annex I, p. 27 (1961). See also, Remarks of ICAO Secretary General, ICAO Assembly, Executive Committee, 13th (Extraordinary) Sess., Doc. 8167 (A13–P/2), p. 58 (1961).
[64] This amendment was adopted in 1954. Assembly Res. A8–4, ICAO Doc. 7499 (A8–P/9) (1954). It gives the Assembly the power to move the permanent seat of the Organization and was prompted by the difficulties ICAO encountered in its negotiations with the Province of Quebec over Provincial tax immunities. See Mankiewicz, *Organisation Internationale de l'Aviation Civile*, [1957] Annuaire Français de Droit International 394–96.
[65] ICAO Assembly, Executive Committee, 8th Sess., Doc. 7501 (A8–EX/MIN. 1–13), p. 72 (1954).

this point is supplied by Article 93 *bis*. It entered into force on 20 March 1961, having on this date been ratified by 28 states—the number specified by the Assembly when the amendment was adopted.[66] By 20 March 1961, the membership of the Organization had increased to 85. The amendment thus entered into force although it had been ratified by less than 50 per cent of the total number of Contracting States.[67]

This curious result is the product of two interpretations bearing on the application of the two-thirds requirement. Both have to do with the meaning ascribed to the last sentence of Article 94(a) that "the number so specified [by the Assembly for the coming into force of the amendment] shall not be less than two-thirds of the total number of contracting States." This provision could be read as providing that in order to enter into force an amendment must be ratified by two-thirds of the total number of Contracting States, which number would be determined by reference to the date of deposit of the latest instrument of ratification.[68] The Assembly has not, however, adopted this interpretation of Article 94(a). Instead, beginning with the first amendment to the Convention which was adopted in 1947, the Assembly has always ascertained the requisite two-thirds number of Contracting States by reference to the total membership of the Organization at the time of the adoption of the amendment.[69] Given this application of Article 94(a), and considering that ICAO's membership has more than tripled since its establishment two decades ago, it is not surprising that some amendments have entered into force even though they were ratified by a very small number of Contracting States.

This result might also have been avoided if Article 94(a) had been interpreted as barring the entry into force of an amendment

---

[66] See Assembly Res. A1–4, ICAO Doc. 4411 (A1–P/45) (1947).

[67] The ICAO Council's ruling that the amendment had entered into force was not challenged. [1961] Report of the Council, ICAO Doc. 8219 (A14–P/4), p. 78 (1962).

[68] The possibility of this interpretation of Article 94(a) was noted in the First Interim Report of the Chairman of Commission No. 1. It pointed out that if the Assembly were to adopt the amendment relating to Article 93 *bis*, it would have "to set up the number of contracting States required for the coming into force of such amendment, and also to specify at what date the minimum number of two-thirds of the contracting States, prescribed as a basis to set up the previous number, should be counted." ICAO Doc. 4117 (A1–CP/24), p. 3 (1947).

[69] See ICAO Doc. C–WP/3456, Annex I, p. 20 (1961).

unless it was ratified by two-thirds of those states that were members of the Organization at the time the amendment was adopted. The influx of new members would thus not have distorted the two-thirds requirement. ICAO has not, however, followed this interpretation of Article 94(a). It has instead consistently been guided by the principle that "the amendment comes into force as soon as the specified number of Contracting States have ratified it, irrespective of whether or not any of the ratifying States was a party to the Convention at the date of the adoption of the amendment." [70]

Since ICAO's membership will henceforth remain relatively stable, this rather liberal interpretation of the two-thirds requirement will not have a significant impact on the entry into force of future amendments. There can be little doubt, however, that this interpretation of Article 94(a), taken together with the relative ease with which amendments can be adopted by the Assembly under Rule 54 of the Assembly's Standing Rules of Procedure, has in the past produced results that are highly questionable as a matter of principle.

DATE OF ENTRY INTO FORCE

Since upon its entry into force an amendment to the Convention that affects the rights and obligations of the Contracting States *inter se* binds only those states which have ratified it, no significance attaches to the fact that the date of entry into force of the amendment and the date on which it becomes binding on a particular state differ. These differences in dates do, however, pose problems in the case of "organizational" amendments which, as ICAO practice indicates, are implemented as soon as they enter into force. [71]

Illustrative is a problem that was discussed by the ICAO Council while it was reviewing the documentation for the Extraordinary

[70] *Ibid.* See also, [1961] Report of the Council, ICAO Doc. 8219 (A14–P/4), p. 78 (1962), where the Council reported that "the first amendment to the Convention . . . came into force on 20 March [1961], when ratification by the Ivory Coast, Mali and Senegal brought the number of States that had ratified to the required twenty-eight." Neither of these states was a Contracting Party when this amendment was adopted.

[71] For a discussion of a similar problem arising under the U.N. Charter, see Schwelb, *Amendments to Articles 23, 27 and 61 of the Charter of the United Nations,* 59 Am. J. Int'l L. 834, 850–51 (1965); Schwelb, *The 1963/1965 Amendments to the Charter of the United Nations: An Addendum,* 60 Am. J. Int'l L. 371 (1966).

Assembly Session that had been called to consider the amendment of Article 50(a). This amendment enlarged the membership of the Council from 21 to 27 Member States.[72] Anticipating its adoption, the Council was called upon to consider what the legal effect of this amendment would be in the period between its entry into force and the election by the Assembly of the new 27-Member Council.[73] The President of the Council wanted to have this question resolved, because the ICAO Legal Bureau had expressed the opinion that as soon as the amendment came into force "the Council had a membership of twenty-seven and the 'two-thirds of the Council' mentioned in Article 90(a) [Adoption of Annexes] was eighteen, not fourteen." [74] Lest states opposing the adoption of an Annex or amendment thereto challenge its legality on the ground that the Council was improperly constituted, the President of the Council "thought that it was better to be on the safe side and to get the Assembly to clarify what the position would be in the interval between the coming into force of the amendment and the first election under the amended Article." [75]

In his opinion, the matter could be satisfactorily resolved in one of three ways. The first was for the Assembly to adopt a resolution stipulating that until the new Council was elected "the number of votes necessary for the purposes of Articles 52 [Voting in Council] and 90(a) would be eleven and fourteen respectively." The second alternative was to incorporate a clause to that same effect in the Protocol of Amendment. Finally, the Assembly might provide that the Protocol specify "that the amendment would take effect (as distinct from come into force) only on the date on which the Assembly held the first election to fill any or all of the twenty-seven seats." [76] The Council debated these alternatives as well as the opinion of the Legal Bureau that the first alternative was *ultra vires* the powers of the Assembly.[77]

Eventually, motivated by the desire to keep the agenda of the extraordinary session as simple as possible, the Council decided not

[72] See Assembly Res. A13–1, ICAO Doc. 8167 (A13–P/2) (1961).
[73] ICAO Council, 42nd Sess. [1961], Doc. 8129 (C/929), pp. 221–24 and 227–29 (1963).
[74] *Id.* at 221.
[75] *Id.* at 222.
[76] *Id.* at 221.
[77] *Ibid.*

to draw the Assembly's attention to this problem.[78] It was thereafter also not raised in the Assembly which, in adopting the amendment to Article 50(a), merely specified the number of ratifications that would be necessary to bring the amendment into force. This amendment entered into force on 17 July 1962. The new 27-Member Council was elected on 28 August 1962. Interestingly enough, in the period between 17 July and 28 August the Council, which was then in its fifty-sixth session, held one short meeting at which only routine business was transacted. Predictably, no Contracting State challenged the legality of any of the actions taken at this meeting.

It is noteworthy that in considering the foregoing problems the Council did not address itself to the question whether states which did not ratify the amendment could object to its application by the Organization. The Council no doubt assumed that, notwithstanding the language of Article 94(a), ICAO was bound by an organizational amendment that had entered into force. If Article 94(a) does not prevent the application by ICAO of organizational amendments as soon as they have entered into force, it must be because Article 94(a) does not deal with this problem. From this it follows that the Convention leaves the Assembly free to fix the date on which such amendment shall be applicable, provided only that this date is subsequent to the date on which the amendment comes into force.

The Application of Article 94(b)

Article 94(b) permits the Assembly to provide, "in its resolution recommending [the] adoption" of an amendment, that any state which fails to ratify the amendment within a specified period after its entry into force "shall thereupon cease to be a member of the Organization and a party to the Convention." This action is authorized only if in the Assembly's "opinion the amendment is of such a nature as to justify this course."

An analysis of Article 94(b) indicates, first, that its provisions may only be invoked by the Assembly in its resolution of adoption. The Assembly accordingly lacks the power to provide in a resolution passed after the adoption of the amendment that Article 94(b) applies to it, even if in retrospect such action appears justified. Second, the Assembly may only implement the sanctions of Article

[78] *Id.* at 225.

94(b) after the amendment has entered into force. Third, Article 94(b) expressly provides not only for the termination of a state's membership in the Organization, but also that the non-ratifying state ceases to be a party to the Convention. Finally, not every amendment adopted by the Assembly is subject to the provisions of Article 94(b). The Assembly must first conclude that the amendment is "of such nature as to justify this course."

The past practice of the Organization in not invoking Article 94(b) justifies the conclusion that only amendments of a fundamental or all-pervasive character that radically alter the basic conception of the Convention will prompt the Assembly to apply Article 94(b). This conclusion is buttressed by the fact that universal membership has been the goal of the Organization from its inception.[79] The Assembly will therefore not risk a decrease in ICAO's membership for any but the most compelling reasons. Thus, neither the possibility of administrative inconvenience nor the likelihood of future legal complications will prompt the Assembly to invoke the sanctions authorized by Article 94(b).

ICAO POLICY RELATING TO AMENDMENTS

The Submission of Proposed Amendments

In 1950 the Assembly adopted Resolution A4–3 setting out ICAO's general policy with regard to amendments of the Convention.[80] This policy statement, which remains in force, provides that "an amendment of the Convention may be appropriate when either or both of the following tests is satisfied: (i) when it is proved necessary by experience; (ii) when it is demonstrably desirable or useful." Regarding the nature of amendments, the Assembly indicated that it was opposed to any plans "in the near future for a general revision of the Convention," and that "modification of the Convention should be accomplished by specific amendment only."

After providing that Article 94 should be maintained in its original form, Resolution A4–3 prescribes two rules to be followed in

[79] See Assembly Res. A1–9, ICAO Doc. 4411 (A1–P/45) (1947), where the Assembly proclaimed that "universal membership in the International Civil Aviation Organization is desirable to achieve its maximum usefulness in promoting safety in the air and the efficient and orderly development of air transport."

[80] Assembly Res. A4–3, ICAO Doc. 7017 (A4–P/3) (1950).

processing proposed amendments to the Convention. The first of these instructs the Council to refrain from initiating proposals for amendments "unless in the opinion of the Council such amendment is urgent in character." The second rule stipulates

> that any Contracting State wishing to propose an amendment to the Convention should submit it in writing to the Council at least six months before the opening date of the Assembly to which it is to be presented. The Council shall consider any such proposal and transmit it to the Contracting States together with its comments or recommendations thereon at least three months before the opening date of the Assembly.

The last sentence of these guidelines has been embodied with minor textual changes in Rule 10(d) of the Assembly's Standing Rules of Procedure,[81] which provides:

> Proposals for the amendment of the Convention, together with any comments or recommendations of the Council thereon, shall be communicated to Contracting States so as to reach them at least ninety days before the opening of the session.

Rule 10(d) has been suspended on two occasions to date. The first suspension occurred in 1954. It enabled the Assembly to vote on a proposal to amend Article 45 of the Convention authorizing ICAO to move its headquarters from Montreal.[82] There was considerable opposition to this amendment in the Assembly [83] and, since

---

[81] ICAO Doc. 7600/2 (1963).

[82] This amendment proposal originated with the ICAO Council, Action of the Council, 21st Sess., ICAO Doc. 7484 (C/872), p. 28 (1954). A draft resolution embodying a proposed amendment of Article 45 was submitted to the Assembly in 1950 by Argentina, Cuba, Mexico, and Venezuela. See ICAO Assembly, Report of the Executive Committee, 4th Sess., Doc. 7007 (A4–EX/2), p. 5 (1950). It was not adopted, however, having failed to receive the requisite two-thirds vote of the 1950 Assembly. See ICAO Assembly, 4th Sess., Doc. 7016 (A4–P/2), p. 88 (1950). The ICAO Council sought this amendment in 1954 to strengthen ICAO's bargaining position in its negotiations with the Province of Quebec for an exemption from the Provincial Income Tax Act. Invoking Assembly Resolution A4–3, which stipulates that the Council should not submit an amendment proposal to the Assembly directly unless the amendment was "urgent in character," the opponents of the amendment argued that it was not urgent and that the Council consequently lacked the power to submit it to the Assembly. See ICAO Council, 21st Sess., Doc. 7464 (C/871), pp. 157–59, 171–76 (1954). The proponents of the amendment nevertheless prevailed in the Council by a vote of 13 to 6, with 1 abstention. *Id.* at 171.

[83] See ICAO Assembly, 8th Sess., Doc. 7505 (A8–P/10), pp. 53–65 (1954).

the ninety-day requirement laid down in Rule 10(d) had not been observed, the opponents of the amendment strenuously objected to its suspension. They argued that the suspension of Rule 10(d) was contrary to the amendment policy enunciated by the Assembly in 1950, and that it was irresponsible for the Assembly to adopt amendments that were not urgent without giving the Contracting States adequate time to consider their advisability.[84] By a vote of 28 to 5, with 4 abstentions, the Assembly nevertheless suspended Rule 10(d).[85]

Rule 10(d) was also suspended in 1965 to permit the Assembly to consider an amendment of Article 93, which would have authorized the Organization to suspend or exclude from ICAO membership any Contracting State practicing a policy of apartheid and racial discrimination.[86] The suspension of Rule 10(d) was necessitated by the fact that the draft resolution proposing the amendment was circulated to the Contracting States for the first time while the Assembly was already in session. Notwithstanding this rather drastic departure from the Assembly's general policy relating to amendments, the 31 states which sponsored this amendment nevertheless obtained the necessary majority of the votes cast to permit suspension of Rule 10(d).[87]

It is thus readily apparent that Rule 10(d) will not prevent the Assembly from considering hastily conceived amendments to the Convention. This is most regrettable. The suspension of Rule 10(d) not only deprives the Contracting States of the time needed to consider the advisability of such amendments, but it also makes it impossible for the Organization's legal staff to study the draft proposals with the care needed to prevent the adoption of poorly drafted amendments.

The Protocol of Amendment

When adopting an amendment to the Convention, the Assembly at the same time instructs the ICAO Secretary General to draw up a Protocol embodying the amendment. The Assembly's current prac-

[84] *Id.* at 34–39.

[85] *Id.* at 39.

[86] This draft resolution is reproduced in ICAO Assembly, Report of the Executive Committee, 15th Sess., Doc. 8522 (A15–EX/43), pp. 30–31 (1965).

[87] See ICAO Assembly, 15th Sess., Doc. 8516 (A15–P/5), p. 139 (1965). The amendment itself was defeated. *Id.* at 142.

tice is to set forth all matters relating to the Protocol in the resolution of adoption.[88] This is a departure from the procedure that was followed when the first amendment to the Convention was adopted in 1947. On that occasion the Assembly adopted a separate resolution relating to the preparation of the Protocol.[89]

The instructions to the Secretary General are usually embodied in a clause that might read as follows:

> THE ASSEMBLY . . . RESOLVES that the Secretary General of the International Civil Aviation Organization draw up a Protocol, in the English, French and Spanish languages, each of which shall be of equal authenticity, embodying the proposed amendment above mentioned and the matter hereinafter appearing.[90]

The "matter hereinafter appearing" consists of a number of clauses relating, *inter alia*, to the ratification of the amendment, its entry into force, and the functions of the ICAO Secretary General as depositary of the instruments of ratification. These clauses customarily provide that the Protocol may be ratified by the Contracting Parties to the Convention; they specify the number of ratifications required for its entry into force "in respect of the States that have ratified it"; and contain a stipulation that "with respect to any Contracting State ratifying the Protocol after the date aforesaid [its entry into force], the Protocol shall come into force upon

[88] See, *e.g.*, Assembly Res. A14–5, ICAO Doc. 8268 (A14–P/20) (1962).

[89] See Assembly Res. A1–4, ICAO Doc. 4411 (A1–P/45) (1947).

[90] See, *e.g.*, Assembly Res. A13–1, ICAO Doc. 8167 (A13–P/2) (1961). The Assembly's practice of instructing the Secretary General to draw up a Protocol in the three official languages of the Organization deserves attention because until recently there did not exist an official trilingual text of the Convention. The final clause of the Convention reads in part as follows:

> Done at Chicago the seventh day of December 1944, in the English language. A text drawn up in the English, French, and Spanish languages, each of which shall be of equal authenticity, shall be opened for signature at Washington, D.C.

Such a trilingual text was not drawn up, however, because the United States, which had attempted to prepare it, encountered considerable difficulty in doing so. See generally, ICAO Doc. C–WP/4031 (1964).

An authentic French and Spanish text of the Convention has now been appended to a PROTOCOL ON THE AUTHENTIC TRILINGUAL TEXT OF THE CONVENTION ON INTERNATIONAL CIVIL AVIATION (*Chicago*, 1944), which was open for signature at Buenos Aires on 24 September 1968. The Protocol is reproduced in T.I.A.S. No. 6605.

deposit of its instrument of ratification with the International Civil Aviation Organization." [91]

The Protocol is not opened for signature by the Contracting States. Instead, it is merely signed by the President and the Secretary General of the Assembly session at which the amendment was adopted. Certified copies of the Protocol are then transmitted by the ICAO Secretary General, in accordance with the Assembly's instructions, to all Contracting States and all new states adhering to the Convention.[92]

Conclusion

Over the years, ICAO has demonstrated an unusual capacity for reshaping many provisions of the Convention without formally amending them. This approach, compelled by the difficulties the Organization encountered with the amendment process prescribed in Article 94, capitalizes on the readily observable phenomenon that modifications which cannot be achieved directly by amendment can often be obtained through acquiescence to certain practices that bring about these modifications. Because amendments as a rule require domestic legislative or executive assent, an amendment proposal triggers a process which begins with national delegations requesting instructions from their governments and concludes with a government decision on the amendment. Since a multitude of considerations enter into the making of this decision—some of them having nothing to do with the merits of the amendment—it is more likely that the amendment will be rejected than that it will be accepted.

The converse is probably true where modifications of a provision of the constitutive instrument of an international organization are accomplished in the course of the organization's day-to-day practice. This tends to be a very gradual and sometimes imperceptible

[91] See, *e.g.*, Assembly Res. A13–1, ICAO Doc. 8167 (A13–P/2) (1961).

[92] The Assembly in its resolution of adoption customarily directs the Secretary General of the Organization to transmit certified copies of the Protocol to all Contracting States. Specific instructions to this effect appear in all but one such resolution. See Assembly Res. A13–1, ICAO Doc. 8167 (A13–P/2) (1961). It was probably omitted in this case, because the Assembly directed the Secretary General in a companion resolution to bring the amendment to the attention of the Contracting States with a view toward their expeditious ratification of the amendment. Assembly Res. A13–2, ICAO Doc. 8167 (A13–P/2) (1961).

process. As a result, states are often not alerted by their representatives to the modifications that have been wrought until a given practice has become well established, by which time they may be deemed to have assented to it.

A striking example of the manner in which this process operates is presented by the transformation that Article 94(a) itself has undergone. Although the various attempts to amend Article 94(a) failed, substantially all the modifications of that provision sought to be achieved by its amendment were subsequently read into it by the Organization. This result has probably been facilitated by the fact that very few lawyers serve on the ICAO Council or on national delegations to the ICAO Assembly. Since those not trained in the law are often unaware that their acquiescence to a given practice may have legal consequences, they tend to be oblivious to the legal effect that might be ascribed to their conduct. One would suppose, therefore, that they would not as a rule seek instructions from their governments on whether to acquiesce to a "practical" solution that is presented in the course of the Organization's deliberation, whereas that same solution, should it be couched in the form of an amendment, would obviously present a "legal" question to them on which they would want to consult their governments.

In the absence of sound empirical data on the behavior of ICAO Council Representatives and national delegations to the Assembly, it is difficult to say how valid this hypothesis is. It does, however, seem to explain the curious phenomenon that none of the states which were opposed to the formal amendment of Article 94(a) objected to its *de facto* amendment along substantially similar lines. It is arguable that Article 94(a) did not have to be amended, because the manner in which it was subsequently applied by the Organization is compatible with its provisions. Even if this be true—and it may well be that it is—the fact remains that those who supported the amendment proposals, and those who were opposed to them, proceeded on the assumption that the result sought to be accomplished required an amendment of Article 94(a). Yet when the Organization subsequently applied Article 94(a) as if it had been amended, no objections were raised. This would seem to indicate that the representatives of some states must not have been alerted to or failed to grasp the legal consequences of their acquiescence.

The transformation that Article 94(a)—and, for that matter,

many other provisions of the Convention—has undergone over the years, indicates that the admittedly much slower process of law-making by precedent-setting practice has proved to be more effective than formal amendment in resolving many of the constitutional problems that ICAO has had to cope with. These findings are by no means surprising once it is recognized that the constitutive instrument of an international organization is the functional equivalent of a domestic constitution, with which it shares an inherent potential for constitutional evolution.

General Conclusion

The findings that have emerged from the foregoing study have already been discussed in the individual conclusions to each of the four parts comprising it. Little would therefore be gained by restating these findings again. Here it may be useful, however, to call attention to the single most important conclusion that has emerged from this study: ICAO's unusual capacity for adapting its constitutive instrument to the demands which have been made on it over the two decades of its existence.

ICAO's experience indicates that the charter of an international organization is potentially no less capable of evolution than is a national constitution. This evolution, whether it occurs on the domestic or international plane, presupposes a level of institutional maturity whose basic ingredient is the existence of a broad consensus regarding the ultimate aims or functions of the particular constitutional system. By cultivating this consensus ICAO has attained a high degree of institutional stability, which in turn has enabled it to apply and evolve legal rules in a manner that is calculated to advance rather than to hinder the long-range goals of the Organization.

The transformation which the Convention has undergone has been achieved by a gradual process in which formal legal rulings have been rare. This is not to say that constitutional objections are not accorded the hearing they deserve, or that considerations of legality have not influenced the resolution of legal problems. The contrary is probably true, because ICAO's institutional stability is sustained in large measure by the confidence that the Contracting States have in the manner in which the Organization exercises its powers. The Organization has therefore taken great care to explore and to take account of the legal and constitutional ramifications of a given problem before deciding on how to resolve it.

ICAO avoids formal legal rulings, probably because they could force decisions that might be unacceptable to some states for political or economic reasons. Since the decision-making process of ICAO, and consequently its law-making process, is predicated on obtaining compromise solutions, law is used primarily as an instrument to legitimate action or to encourage compromise. If law were used to compel action not acceptable to many states, it would lose much of its legitimating and persuasive influence. When an international organization succeeds, as ICAO has done, in developing a decision-making process in which law does perform an important function, it has in effect created a viable constitutional framework for the accommodation of competing economic or political claims.

ICAO has demonstrated considerable genius for preserving and evolving a legal order which is particularly well-suited for an organization whose tasks are many and complex, but whose powers are extremely limited. The relative success of its law-making techniques demonstrates that it is by no means impossible for an organization of some 116 states to make considerable progress in regulating the conduct of governments.

Note on ICAO Documentation

Serious research relating to the activities of the International Civil Aviation Organization is hampered by the fact that, with the exception of the Organization's own library which is located in Montreal, few libraries have complete or substantially complete ICAO document collections.

DOCUMENTS AND WORKING PAPERS

ICAO publications consist of *documents* (Symbol: Doc.) and *working papers* (Symbol: WP). The Organization's Publications Regulations define a *document* as "a publication which is considered to have permanent character or special importance and which for this reason is suitable for distribution to all Contracting States." A *working paper*, on the other hand, is "a publication intended to serve primarily as a basis for discussion in, or source of information for, a meeting of the Organization." Its distribution is normally limited only to the members of the body for which the working paper was prepared.

The experience of the present writer is that it is impossible to obtain a thorough understanding of the practice and institutional personality of ICAO without having access to Assembly and Council working papers. The reason for this is that ICAO Assembly and Council action is in most cases directly related to certain proposals or findings embodied in working papers which are usually not summarized in the relevant minutes or reports of these bodies.

ICAO REFERENCE SYMBOLS

Documents

Those ICAO documents which contain information bearing on the activities of the Organization as a whole are usually assigned only the general ICAO document serial number.

Example: Index of ICAO Publications, 1958 Cumulated Edition, Doc. 7907.

All other ICAO documents bear a reference symbol which consists of the general ICAO document serial number, code letters identifying the ICAO category of activity to which the document relates, or the ICAO organ

231

that issued the document, followed by the serial number that was assigned to the document within the category to which it belongs.

Example: Doc. 7525–C/874

Doc. 7525 [General ICAO document serial number] –C [Category of activity, Council] /874 [Category serial number]

Example: Doc. 8724 (A16–P/3)

Doc. 8724 [General ICAO document serial number] (A16 [Category of activity, Assembly, 16th Session] –P [Sub-category of activity, plenary meeting] /3) [Sub-category serial number]

Working Papers

ICAO working papers are assigned a reference symbol that consists of code letters identifying the ICAO category of activity to which the working paper relates, and the category serial number.

Example: C–WP/2371

C [Category of activity, Council] –WP [Working paper] /2371 [Category serial number]

Example: A15–WP/15 (TE/6)

A15 [Category of activity, Assembly, 15th Session] –WP [Working paper] /15 [Category serial number] (TE [Sub-category of activity, Technical Commission] /6) [Sub-category serial number]

List of Main Category Symbols

General

A   Assembly
C   Council
AD   Administrative Commission
AN   Air Navigation
ANC   Air Navigation Commission
AN Conf Air Navigation Conference
AT   Air Transport
ATC   Air Transport Commission
EC   Economic Commission
ECAC   European Civil Aviation Conference
EX   Executive Committee
FI   Finance Committee
JS   Joint Support
LC   Legal Committee
LE   Legal Commission
LGB   Legal Bureau
P   Plenary Meetings
TE   Technical Commission

Divisions of the Air Navigation Commission

AGA   Aerodromes, Air Routes and Ground Aids
AIG   Accident Investigation
AIS   Aeronautical Information Services
COM   Communications
MAP   Aeronautical Maps and Charts
MET   Meteorology
OPS   Operations
PEL   Personnel Licensing
RAC   Rules of the Air and Air Traffic Services
SAR   Search and Rescue

Air Navigation Regions

AFI   Africa-Indian Ocean
CAR   Caribbean
EUM   European-Mediterranean
MID   Middle East
NAM   North American
NAT   North Atlantic
PAC   Pacific
SAM   South American (formerly SAM/SAT)
SEA   South East Asia

Divisions of the Air Transport Committee

FAL   Facilitation of Air Transport
STA   Statistics

INDEX TO ICAO PUBLICATIONS

An indispensable guide to ICAO documentation is the *Index of ICAO Publications* which is cumulated annually. It lists all ICAO documents and working papers issued in a particular year, and arranges them alphabetically under appropriate subject headings.

The *Index* is usually about a year behind schedule. An up-to-date listing of ICAO publications is provided by the *Weekly List of Publications*.

ASSEMBLY DOCUMENTATION

Salable Publications

ICAO currently issues, as salable documents, the following publications relating to the work of the Assembly:

MINUTES OF THE PLENARY MEETINGS OF THE ASSEMBLY

Full citation: Minutes of the Plenary Meetings, Fifteenth Session of the Assembly, Montreal, 22 June–16 July 1965, ICAO Doc. 8516–A15–P/5.

Citation used in this book: ICAO Assembly, 15th Sess., Doc. 8516 (A15–P/5) (1965). *Note:* For the first five sessions (1947–1951) of the Assembly ICAO issued, as a salable document, a publication entitled *Proceedings of the Assembly.* This very useful publication contained a detailed description of the activities of the Assembly and its various subsidiary organs.

REPORTS OF ALL ASSEMBLY COMMITTEES AND COMMISSIONS

Full citation: Report of the Executive Committee, Fifteenth Session of the Assembly, Montreal, 22 June–16 July 1965, ICAO Doc. 8522–A15–EX/43. *Citation used in this book:* ICAO Assembly, Report of the Executive Committee, 15th Sess., Doc. 8522 (A15–EX/43) (1965).

ASSEMBLY RESOLUTIONS

Full citation: Resolution A15–1, Resolutions Adopted by the Assembly and Index to Documentation, Fifteenth Session of the Assembly, Montreal, 22 June–16 July 1965, ICAO Doc. 8528–A15–P/6. *Citation used in this book:* Assembly Res. A15–1, ICAO Doc. 8528 (A15–P/6) (1965). *Alternate Source:* The resolutions adopted by the Assembly between 1947 through 1962 have been compiled in a two-volume publication that was issued as ICAO Doc. 7670.

Non-Salable Publications

Among the non-salable publications of the Assembly are:

THE MINUTES OF THE VARIOUS ASSEMBLY COMMITTEES AND COMMISSIONS, EXCLUDING THE MINUTES OF THE LEGAL COMMISSION WHICH ARE REPRINTED IN THE REPORT OF THE LEGAL COMMISSION

Full citation: Minutes of the Executive Committee, Fifteenth Session of the Assembly, Montreal, 22 June–16 July 1965, A15–WP/213 MIN–EX/1–13. *Citation used in this book:* ICAO Assembly, Executive Committee, 15th Sess., Doc. A15–WP/213 (MIN–EX/1–13) (1965).

ALL ASSEMBLY WORKING PAPERS

This includes working papers of the plenary meetings of Assembly, *e.g.,* A15–WP/1 P/4 (1965), and those of the various Committees and Commissions, *e.g.,* A15–WP/38 EX/5 (1965).

COUNCIL DOCUMENTATION

Salable Publications

The most important salable publications relating to the work of the ICAO Council are:

THE ANNUAL REPORTS OF THE COUNCIL TO THE ASSEMBLY

These Reports describe the activities of the Organization in considerable detail, provide important statistical data, and at times contain information relating to ICAO that is not otherwise available in published form. *Full citation:* Annual Report of the Council to the Assembly for 1967, Supporting Documentation for the Sixteenth Session of the Assembly, Buenos Aires, September 1968, ICAO Doc. 8724–A16–P/3 (April 1968). *Citation used in this book:* [1967] Report of the Council, ICAO Doc. 8724 (A16–P/3) (1968).

ACTION OF THE COUNCIL

Inaugurated in 1951, this publication summarizes the deliberations of the ICAO Council and records the decisions adopted by it. It is, more often than not, much too sketchy to provide a useful description of the work of the Council. A very thorough description used to be provided in the *Proceedings of the Council,* which were unfortunately published only for the first thirteen sessions (1947–1951) of the Council. *Full citation:* Action of the Council, Sixty-first Session, Montreal, 25 April–28 June 1967, ICAO Doc. 8693–C/973. *Citation used in this book:* Action of the Council, 61st Sess., ICAO Doc. 8693 (C/973) (1967).

Non-Salable Publications

The most important non-salable publications relating to the work of the Council are:

MINUTES OF THE COUNCIL

Since the *Proceedings of the Council* are no longer published, it is today impossible to study the work of the Council meaningfully without consulting the *Minutes. Full citation:* Council, Twenty-third Session, Montreal, 28 September–15 December 1954, Minutes with Subject Index, ICAO Doc. 7525–C/874 (December 1955). *Citation used in this book:* ICAO Council, 23rd Sess. [1954], Doc. 7525 (C/874) (1955).

COUNCIL WORKING PAPERS

The Council *working papers* frequently contain valuable studies and information which must be taken into account when assessing the scope of a Council decision or the factors motivating it. *Full citation:* C–WP/2452 (6/6/57). *Citation used in this book:* ICAO Doc. C–WP/2452 (1957).

SELECTED ICAO REFERENCE DOCUMENTS

Aims of ICAO in the Field of Facilitation, ICAO Doc. 7891 (C/906/2) (1965).

Convention on International Civil Aviation, ICAO Doc. 7300/3 (1963). Contains official English text of Convention together with amendments adopted thereto, as well as unofficial French and Spanish texts of the Convention.

Directives of the Council Concerning the Conduct of ICAO Meetings, ICAO Doc. 7986 (C/915) (1959).

Directives to Panels of the Air Navigation Commission, ICAO Doc. 7984/2 (1962).

International Civil Aviation Conference, Chicago, Illinois, 1 November–7 December 1944, Final Act and Appendices, ICAO Doc. 2187. Contains texts of the Interim Agreement on International Civil Aviation, the Convention on International Civil Aviation, the International Air Services Transit Agreement, and the International Air Transport Agreement.

ICAO Publications Regulations, ICAO Doc. 7231/4 (1960).

ICAO Secretariat, MEMORANDUM ON ICAO (5th ed. 1966). Very useful description of the history and activities of ICAO.

Legal Committee, Constitution, Procedure for Approval of Draft Conventions, Rules of Procedure, ICAO Doc. 7669 (LC/139) (1956).

Protocol on the Authentic Trilingual Text of the Convention on International Civil Aviation (Chicago, 1944), T.I.A.S. 6605. Contains authentic French and Spanish language texts of the Convention, which was signed at Buenos Aires on 24 September 1968.

Rules for the Settlement of Differences, ICAO Doc. 7782 (1959).

Rules of Procedure for Standing Committees of the Council, ICAO Doc. 8146 (C/930) (1961).

Rules of Procedure for the Air Navigation Commission, ICAO Doc. 8229 (AN/876) (1962).

Rules of Procedure for the Conduct of Air Navigation Meetings and Directives to Divisional-Type Air Navigation Meetings, ICAO Doc. 8143 (AN/873) (1961).

Rules of Procedure for the Conduct of Air Navigation Meetings and Directives to Regional Air Navigation Meetings, ICAO Doc. 8144 (AN/874) (1961).

Rules of Procedure for the Council, ICAO Doc. 7559/3 (1959).

Standing Rules of Procedure of the Assembly of the International Civil Aviation Organization, ICAO Doc. 7600/2 (1963).

The ICAO Financial Regulations, ICAO Doc. 7515/5 (1963).

Bibliography

BOOKS

BOWETT, DEREK, W. THE LAW OF INTERNATIONAL INSTITUTIONS. New York, Praeger, 1963, 347 p.

BRANDT, LEO WOLFGANG (ed.). BEITRÄGE ZUM INTERNATIONALEN LUFT-RECHT (FESTSCHRIFT ZU EHREN VON ALEX MEYER). Düsseldorf, Droste-Verlag, 1954, 160 p.

CARLSTON, KENNETH SMITH. THE PROCESS OF INTERNATIONAL ARBI-TRATION. New York, Columbia Univ. Press, 1946, 318 p.

CHENG, BIN. THE LAW OF INTERNATIONAL AIR TRANSPORT. London, Stevens, 1962, 726 p.

COOPER, JOHN COBB. THE RIGHT TO FLY. New York, H. Holt, 1947, 380 p.

DETTER, INGRID. LAW MAKING BY INTERNATIONAL ORGANIZATIONS. Stockholm, P. A. Norstedt, 1965, 353 p.

ERLER, JOCHEN. RECHTSFRAGEN DER ICAO: DIE INTERNATIONALE ZIVILLUFTFAHRTORGANISATION UND IHRE MITGLIEDSTAATEN. Berlin, Heymann, 1967, 223 p.

HAMBRO, EDWARD ISAK. L'EXÉCUTION DES SENTENCES INTERNATIONALES. Paris, Librairie du Recueil Sirey, 1936, 148 p.

HOYT, EDWIN CHASE. THE UNANIMITY RULE IN THE REVISION OF TREATIES: A RE-EXAMINATION. The Hague, M. Nijhoff, 1959, 264 p.

HUDSON, MANLEY OTTMER. THE PERMANENT COURT OF INTERNATIONAL JUSTICE 1920–1940. New York, The Macmillan Co., 1943, 807 p.

INSTITUTE FÜR AUSLÄNDISCHES ÖFFENTLICHES RECHT UND VÖLKER-RECHT, STATUT ET RÈGLEMENT DE LA COUR PERMANENTE DE JUSTICE INTERNATIONALE: ÉLÉMENTS D'INTÉRPRETATION. Berlin, Heymann, 1934, 498 p.

INTERNATIONAL CIVIL AVIATION CONFERENCE, FINAL ACT AND RELATED DOCUMENTS. Washington, U.S. Gov't Print. Off., 1945, 284 p.

INTERNATIONAL LAW ASS'N, THE EFFECT OF INDEPENDENCE ON TREAT-IES: A HANDBOOK. London, Stevens, 1965, 391 p.

KISTLER, PETER. DAS RÖMER HAFTUNGSABKOMMEN VON 1952. Winter-thur, H. Schellenberg, 1959, 107 p.

LECA, JEAN. LES TECHNIQUES DE RÉVISION DES CONVENTIONS INTERNATIONALES. Paris, Librairie générale de droit et de jurisprudence, 1961, 330 p.

MATEESCO MATTE, NICOLAS. TRAITÉ DE DROIT AÉRIEN-AÉRONAUTIQUE. Paris, A. Pedone, 2d ed. 1964, 1021 p.

MCNAIR, LORD ARNOLD. THE LAW OF THE AIR. London, Stevens, 3rd ed., 1964, 588 p.

O'BRIEN, WILLIAM VINCENT (ed.). THE NEW NATIONS IN INTERNATIONAL LAW AND DIPLOMACY. New York, Praeger, 1965, 323 p.

O'CONNELL, DANIEL T. STATE SUCCESSION IN MUNICIPAL LAW AND INTERNATIONAL LAW. Cambridge, Cambridge University Press, 1967, Vol. I, 592 p., Vol. II, 430 p.

RIESE, OTTO. LUFTRECHT. Stuttgart, K. F. Koehler, 1949, 556 p.

RIESE, OTTO, AND LACOUR, JEAN. PRÉCIS DE DROIT AÉRIEN. Paris, Librairie générale de droit et de jurisprudence, 1951, 374 p.

ROHKAM, WILLIAM, JR. and PRATT, ORVILLE C. STUDIES IN FRENCH ADMINISTRATIVE LAW. Urbana, The Univ. of Illinois Press, 1947, 109 p.

ROPER, ALBERT. LA CONVENTION INTERNATIONALE DU 13 OCTOBRE 1919 PORTANT RÉGLEMENTATION DE LA NAVIGATION AÉRIENNE. Paris, Librairie du Recueil Sirey, 1930, 379 p.

ROSENNE, SHABTAI. THE INTERNATIONAL COURT OF JUSTICE. Leyden, A. W. Sijthoff, 1957, 592 p.

———. THE LAW AND PRACTICE OF THE INTERNATIONAL COURT. Leyden, A. W. Sijthoff, 1965, 2 vols., 998 p.

SAND, PETER. AN HISTORICAL SURVEY OF THE LAW OF FLIGHT. Montreal, Institute of Air and Space Law, McGill Univ., 1961, 74 p.

SCHENKMAN, JACOB. INTERNATIONAL CIVIL AVIATION ORGANIZATION. Genève, H. Studer, 1955, 410 p.

SHIHATA, IBRAHIM F. THE POWER OF THE INTERNATIONAL COURT TO DETERMINE ITS OWN JURISDICTION. The Hague, M. Nijhoff, 1965, 400 p.

SIMPSON, JOHN LIDDLE, and FOX, HAZEL. INTERNATIONAL ARBITRATION: LAW AND PRACTICE. London, Stevens, 1959, 330 p.

SINGH, NAGENDRA. TERMINATION OF MEMBERSHIP OF INTERNATIONAL ORGANISATIONS. London, Stevens, 1958, 209 p.

STABREIT, IMMO. DIE REVISION MULTILATERALER VÖLKERRECHTLICHER VERTRÄGE DURCH EINE BEGRENZTE ANZAHL DER VERTRAGSPARTEIEN. Diss., Heidelberg, 1964, 223 p.

STUDI IN ONORE DI ANTONIO AMBROSINI. Milano, A. Giuffrè, 1957, 911 p.

TUNÇEL, ERHAN, L'EXÉCUTION DES DÉCISIONS DE LA COUR INTERNATIONALE DE JUSTICE SELON LA CHARTE DES NATIONS UNIES. Thèse, Neuchâtel, 1960, 135 p.

U.S. DEPARTMENT OF STATE, PROCEEDINGS OF THE INTERNATIONAL CIVIL

Aviation Conference, Chicago, Illinois, November 1–December 7, 1944. Washington, United States Government, 1948, 2 vols., 1509 p.

U.S. Senate Committee on Commerce, Air Laws and Treaties of the World. Washington, United States Government Printing Office, 1965, 3 vols., 4483 p.

Wassenbergh, H. A. Post-War International Civil Aviation Policy and the Law of the Air. The Hague, M. Nijhoff, 2d rev. ed., 1962, 197 p.

Wheatcroft, Stephen. The Economics of European Air Transport. Manchester, Manchester Univ. Press, 1956, 358 p.

Winterhager, Eva Marie. Die Revision von Gründungsverträgen Internationaler und Supranationaler Organisationen. Diss., Frankfurt/Main, 1963, 87 p.

Periodical Literature

Alexandrowicz, C. H. *The Convention on Facilitation of International Maritime Traffic and International Technical Regulations: A Comparative Study.* 15 Int'l & Comp. L.Q. 621 (1966).

Anderson, D. R. *Reservations to Multilateral Conventions: A Re-Examination.* 13 Int'l & Comp. L.Q. 450 (1964).

Aufricht, H. *Supersession of Treaties in International Law.* 37 Cornell L.Q. 655 (1951–52).

Bärmann, J. *Art. 93 des Abkommens von Chicago und das Völkerrecht.* 2 Zeitschrift für Luftrecht 1 (1953).

Bhatti, Drion, and Heller. *Prohibited Areas in International Civil Aviation —the Indian-Pakistani Dispute.* [1953] U.S. & Can. Av. 109.

Bishop, W. W. *Reservations to Treaties.* 103 Recueil des Cours 245 (1961).

Bowen, H. A. *The Chicago International Civil Aviation Conference.* 13 Geo. Wash. L. Rev. 308 (1945).

Buergenthal, T. *Appeals for Annulment by Enterprises in the European Coal and Steel Community.* 10 Am. J. Comp. L. 227 (1961).

Carroz, J. *International Legislation on Air Navigation over the High Seas.* 26 J. Air L. & Com. 158 (1959).

Cheng, B. *Centrifugal Tendencies in Air Law.* 10 Current Legal Problems 200 (1957).

Codding, G., Jr. *Contributions of the World Health Organization and the Civil Aviation Organization to the Development of International Law.* [1965] A.S.I.L. Proceedings 147.

Cooper, J. C. *New Problems in International Civil Aviation Arbitration Procedure.* 2 Arb. J. 119 (1947).

Cooper, J. C. *The Chicago Convention—After Twenty Years.* 14 ZEITS-CHRIFT FÜR LUFTRECHT UND WELTRAUM-RECHTSFRAGEN 273 (1965).

Domke, M. *International Civil Aviation Sets New Pattern.* 1 INT'L ARB. J. 20 (1945).

Drion, H. *The Council of I.C.A.O. as International Legislator over the High Seas,* in STUDI IN ONORE DI ANTONIO AMBROSINI. Milano, A. Giuffrè, 1957, 911 p.

Fitzmaurice, Sir G. *Reservations to Multilateral Conventions.* 2 INT'L & COMP. L.Q. 1 (1953).

Fuller, W. E. *I.C.A.O. International Standards in the Technical Annexes— Their Effect within the U.S. and Validity under the Constitution.* 21 GEO. WASH. L. REV. 86 (1952).

Garnault, A. *Les Conventions et Résolutions de Chicago.* 1 REVUE FRANÇAISE DE DROIT AÉRIEN 25 (1947).

Goedhuis, D. *Problems of Public International Air Law.* 81 RECUEIL DES COURS 205 (1952).

Guggenheim, P. *L'élaboration d'une clause modèle de compétence obligatoire de la Cour internationale de Justice.* 44/1 ANNUAIRE DE L'INSTITUT DE DROIT INTERNATIONAL 458 (1952).

Guildimann, W. *La Méthode de travail du Comité juridique de l'OACI.* 14 REVUE FRANÇAISE DE DROIT AÉRIEN 1 (1960).

Hexner, E. *Interpretation by Public International Organizations of their Basic Instruments.* 53 AM. J. INT'L L. 341 (1959).

Hingorani, R. C. *Dispute Settlement in International Civil Aviation.* 14 ARB. J. 14 (1959).

Jenks, C. W. *Due Process of Law in International Organizations.* 19 INT'L ORG. 163 (1965).

———. *Some Constitutional Problems of International Organizations.* 22 BRIT. YB. INT'L L. 11 (1945).

Jennings, R. Y. *International Civil Aviation and the Law.* 22 BRIT. YB. INT'L L. 191 (1945).

———. *Some Aspects of International Air Law.* 75 RECUEIL DES COURS 513 (1949).

Jessup, P. C. *Parliamentary Diplomacy: An Examination of the Legal Quality of the Rules of Procedure of Organs of the United Nations.* 89 RECUEIL DES COURS 185 (1956).

Jones, H. H. *Amending the Chicago Convention and its Technical Annexes.* 16 J. AIR L. & COM. 185 (1949).

Kos-Rabcewicz-Zubkowski, *Le Règlement des différends internationaux relatifs à la navigation aérienne civile.* 2 REVUE FRANÇAISE DE DROIT AÉRIEN 340 (1948).

LaPradelle, A. de. *La Conférence de Chicago—Sa place dans l'évolution politique, economique et juridique du monde.* 9 Revue Générale de l'Air 107 (1946).

Latchford, S. *Comparison of the Chicago Aviation Convention with the Paris and Habana Conventions,* 12 Dep't State Bull. 411 (1945).

LeGoff, M. *Les Annexes Techniques à la Convention de Chicago.* 19 Revue Générale de l'Air 146 (1956).

———. *L'Organisation Provisoire de Chicago sur l'Aviation Civile.* 9 Revue Générale de l'Air 600 (1946).

McMahon, J. F. *The Legislative Techniques of the International Labour Organization.* 41 Brit. Yb. Int'l L. 1 (1965–66).

Malintoppi, A. *La Fonction "Normatif" de l'O.A.C.I.* 13 Revue Générale de l'Air 1050 (1950).

Mankiewicz, R. H. *Air Law Conventions and the New States.* 20 J. Air L. & Com. 52 (1963).

———. *L'adoption des annexes à la Convention de Chicago par le Conseil de l'Organisation de l'Aviation Civile Internationale, in* Brandt, Beiträge zum Internationalen Luftrecht (Festschrift zu Ehren von Alex Meyer) (1954).

———. *Organisation Internationale de l'Aviation Civile.* [1956] Annuaire Français de Droit International 643.

———. *Organisation Internationale de l'Aviation Civile.* [1957] Annuaire Français de Droit International 383.

———. *Organisation de l'Aviation Civile Internationale.* [1962] Annuaire Français de Droit International 675.

———. *L'Organisation de l'Aviation Civile Internationale.* [1965] Annuaire Français de Droit International 630.

———. *The [ICAO] Legal Committee—Its Organization and Working Methods.* 32 J. Air L. & Com. 94 (1966).

Merlin, E. R. *Ten Years of Technical Assistance Co-operation in Civil Aviation.* 16 ICAO Bull. 8 (1961).

O'Connell, D. P. *Independence and Problems of State Succession, in* O'Brien, The New Nations in International Law and Diplomacy (1965).

Osterhout, H. *A Review of the Recent Chicago International Air Conference.* 31 Va. L. Rev. 376 (1945).

Pépin, E. *Development of the National Legislation on Aviation since the Chicago Convention.* 24 J. Air L. & Com. 1 (1957).

———. *ICAO and Other Agencies Dealing with Air Regulations.* 19 J. Air L. & Com. 152 (1952).

———. *Le Droit Aérien.* 71 Recueil des Cours 477 (1947).

———. *The Law of the Air and the Articles Concerning the Law of the Sea Adopted by the International Law Commission at its Eighth Session.* U.N. Doc. A/Conf. 13/4 (1957).

Phillips, L. H. *Constitutional Revision in the Specialized Agencies.* 62 AM. J. INT'L L. 654 (1968).

Riese, O. *Das mehrseitige Abkommen über gewerbliche Rechte im nicht-planmässigen Luftverkehr in Europa.* 8 ZEITSCHRIFT FÜR LUFTRECHT 127 (1959).

Rinck, G. *Damage Caused by Foreign Aircraft to Third Parties.* 28 J. AIR L. & COM. 405 (1961–62).

Ros, E. J. *Le Pouvoir Législatif International de l'O.A.C.I. et ses Modalités.* 16 REVUE GÉNÉRALE DE L'AIR 25 (1953).

Rosenne, S. *The Depositary of International Treaties.* 61 AM. J. INT'L L. 923 (1967).

Saba, H. *L'activité quasi-législative des institutions spécialisées des Nations Unies.* 111 RECUEIL DES COURS 607 (1964).

Schachter, O. *Enforcement of International Judicial and Arbitral Decisions.* AM. J. INT'L L. 1 (1960).

———. *Question of Treaty Reservations at the 1959 General Assembly.* 54 AM. J. INT'L L. 372 (1960).

Schwelb, E. *Amendments to Articles 23, 27 and 61 of the Charter of the United Nations.* 59 AM. J. INT'L L. 834 (1965).

———. *The Amending Procedure of Constitutions of International Organizations.* 31 BRIT. YB. INT'L L. 49 (1954).

———. *The 1963/1965 Amendments to the Charter of the United Nations: An Addendum.* 60 AM. J. INT'L L. 371 (1966).

Seyersted, F. *Settlement of internal disputes of intergovernmental organizations by internal and external Courts.* 27 ZEITSCHRIFT FÜR AUSLÄNDISCHES ÖFFENTLICHES RECHT UND VÖLKERRECHT 1 (1964).

Sheffy, M. *The Air Navigation Commission of the International Civil Aviation Organization.* 25 J. AIR L. & COM. 281 AND 428 (1958).

Skubiszewski, K. *Enactment of Law by International Organizations.* 41 BRIT. YB. INT'L L. 198 (1965–66).

Sohn, L. B. *Expulsion or Forced Withdrawal from an International Organization.* 77 HARV. L. REV. 1381 (1964).

———. *The Function of International Arbitration Today.* 108 RECUEIL DES COURS 9 (1963).

———. *The Role of International Institutions as Conflict-Adjusting Agencies,* 28 U. CHI. L. REV. 205 (1961).

Vulcan, C. *L'Exécution des Decisions de la Cour Internationale de Justice d'Après la Charte des Nations Unies.* 51 REVUE GÉNÉRALE DE DROIT INTERNATIONAL PUBLIC 187 (1947).

Warner, E. P. *PICAO and the Development of Air Law.* 14 J. AIR L. & COM. 1 (1946).

———. *The Chicago Air Conference,* 23 FOR. AFF. 406 (1944–45).

Index

tion, 86; implementation problems, 109–10; implementation techniques, 110–12

Finance Committee: composition, 11; function, 11

Food and Agriculture Organization: amendments, 206n26

Former Enemy States. *See* Admission of

Freedoms of the Air: Two Freedoms, 154; Five Freedoms, 154–55

General Declaration. *See* Facilitation SARPS

Gibraltar: United Kingdom v. Spain, 123n1

Guatemala: withdrawal of denunciation, 35

High Seas: compulsory character of ICAO legislation, 80–85

India: IMCO reservation, 29n65; dispute with Pakistan, 129, 137–39, 140, 156

Inter-Governmental Maritime Consultative Organization (IMCO): reservation by India, 29n65

Interim Agreement on International Civil Aviation: establishment of Provisional International Civil Aviation Organization (PICAO), 5; disputes under, 180

International Air Services Transit Agreement: relation to Convention on International Civil Aviation, 5; disputes under, 123, 137, 155–58; India v. Pakistan, 137, 156; complaints under, 155, 158–66; sanctions under, 156–58, 164–66; choice of remedy, 159–61; Jordan v. Syria (U.A.R.), 162–64; rules of procedure, 182, 192–93

International Air Transport Agreement: relation to Convention on International Civil Aviation, 5; disputes under, 123, 155–58; complaints under, 155, 158–66; sanctions under, 156–58, 164–66; choice

of remedy, 159–61; rules of procedure, 182, 192–93

International Bank for Reconstruction and Development: amendments, 209n35

International Civil Aviation Conference (Chicago Conference): establishment of ICAO, 2–3

International Civil Aviation Organization (ICAO): establishment of, 3; function, 5–6; institutional structure, 6 12; documentation explained, 231–36; *See also* specific subject headings

International Commission for Air Navigation: powers under Paris Convention, 118

International Court of Justice: appeal to, 125, 141, 142, 143–44; interpretation of judgment, 147, 148, 149; advisory opinion, 148, 187; revision of judgment, 148, 149; non-compliance with judgment, 152–53, 154; adjudication *ex aequo et bono*, 161

International Labour Organisation: reservation by U.S.S.R., 29n66

International Monetary Fund: amendments, 209n35

International Standards and Recommended Practices (SARPS): power to adopt, 58–59; procedures, 59, 81n74; Annex designation, 60; recommended practices defined, 60, 61; standards defined, 60, 61; air navigation SARPS defined, 60–61; facilitation SARPS defined, 61; development of, 62–63; adoption of, 63–64; deviations from, 88–94; domestic law status, 102–06; implementation problems, 107–14; *See also* Annexes; Notification of Differences

Joint Financing Agreements: disputes under, 167–68

Joint Support of Air Navigation Services: Agreements on Financing, 166–68; *See also* Committee on Joint Support of Air Navigation Services